ers

EPH

College Library

CARPENTER'S
WORLD TRAVELS

—

*Familiar Talks About Countries
and Peoples*

WITH THE AUTHOR ON THE SPOT AND
THE READER IN HIS HOME, BASED
ON THREE HUNDRED THOU-
SAND MILES OF TRAVEL
OVER THE GLOBE

"READING CARPENTER IS SEEING THE WORLD"

ALASKA
OUR NORTHERN WONDERLAND

OUR NORTHERN WONDERLAND

Alaska is no land of perpetual ice and snow. Wild flowers bloom everywhere; delicious fruits and vegetables grow to great size and ripen quickly in the days of the long sun, and its scenic beauties are unsurpassed.

CARPENTER'S WORLD TRAVELS

ALASKA
OUR NORTHERN WONDERLAND

BY
FRANK G. CARPENTER
LITT. D., F. R. G. S.

WITH 123 ILLUSTRATIONS
FROM ORIGINAL PHOTOGRAPHS
AND TWO MAPS IN COLOUR

GARDEN CITY   NEW YORK
DOUBLEDAY, PAGE & COMPANY
1925

ACKNOWLEDGMENTS

IN THE publication of this volume on Alaska I wish to thank the officials of our Government at Washington for letters which have given me the invaluable assistance of our authorities in the Territory. I thank also those men of Alaska at the head of its great productive undertakings for their generous courtesies in enabling me to study what has been achieved in our northern wonderland and according me privileges seldom available to the traveller.

I acknowledge, too, the assistance and coöperation rendered by Mr. Dudley Harmon, my editor, and Miss Ellen McB. Brown and Miss Josephine Lehmann in the revision of notes dictated or penned by me on the ground.

While most of the illustrations are from my own negatives, certain photographs have been supplied by the United States Department of Agriculture, the Forest Service, the Bureau of Education, the Coast & Geodetic Survey, the Bureau of Fisheries, the Alaskan Engineering Commission, the International News Reel Corporation, the Publishers' Photo Service, and Dr. L. S. Sugden and the Canadian Pacific Railway.

F. G. C.

CONTENTS

CHAPTER   PAGE

I   JUST A WORD BEFORE WE START   1

II   KETCHIKAN   5

III THE TOWN OF THE GOOD INDIANS   13

IV   ALASKA'S GOLDEN FISHERIES   21

V   THE STORY OF "SEWARD'S ICE BOX" . .   32

VI   THE THLINGETS AND THE HYDAHS . . .   44

VII TOTEM INDIANS AND THEIR CUSTOMS . .   52

VIII FARM LANDS OF THE FUTURE   60

IX   AT JUNEAU   69

X   TREASURES UNDER THE SEA   78

XI   THE WORLD'S GREATEST GLACIERS . .   87

XII SKAGWAY, THE GATE TO THE KLONDIKE .   96

XIII OVER THE GOLD-SEEKERS' TRAIL . . 106

XIV IN THE YUKON FLATS 115

XV   WINTER TALES OF TANANA 124

XVI HOT SPRINGS IN COLD LANDS 133

XVII FAIRBANKS, THE CHICAGO OF ALASKA . . 139

XVIII HOMESTEADING UNDER THE ARCTIC CIRCLE 148

XIX THAWING FORTUNES OUT OF THE ICE . . 156

XX   STORIES OF GOLD AND GOLD MINERS . . 162

ix

CONTENTS

CHAPTER		PAGE
XXI	AMONG THE OLD TIMERS	169
XXII	FROM FORT GIBBON TO THE SEA . .	178
XXIII	THE CITY OF GOLDEN SANDS . . .	183
XXIV	CREEKS THAT MADE MILLIONAIRES .	191
XXV	THE DOG DERBY OF ALASKA . . .	197
XXVI	REINDEER MEAT FOR AMERICAN MARKETS	205
XXVII	AMONG THE ESKIMOS	214
XXVIII	SCHOOL REPUBLICS OF THE ARCTIC . .	222
XXIX	FUR SEALS AND FOX FARMS	230
XXX	THE ALEUTIAN ISLANDS	239
XXXI	THE CITY OF SEWARD	250
XXXII	ACROSS KENAI ON HORSEBACK . . .	256
XXXIII	OUR NORTHERN GAME PRESERVE . .	263
XXXIV	THE BIGGEST THING IN ALASKA . .	271
XXXV	MOUNT MCKINLEY, THE "MOST HIGH"	281
XXXVI	THE STORY OF KENNECOTT	289
XXXVII	ON THE COPPER RIVER RAILROAD . .	296
XXXVIII	WOMEN ON AMERICA'S LAST FRONTIER	302
BIBLIOGRAPHY.		311
INDEX		315

LIST OF ILLUSTRATIONS

In Our Northern Wonderland . . . *Frontispiece*

FACING PAGE

Eddystone Rock. 4
Ketchikan Mountain-side 5
Making Soundings 12
Father Duncan 13
Salmon in Ketchikan 20
Indian Village 21
A One-hundred-pound Halibut 28
Drying Salmon 29
Salmon at the Spawning 29
Sitka Harbour 36
Indians at Sitka 36
Battle-scarred Blockhouse 37
"The Lady of Kazan" 44
Chilkat Blanket 45
Tools of Indian Magic 45
School Gardens 48
Indian Coöperative Store 48
Indians in Native Garb 49
Totems in Marble 52
Indian Canoe 53
Strawberry Patch 60
Pastures Near a Glacier 61
Alaska's Rich Harvest 61
Alaska Spruce 64

ILLUSTRATIONS

FACING PAGE

The Pack Horse 65
Arctic Oil 68
Juneau 69
The Governor's Residence 76
Repairing the Planked Streets 76
Mills at Gastineau 77
A Glacial Lake and Falls 84
Beside a Glacier 85
Taku Glacier 92
Flowers and Ice 92
Where Glaciers Come from 93
To a Glacier by Automobile 93
Skagway 100
Fourth of July Celebration 100
In the "Flower City" 101
"Soapy" Smith's Memorial 104
Mrs. Pullen 105
Staking out a Corner 108
Athapascan Mother and Child 109
"Calico Bluffs" 116
International Boundary 117
On the Yukon Flats 117
Taking on Fuel 124
Prehistoric Ivory 124
Bear Drinking Pop 125
An Outdoor Cache 132
When the Ice Breaks 132
At the Hot Springs 133
Mt. McKinley at Night 133
Library at Fairbanks 140
A Snug Home 140

ILLUSTRATIONS

FACING PAGE

Winter Bridge at Fairbanks 141
The Homesteader 148
Pitching Hay 149
Roadhouse on the Creeks 156
Over the Winter Trail 156
Rex Beach's Cabin 157
The "Sourdough's" Dog Team 157
Thawing with Steam Points 164
A Sluice Box 165
Miner's Shack 172
Cleaning Gold 172
Nenana Coal 173
Hiding from the Camera 180
Ruby 181
Iditarod 181
Going Ashore at Nome 188
Nome's Log Cabin Club 189
Going to the Dance 192
Hydraulic Mining 193
Panning Gold 196
The Alaskan Husky. 197
Carrying the Mail 204
Dog-team Delivery 204
Alaskan Puppies. 205
Pupmobile 205
Eskimo and Reindeer 208
A Reindeer Herd 209
Reindeer Awaiting Slaughter 209
St. John's in the Wilderness 212
Eskimo Children 213
Eskimo Dress 220

ILLUSTRATIONS

FACING PAGE

The Kayak 221
Native Dances 221
Going to School 224
Kivalina Community Council 225
Manual Training at Selawik 225
Hospital at Kanakanak 228
Young Eskimos 228
White Fox Furs 229
Seal on the Pribilofs 236
Silver-gray Fox Pups 237
Basket Weaving 240
Whale Dance 241
Waiting for a Seal 244
The Beluga Whale 244
Kodiak 245
An Old Aleut Home 245
Resurrection Bay 252
Seward 253
View near Resurrection Bay 253
Going through Kenai 260
Fishing in a Kenai Stream 261
A Caribou 268
The Lynx 269
Railroad through the Mountains 276
Snow Sheds on the Railroad 277
View of Mt. McKinley 284
Climbing Mt. McKinley 285
Bridge at Hurricane Gulch 288
Cordova 289
Camp in the Snow 292
The Bonanza Mines 293

ILLUSTRATIONS

FACING PAGE

Glaciers along Copper River 300
Keystone Canyon 301
Driving the First Spike. 304
Homesteading 305
The "Two Girls' Waffle House" 305

MAPS

Alaska and the Klondike 24
Alaska and the United States Compared. . . . 56 — missing
cap 1-96

ALASKA
OUR NORTHERN WONDERLAND

ALASKA
OUR NORTHERN WONDERLAND

CHAPTER I

JUST A WORD BEFORE WE START

OF ALL the countries I have visited, our Polar Wonderland is among the most interesting. Lying as it does at the northwestern end of the continent, so close to Asia that one might fly from Alaska to Siberia within fifteen minutes, and so near the North Pole that an airplane might make the trip between breakfast and dinner, it forms a part of our union with British America, tying us as it were to Europe and Asia, and hooking us on to the topmost peak of the world.

Alaska is truly a land of surprises. In some parts the winters are as mild as those of Virginia and in others as severe as in Sakhalin or Kamchatka. It has summers as hot at midday as Bangkok and Rangoon, and so cool at night that one welcomes blankets. It has seasons when the sun shines at midnight, and winter days so dark that the electric light can be turned off in the schools and the homes only from eleven to one. It is a land of jungles that vie with the Himalayas in their dense vegetation, and of scanty mosses springing from desert beds of perpetual ice. It has gorgeous wild-flowers, mighty forests, vast glaciers, mountains capped with snow, and

1

valleys out of which spout by the thousands the vents of volcanoes. It is beyond conception among the grandest of all nature's wonderlands.

A most interesting feature was the virgin newness of all my surroundings. I travelled for days through the wilds, seeing hardly a cabin. I sailed on the rivers through long stretches where not a vestige of man could be seen, and I could easily imagine myself a Columbus or a Hernando de Soto discovering a world. When I crossed Bering Sea on the edge of the winter I felt like an Arctic explorer, and in the Aleutian Islands the perpetual mists chilled my soul with the fear that I had on the Grand Banks of Newfoundland when the fog horn blew day and night.

The talks of this book are the notes made during my travels. They were written on steamer and on train, on foot and on horseback, now in motor cars riding from one mining camp to another, now on the top of glacier-clad mountains, and now in tunnels where men were getting out gold from under the earth. They represent chats with the hardy pioneers of our farthest North; men who of all our citizens are the most patriotic Americans; men who can see straight and shoot straight; the survivors of stampedes to many a far-away camp, true men, and strong men, the weaklings having died on the way. Indeed, I met no one in my journeys who, to use an Alaskan expression, had "a wishbone where his backbone should be."

When I started north I had a stomach, and lungs, and liver, and lights. All seemed to be ailing as I climbed the gang plank of the ship at Seattle. I lost them that night; and for four months and more, as far as I knew, they had no existence. I ate buckwheat cakes and "sour dough," and bear meat and fat pork in the heart of midsummer;

2

JUST A WORD BEFORE WE START

I breathed champagne in the air of the mountains; my liver worked like a seventy-horsepower automobile, and as for my lights, whatever and wherever they are, they were dormant.

Our Northland is undergoing a change. The Government is adopting a more liberal policy as to the territory. The forest and oil fields are being exploited. The fisheries are protected and the catch will increase. Fox farming is rapidly becoming a substantial industry, with over a hundred farms, the majority of which are on islands along the coast. The railway from Seward to Fairbanks has opened vast areas of arable land to the homesteader, and the best of hard wheat is now grown and milled in the Tanana Valley. I rode through grasslands where the spears on the ends of the stalks tickled the ears of my horse, ate strawberries on the Arctic Circle, and at Skagway saw dahlias as big as a dinner plate.

In the gardens along the Yukon and Tanana I dug potatoes of twenty-seven varieties, cut off cabbages as big as the head of a bull, and pulled up turnips that would surprise the best soil of the Temperate Zone. I visited several successful dairies near Fairbanks, and on Kodiak Island found a government experiment station where they are raising fine cattle and sheep. Near the mouth of the Yukon I saw hundreds of reindeer, and at Nome visited packing plants where they were being killed and frozen for export to the markets of our larger cities.

At the same time new mineral areas are being prospected, iron of good grade is known to exist, and the coal deposits cover a region almost as big as the mine fields of Pennsylvania. The nickel of Chichagof Island is supposed to surpass that of Canada or New Caledonia, and high-

3

grade tin is being mined on the Seward Peninsula near Bering Strait. The government geologists and others are finding new wells of petroleum, and the coal beds opened up by the railroads promise a new supply of fuel for the fleets of the eastern Pacific. The copper output is now worth tens of millions of dollars a year, and rich silver mines are being worked just over the international boundary near the Portland Canal. There are still fortunes in gold underlying the beds of prehistoric ice, and more quartz gold is being discovered. Indeed, the future of Alaska is bright.

Eddystone Rock is not as great a menace to ships on the southeastern coast of Alaska as the many similar pinnacles which lie hidden under the water.

Ketchikan is built on the steep mountainside rising up from the water. The streets are planks laid on piles, and a four-horse dray or heavy motor truck jars a whole block.

CHAPTER II

KETCHIKAN

I AM in Ketchikan, the first port at which our steamers call in entering Alaska. It is at the southern end of the Panhandle, the strip of islands and mainland at the lower end of our territory that seems to be cut out of British Columbia. The Panhandle begins just above Skagway near the pass over the mountains to the Klondike and Dawson, and extends south for more than three hundred miles. It consists of many large islands and a strip of mainland about thirty miles wide which runs from the Pacific Ocean to the crest of the coast mountain range, the whole making a territory as big as South Carolina. This district is known as Southeastern Alaska. It has its own climate, its own vegetation, and its own peculiar products and resources. It is covered with green from one year's end to the other and differs from the great Alaskan interior as much as Maine differs from Florida. I shall be travelling within it for some weeks to come.

The town of Ketchikan lies not far from the international boundary. It is only forty miles north of the Canal and within six hours' sail of Prince Rupert, the terminus of the Grand Trunk Pacific Railway and the port which the Canadians are developing as the gateway to the shortest route to Japan and the Orient.

Ketchikan is as far north of Seattle as the distance

5

between New York and Toledo. After leaving Seattle, I sailed for more than five hundred miles through Canadian waters before I came to the edge of Alaska, and from there made my way in and out among the islands to Revilla Gigedo, on the shores of which lies Ketchikan. The trip took me over two days.

I despair of giving you any idea of the beauties of this voyage, they are so many and so varied. The route from Seattle to Skagway is known as the Inside Passage. It is a winding in and out among half-submerged mountains. It is floating through great lakes studded with islands. It is travelling along and within fiords like those of west Norway. Now you have the wonders of the Swiss lakes, now those of the Inland Sea of Japan, and now scenery like that on the coasts of New Zealand. There are all sorts of combinations of sea and sky, of evergreen slopes and snow-capped mountains. There are ever-shifting colour effects and marvellously beautiful sunsets.

These are the characteristics of Southeastern Alaska. The whole district between the Portland and Lynn canals is composed of islands covered with evergreen trees many of which are four or five feet thick. A number of the islands have snow-capped mountains whose green walls rise almost straight up from the water. Most of the mainland is also one mighty wall of green.

The islands, which are of all shapes and sizes, float upon sapphire seas. When the tide is low—and the tide here rises and falls to the height of a two-story house—these islands seem like floating gardens. Then vegetation does not begin until fifteen or twenty feet above the water, and there are only precipices of black rock below. The islands are bedded upon the rocks and as the water falls

6

the living earth seems to be lifted up. The forests sit aloft on pedestals of stone, and mountains of green and white tower above their rocky bases. Here bold cliffs, brown and gray walls several hundred feet high, rise sheer from the blue waves; there the bare rocks thrust out from the growth of pines on the hillsides.

As you sail on to the northward the channels vary. Now they widen into great lakes, now they are rivers as narrow as the Hudson or the Rhine. Sometimes the way lies through gorges between the islands and the mainland. In places the waters are a thousand feet deep. In others, there are great rocks as steep, as high, and as sharp as the Washington Monument, which come within twenty or thirty feet of the surface. These are the terrible pinnacle rocks that rip open the hulls of the steamers. They are constantly being searched for and marked with buoys by the wire drag of our Coast and Geodetic Survey.

Indeed, the seas about Alaska are so dangerous that they are sometimes called the "Graveyard of the Pacific." The commerce of the territory is rapidly increasing in importance, yet fifty years after our purchase the United States Coast Survey admitted that ninety-two per cent. of its waters were unsurveyed and that it would take two vessels fifty-nine years to complete a first survey of the exposed areas, in addition to the wire-drag and inshore parties necessary in the sheltered portions. The Government's ships are keeping everlastingly at it, however, and I have been out with one of the wire-drag boats and have seen how the needle-tipped peaks of the Panhandle coast are detected. A wire cable with buoys attached is slung between two ships and set at a fixed depth. As the vessels sail along the buoys are pulled under like a fish-line bob when the wire strikes a hidden rock, which is then marked by a float and its position recorded. Over a thousand pinnacle rocks, terrible menaces to navigation and undiscovered by the ordinary survey methods, have been found by the use of the wire drag.

But let us come back to Ketchikan. The town is situated on the southern shore of Revilla Gigedo Island, in a region where the salmon come in great hordes every summer and near banks from which are taken most of the halibut sent from Alaska to the United States and to Canada. Revilla Gigedo is about one third as large as Porto Rico. It is fifty miles long and twenty miles wide and is made up of mountains which for much of the time have their heads in the clouds.

Ketchikan lies right on the water against a background of towering green mountains crested with snow. The harbour is the shape of a half-moon protected by islands. It has no beach to speak of and the business district rests upon piles. The streets are plank roadways built upon posts, and much of the freight is carried about on trucks and carts pushed by men. Horses are unpopular, for their shoes roughen the planks and they shake the town as they trot through the streets, so they are being replaced by automobiles and motor delivery trucks.

The residential section of the city clings to the sides of the cliffs higher up. It is so steep that one has to climb stairways to reach some of the streets, while others have winding roadways of boards upon which slats have been nailed to keep one from slipping. The Ketchikaners make one think of tree dwellers, who climb ladders to get to their homes.

The best houses, which are high on the cliffs, far above

the harbour, seem to grow out of the rocks. Nevertheless, nearly every home has its little lawn with shrubs and flowers and a tiny garden patch, although the soil has to be sprinkled with gold dust to make them.

In this connection the captain on my steamer coming up told me a story of a Ketchikan man who sailed with him last month. This man was sitting at the captain's right hand at dinner. During one meal he was in a brown study. Course after course passed and he ate but little. At last he burst out in an agonized soliloquy:

"I knew I'd forget it! I knew I'd forget it! I knew I'd forget it!"

"What," said the captain, "have you forgotten something your wife told you to bring back from outside?"

"Yes, I have," was the reply. "And I knew I'd forget it. She made me promise to bring seven sacks of good soil to lay on the rocks and make her a garden. And now I've forgot it."

Some of the Ketchikaners raise vegetables and berries. In the garden of H. C. Strong I saw raspberry bushes as high as my shoulder, which for more than two months during the summer, give him all of that fruit he can eat. The berries, which are large and of a fine flavour, never become mushy when ripe. Ketchikan also raises currants, salmon berries, and many beautiful flowers. There is so much moisture that the plants will grow on the rocks with very little soil.

It has been raining steadily ever since I arrived, and to-day during a downpour I asked one of the citizens:

"Does it never stop raining in Ketchikan?"

He replied, with a laugh: "I hardly know, I have lived here only fifteen years."

ALASKA—OUR NORTHERN WONDERLAND.

The city really has rain for more than two-thirds of the year and an annual precipitation of over thirteen feet. The leaves of the trees drip almost as steadily as those of the famous forest sprinkled by the mist of the Zambesi Falls in Central Africa.

Indeed, the southern coast of Alaska is one of the rainiest parts of the world. Juneau, the capital, is much like Ketchikan, while on some of the Aleutian Islands a day of sunshine is a rarity. But the people go about regardless of the wet. They wear oilskin hats and rubber coats or slickers, and if they tramp up the mountains they put on rubber boots reaching to the waist. Some of the ladies even have slicker suits consisting of skirts and jackets. No one thinks of staying away from a party or tea on account of the weather, and women go visiting clad in oilskins covering dresses fit for a party in New York or Washington.

Some people here tell me, however, that Ketchikan has many bright days and that its climate is unsurpassed by any other part of our country. The inhabitants are healthy. The children have bright eyes and rosy cheeks. They play about everywhere, notwithstanding the rain. In the winter they coast down the board roads which in places run for more than a mile up and down the hills. The town has but little snow at any time of the year, but then the frosts are so heavy that there is splendid sledding until 9 or 10 o'clock in the morning. If there is not enough frost, the roads can be sprinkled at night and will be covered with ice in the morning.

Many people of the United States think of all Alaska's winter as bitterly cold. Their idea of the country is expressed in Bret Harte's "Arctic Vision":

KETCHIKAN

Where the short-legged Eskimo
Waddles in the ice and snow,
And the playful polar bear
Nips the hunter unaware.

Ketchikan has neither Eskimos nor polar bears and there is little ice and snow. The thermometer seldom falls to zero, and the climate is as mild as that of Atlanta or Richmond.

The stores here are excellent. Most of them are on the water front built upon piles that rest on the rocks. The shops have plate-glass windows and the goods are well displayed. In one window I saw a full line of electrical apparatus, including electric irons, toasters, and heaters. Another shows a large supply of thermos bottles and baby carriages. The butcher shops have quarters of red beef just in from Seattle, and the fruit stores sell raspberries and strawberries grown in Alaska, oranges and figs from California, and apples from Oregon and British Columbia. The supply of eatables is quite as good as that of the provision stores in the States, and the prices are not much higher. Indeed, I believe one can live almost as cheaply in Ketchikan as in Cleveland, Kansas City, or Kalamazoo.

I have a room and bath at the Revilla Hotel, one of the two leading taverns. The Revilla is a three-story frame building within a stone's throw of the sea. The hotel office is a loafing place and poolroom as well, and the guests and outsiders are knocking the billiard balls over the tables at all hours of the night. As the hotel serves no meals I have to go out to the restaurants. I am eating at the Poodle Dog grill, where I sit on a stool at the lunch counter and eat my ham and eggs or other meat from a great oval platter. The Poodle Dog advertises these hot platters as its specialty and serves food in no other way.

The town has an excellent and abundant water supply from a lake high up in the mountains. Any one who wants a drink of pure mountain water has only to fit his mouth over the little porcelain bowls of the sanitary drinking fountains at every street corner and take in all he will.

In addition to the lake, Ketchikan has a rushing stream flowing in cascades and rapids right through it. In the salmon season this stream is one pink-and-silver mass of fish. The fish come by the thousands and swim up the stream to spawn, toiling their way through the rapids and jumping the falls. At that season any one may have fish for the taking, and quantities are caught for the canneries.

This stream furnishes the city its electric power and runs the street lights and telephones. It gives electric heat to some of the houses. During my stay I have had dinner with one of the leading citizens whose home is a beautiful house of ten rooms lighted and heated by electricity. The cooking is done on an electric stove, and hot water is supplied in the same way. Yet he tells me that his fuel and light bills, even in midwinter, are not more than eighteen dollars a month.

Large areas of Alaskan waters are still unsounded. The United States revenue cutters are equipped with modern sounding apparatus, but sometimes a sailor will merely be swung over the ship's side to "heave the lead" and plumb the depth.

TOWN LIBRARY

Under Father William Duncan, the Tsimpseans attained in thirty years a degree of civilization that it has taken other savages centuries to achieve. When he started his mission the Indians were addicted to cannibalism and Father Duncan's life was in danger.

CHAPTER III

ON ANNETTE ISLAND, just south of Ketchikan, is Metlakahtla, the seat of one of the most remarkable experiments in the civilization of the Red Man. This is the town of the Good Indians established by Father William Duncan, whose wonderful work with these natives justified his title of the "Apostle of Alaska."

Father Duncan began life as a commercial traveller in England, and at twenty-one was well on his way toward a salary of five thousand dollars a year. He decided, however, to give up his work and become a missionary. He went to college expecting to be sent out to India, but instead he was ordered to the western coast of British Columbia to work with a tribe of Indians known as the Tsimpeans.

These Tsimpean Indians were then among the most barbarous of any on the North American continent. They believed in witch doctors and practised cannibalism. They were hunters and fishers and clothed themselves in the skins of bears and wolves. In their weird dances they put the skulls of bears on their heads. Their medicine men wore hideous masks and tried to frighten off disease with horrible noises. If the demon of disease did not leave, the witch doctors would hack away the sore places with their knives, or suck or burn away the

13

ailing flesh. Any one they pointed out as possessed of evil spirits or as a witch was killed by his tribe.

The Tsimpseans had also curious ideas regarding the treatment of their women. Young girls approaching womanhood were confined far away in isolated cabins, and when brought back were supposed to have dropped down from the moon and to be ready for marriage. On such occasions there were great feasts at which the youths of the tribe were initiated into dog eating, cannibalism, and devil dancing. The Indians believed in spirits and the transmigration of souls.

When Father Duncan arrived in Victoria on his way to this work he was told by the agent of the Hudson's Bay Company that if he went he would beyond doubt be killed. When Duncan still insisted, he said: "Well, my good man, if you are to be killed and eaten I suppose you are the one most interested, and we shall have to let you do as you wish."

With this permission, Father Duncan was allowed to go to Fort Simpson, in British Columbia, not far from Prince Rupert. On his way up the beach to speak to the officer in charge at the fort stockade he came to a place where the remains of a number of human beings were scattered about and was told that the bodies he saw had been hacked to pieces and thrown on the sand in a fight between two parties of savages a few days before.

At that time many of the tribes along the coast of British Columbia were cannibals and Father Duncan actually saw a band of Indians on the beach eating a boy who had died of tuberculosis, and he had every reason to believe that a woman he saw killed was disposed of in the same fashion. Here is his own account of the latter incident:

THE TOWN OF THE GOOD INDIANS

"I had heard of the cannibalism, and one day an officer of the fort ran into my house and told me that the Indians were about to kill one of their women. He warned me to keep indoors and said that I would surely be killed if I attempted to interfere. A moment later another man rushed in and said that the woman had already been killed. We went out to the beach where there was a crowd of Indians. They were divided into two bands, each led by a stark-naked brave. All were howling horribly. They had killed a woman and cut her in two and each of the nude Indian leaders was carrying half of the woman's body by his teeth. As we came up the bands separated, each gathering around its leader. They sat down on the sand so crowded together that I could not see. When they got up not a vestige of the woman was to be seen. What became of the flesh I do not know, but I believe it was devoured. I doubt, however, whether it agreed with them, for the officers of the Hudson's Bay Company fort near by told me that it was the custom of the Indians after every such cannibal feast to come into the post the day following and buy large quantities of epsom salts."

In those early days there were several attempts to kill Father Duncan. On one occasion a tribal chief demanded that the mission school be closed because his beautiful daughter was just about to drop down from the moon to be married. The chief said that she had gone away and would come back in great state. She would drop from the moon into the sea and would rise out of the water with a bearskin over her shoulders and thus appear to the people. At this time there would be many ceremonies that would prevent the school being kept open.

15

Father Duncan refused to close the school and the chief persisted in his demands. At last, on the day before the feast, he sent two men with long knives to kill the missionary, whose life was saved by a friendly Indian who had taught him the native language. The school was kept going.

The missionary kept steadily at his work until he had converted eight or nine of these tribes to the Christian religion and made them about the most law-abiding and civilized people of the Indian race. To belong to Father Duncan's community the Indians did not have to promise to become Christians but they did have to agree that they would drink no liquor, that there should be none of the performances of the medicine men over the sick, and that they would do no work on Sunday. They had their own council and governed themselves. They had their own boats, and they established a canning factory and put up salmon for shipment. They learned to make ropes and brushes, to weave, and to spin. Father Duncan went to England and brought back musical instruments and they established a brass band. They had a schoolhouse and a church with an organ, which some of them were able to play. They had their market house, their shops, their carpenters, tinners, coopers, and other mechanics. What it has taken ages to accomplish with other uncivilized peoples these Indians, under Father Duncan, achieved in less than thirty years.

Then the Church of England began to meddle with Duncan's mission, sending a bishop to rule over him and the Indians. Finding that his work was being undone, Father Duncan asked the United States to allow his Indians to settle on our territory. That was in 1887.

The matter was much agitated in the United States. Father Duncan was supported by Henry Ward Beecher, Phillips Brooks, and others, and through their efforts a territory was allotted to him and his Indians on the northwestern side of Annette Island. They came in August, and the first thing they did was to erect a flagpole and hoist the Stars and Stripes. They had speeches by the United States Commissioner of Education and by Father Duncan, and later on divine service consisting of song and praise in the Tsimpsean language.

The next day a portable sawmill was unloaded, and the people began at once to clear the forests and erect buildings for their new homes. They built a cannery, and year by year added to their structures until they had a town hall, a church, a schoolhouse, a store, a public library, and the other buildings necessary to a civilized community. The settlement was called the New Metlakahtla and since then the Indians have been known as the Metlakahtlans. In 1891 Annette Island was set aside by Congress as a reservation for them and it was provided that it should be used by them in common under such rules and regulations as might be prescribed by the Secretary of the Interior.

Annette Island is one of the most beautiful parts of Southeastern Alaska. It is fifteen miles long and ten miles wide, and is formed by a long wooded mountain on the backbone of which are a number of beautiful lakes. About the harbour of Metlakahtla the land slopes gently down to the sea. Here the trees have been cut away and a few hundred acres have been cleared and divided up into town lots. On the left of the harbour a silvery cascade tumbles down the side of the mountain.

It comes from Lake Chester a short distance inland and eight hundred and fifty feet above the sea.

The most conspicuous building in Father Duncan's settlement is a great white frame structure with two towers. This is the Westminster Abbey of Metlakahtla. It is Father Duncan's church and was built by the Indians at a cost of twelve thousand dollars. It is the largest church in Alaska and seats five hundred people.

On the left of the church is the public school erected by the United States, and still farther away are Father Duncan's twelve-room guest house, his office, his school, and the great store he built to supply the needs of the people.

Right at the dock is a salmon cannery with a capacity of about a million cans a year, which has at times been a very profitable undertaking, giving work to all the people and bringing in a good revenue to the colony. Connected with it is a box factory which turns out the twenty thousand cases or boxes used for shipping the fish. At times as many as ten thousand salmon have been handled in a day.

One of the striking buildings of the new Metlakahtla is the library and jail. This is painted in the colours of the American flag. The first story is bright red; it is the jail. The second story is snow-white; it is the library. The cupola on the top is blue.

Close to the beach and running back from it toward the public buildings are the homes of the people. There are several hundred of them, all built by the Indians with money earned in the community enterprises established by Father Duncan. The houses are cottages of one and two stories. They have glass windows, porches, and comfort-

able surroundings. Each has a lot about eighty feet
front and ninety feet deep, and every family has its
garden.

The community has its own preachers and public
speakers. Some of the sermons, in the Tsimpsean language, are full of eloquence and beauty. Here, for
instance, is one urging the people to believe that the
Saviour will take care of them:

"Brethren and sisters: You know the eagle and its ways.
The eagle flies high. The eagle rests high. It always
rests on the highest branch of the highest tree. We should
be like the eagle. We should rest on the highest branch
of the highest tree. That branch is Jesus Christ. When
we rest on him all our enemies will be below and far
beneath us."

Another preacher who had formerly been vicious and
high-tempered, speaking of himself, said:

"I will tell you what I feel myself to be. I am like a
bundle of weeds floating down the stream. I was going
down with all my sin, like the weeds, covered with earth
and filth; but I came to the rapids, when lo! there was a
pole stuck fast and firm in the rock, and I clutched at the
pole, and there I am now. The stream is passing by and
washing away my filth. Christ to me is the pole; I hold
to him and am safe."

I might cite other quotations to show the civilization,
intelligence, and piety of the Metlakahtlans. They are
far above the average of their race and they are now
aspiring to a higher education, to full United States
citizenship, and to ownership of land in severalty. Under
the regulations fixed by the Secretary of the Interior
the Indians govern their colony through a council of

twelve, elected annually, and their church is directed by twelve elders, also chosen by vote of the people.

From reading the following translation of the Lord's Prayer into Tsimpsean one gets some idea of what it means to work with these Indians in their own language:

Wee-Nahgwah-dum koo tsim lachahgah, Nclootiksh ah Noo-wahnt, Shahaksheah ntsabbany, Shah-koad-kan tum wahl ah halletsohamee. Ne-wahltksh tsim lachah-gah. Kinnam klahgam ah chah quah ahm shkabboo wenayah. Kamkoadan ah naht-ahtackamee, new-ahl-dah dee willah ham hoadamum ah haht-ach-ah-deah gam; Killohmdʒah tahtaink umt shpiet t'in shpahlt koadumt; addah mah al tillahmantkum ah haht-achahdat; Ahwill n'tsabbanıat, addah nahkat kettandat, tilth n'cloadant, addah tum clah-willah wahl. Amen.

A beautiful rushing stream flows right through Ketchikan. In spring it is pink and silver from bank to bank with the hordes of salmon that jump the falls on their way upstream to spawn.

Getting nine tenths of their living from the sea, the Indians locate their villages on the narrow beach between the water and mountainside. They have learned to use tools and put up frame houses in place of rude huts.

CHAPTER IV

ALASKA'S GOLDEN FISHERIES

DURING the last two weeks I have visited several fishing centres of Southeastern Alaska, and have gone through many of the canneries where they are putting up salmon for shipment to all parts of the world. There are more than seventy-five such canneries in Southeastern Alaska alone and nearly twice that number in the whole territory. I have also gone through the cold storage plants at Ketchikan and elsewhere, where they are freezing salmon for export, and have seen the various processes of mild-curing and smoking and pickling the fish for the market.

But few people appreciate what Uncle Sam is now getting out of the waters of this territory. The fishing industry is the most important business in Alaska. So far the seas have proved almost as valuable as the land. Including the operations of the seal fisheries, we have realized more than half a billion dollars from them. We are now getting almost six times as much annually from Alaskan fish as the sum we paid for the whole territory when we bought it from the Russians, and we have received more than seventy times that amount since the purchase was made. If the industry is properly protected and fostered it should produce at that rate for all time to come.

Indeed, the waters of Alaska have to be reckoned among

the big sources of our food supply. They produce hundreds of millions of pounds of food every year, and the canned salmon alone is enough to give ten meals to every family in the United States and still leave some for export. The fresh salmon sold in a year runs upward of three million pounds, while the salmon frozen, mild-cured, and pickled comes to fifteen million pounds. The annual halibut export amounts to about seven million pounds, and the codfish to ten million. In addition to this there are many other kinds of fish in these waters that will eventually be caught and shipped, so that in some respects the industry is at its beginning.

In the water divisions which the United States Bureau of Fisheries has made of the territory, Southeastern Alaska is known as Fishing District Number One. It is by far the most important of the water regions of our territory, having something like ten thousand men engaged in fishing. This district has great halibut banks off its many islands and is the seat of the fresh fish industry of Alaska. The fishing investments there amount to something like thirty million dollars, most of which is in salmon.

The second fishing district is known as that of Central Alaska. This begins at Yakutat Bay and includes the great Gulf of Alaska and all of the waters south of the mainland and along the Aleutian Islands, which run almost to Asia. The ocean bed of a great part of this enormous district is paved with fish. The bulk of the catch is salmon, but there is also an annual export of cod, amounting to millions of pounds, from the extensive cod banks south of the Alaska Peninsula and the Aleutian Islands.

These banks compare with those of Newfoundland. Some of them are one hundred and twenty miles long and of great width. They are so situated that the Arctic and the Japanese currents bring them a great deal of fish food and the cod come there by the millions to eat.

The third district, Western Alaska, includes banks swarming with cod. It embraces Bristol Bay, where the salmon run into the streams by the tens of millions a year, the deltas of the Kuskokwim and the Yukon rivers, as well as the coast of Norton Sound and all the waters along Seward Peninsula to Cape Prince of Wales at Bering Strait. We have also an island in the middle of the strait about which some fishing is done. As far as its fisheries are concerned, Western Alaska is next in importance to Southeastern Alaska.

There is a fairly well-authenticated story of how one of the salmon kings started his fortune in the fish industry on the basis of the then-despised light-coloured salmon. This man had put up his cannery at a location past which the fish came in great numbers on their way in to spawn. He was right in his selection of a site, and the salmon were caught in vast quantities. They were all, however, of the light pink variety, and the fisherman was in despair. At that time no light-coloured salmon had been shipped, and the demand everywhere was for salmon of an almost red hue. The man canned his catch and sold it by means of a label which implied that it was the only sanitary fish on the market. The label read: "This salmon is warranted not to turn red in the can." Most of the catch went to the Southern States, and the drummers selling it did their business so well that in some of the towns in that part of

23

the United States to this day you can hardly sell a red salmon. The people think it is spoiled, and has, therefore, turned red in the can.

In interior Alaska both whites and natives are indirectly dependent on dried salmon for their very existence during the winter. One of the most important phases of the salmon industry is the fact that dried salmon is the best food for the "husky," or Alaskan team dog.

Of the seventy million dollars invested in the fishing industry of Alaska sixty-two millions are devoted to catching, canning, and shipping of salmon. There are four species of this fish, all of which are delicious. The largest and most valuable is the king salmon, which has an average weight of twenty-two pounds and sometimes weighs as high as one hundred pounds. This is found in Southeastern Alaska in all months of the year, and in May and June it runs up many of the rivers to spawn. The next in size is the sock-eye, or red salmon, which is about a yard long and has an average weight of five pounds. It is found all over Alaska and runs chiefly from June until the middle of August. The silver or Coho salmon is not so valuable, on account of the paleness of its flesh. It weighs on an average about six pounds, and runs later than the sock-eye. The hump-back is the smallest of our salmon. It is caught by the millions in Southeastern Alaska, and many of the canneries depend upon it. It weighs up to eleven pounds. In addition to these four species Alaska has the dog salmon, which is good for freezing, salting, and smoking, but poor for canning, and is shipped largely to Japan.

Catching the salmon and bringing them to the canneries is a great industry by itself. There are certain weeks or months of the year during which these fish come from the ocean into the fresh waters of the rivers to spawn. The spawning grounds are often a thousand miles or more inland. I have seen the fish fighting their way up the Yukon two thousand miles from its mouth at Bering Sea, and they may be found in great numbers climbing over the rocks of the streams that flow down the mountains of the coast into the Pacific.

When they are four or five years old the instinct to spawn sends the salmon up into the inland creeks and rivers. There seems to be something in the contact with the fresh water coming down into the ocean that causes the fish to run toward it. Usually they pair off. When they have gone far enough from salt water the male, with his tail and snout, digs a broad, shallow nest in the gravelly stream bed in which the female deposits her eggs. After they have been fertilized by the milt of the male, the pair cover them up with sand and gravel, then float down the stream tail first, never swimming or making any effort to get back to sea. In a few days both the male and female die. Four or five months later the young hatch and soon, guided by some instinct, make their way down to the ocean where they stay until they are ready to rush back to fresh water, spawn, and die like their parents before them.

In the spawning season the salmon come up stream in such hordes that they can be caught in traps both stationary and floating, in nets fastened to posts and stakes in the rivers, and in seines which are brought from the beaches and the boats. They are caught also by fish wheels moved by the currents of the river in such a way that the nets of wire or cord attached to the wheels scoop up the fish as they swim against the current and fairly shovel them down into the boats. Fish wheels of this kind are to be seen here and there along the coast, and there are hundreds of them owned by the Indians along the Kuskokwim and Yukon rivers.

The business of the Alaskan canneries is enormous. The one I went through in Ketchikan covers several acres. It will put up seven and one half million cans of salmon this year besides freezing hundreds of thousands of pounds to be sent to the East. When the fish are brought in by the boatloads and dumped out by the thousand they are still alive and flopping, and they are hardly dead as they start into the "iron chink," a machine which cleans each fish, cutting off its head, tail, and fins and taking out its insides within the time of a watch tick. All this work used to be done by hand, and Chinese hands at that. When the machine was invented to take the place of the Chinaman it was nicknamed the "iron chink," and so it is known to this day. The inventor was a cook of Seattle named Smith, who made a fortune out of his invention. His machine will clean thirty thousand fish in ten hours, or as much as was formerly done by fifty of the most expert Chinese. Nevertheless, the whole thing is not much bigger around than a flour barrel and not more than eight feet in height. It consists of a number of knives so arranged that as the fish flies in one knife cuts off the head and at the same time another chops off the tail. As the fish moves on a third knife rips up the belly and other knives take off the fins.

At the end the fish has been split, the backbone taken out, the blood removed, and the salmon is ready for the can. Before being put into the can, however, it is carefully inspected by men who watch the fish as they make their way over endless belts to the chopper.

The chopper automatically cuts the fish into pieces of the right size for the can in such a way that each can gets its own share of the several parts of a fish. There must be some from the back and some from the belly in order to supply the streak of lean and the streak of fat which, as in bacon, are necessary to make the can of salmon just right. The machine puts into each can just sixteen ounces. As the cans move onward they pass through an automatic weighing machine which drops out any that are underweight.

After this the cover of the can is fitted on by machinery in such a way as to allow the steam to escape, and the tins travel on into a furnace or exhaust box where the temperature is two hundred and twelve degrees. Next another machine makes the tops tight, without acid or solder, and the cans are moved on into great retorts where they are cooked for an hour and a half in a heat of two hundred and fifty-four degrees. When they come out they are ready to be labelled and packed into boxes for shipment to all parts of the world.

The halibut is one of the most interesting fish that swims the seas. It is the largest of the flat fish. I have seen many which, if stood upon their tails, would reach high above my head and some which I venture are over three feet in width. The average halibut weighs about one hundred pounds, but some have been caught weighing as much as three hundred. Halibut fishing has nothing gamy or sporting about it. Long lines are dropped down into the sea until the baited hook rests on the bed of the ocean. Sometimes the lines are so long that when loaded with fish it takes the steam engine on the fishing vessel the better part of a day to wind them up. They are divided into sections, each section having a float or buoy that rides on the surface and is marked by a flag in the daytime and by a light at night.

Some halibut fishing is now carried on direct from the ship. A few years ago it was all done in dories or small boats, which were taken out in large vessels. The men would go out in the dories to set the lines and later bring the halibut back to the vessel.

The fishing parties usually stay out from ten days to three weeks. They carry ice with them, and the moment the fish are taken from the hook they are cleaned and packed in the ice. When they reach the cold storage plant they are washed and shipped in cold storage cars direct to the markets.

If they are not to be shipped immediately halibut are put into freezers where they remain for twenty-four hours at a temperature of ten to twenty degrees above zero. Next each one is dipped four or five times in fresh water until it becomes entirely incased in a thin sheet of clear ice. It can then be held in cold storage at a temperature of four degrees below freezing. Finally, the fish get another coating of ice, are wrapped separately in vegetable parchment paper, packed in paper-lined boxes of seventy-five pounds' capacity, and sent eastward in the cold storage trains.

I have gone through some of the big freezing establishments both in Prince Rupert and in Ketchikan. Each town has its cold storage plants where halibut and salmon are frozen. The largest one I visited has a capacity of fourteen million pounds of fish. Its buildings are right

Next in importance to the salmon of Alaska is the halibut. The average halibut weighs about one hundred pounds, but some have been caught weighing as much as three hundred pounds.

The pink flesh of tens of thousands of drying salmon add to the colourful scenes of Alaska. The dried fish are eaten by Indians and white men and are the chief winter food of the sled dogs.

The life story of both the male and female salmon ends with the spawning. The adults leave the ocean for the rivers and streams, but only the young fish survive to make the return journey.

on the harbour, and the fish are frozen stiff as soon as they come from the wharves.

I went into the freezing chambers, the walls and pipes of which were covered with frost. The temperature is far below zero. The smell of the ammonia used to produce refrigeration almost overcame me as I walked between the great masses of fish laid one upon another like so many sticks of cordwood. I took up one of the smaller fish and let it drop on the floor. It was as hard as stone and the noise of its fall was like the crack of a pistol. I examined the fish, but there was no bruise or dent in the flesh. I stood it on end, resting the tail on the floor, and it did not bend in the least.

A great deal of halibut is salted and put in hogsheads for shipment. Each hogshead holds about eight hundred and fifty pounds, and when full is worth around a hundred dollars. The halibut intended for salting is dressed before it is packed. It is hung by the gills to a hook then sliced in two, the back and the front forming great slabs of snow-white meat. The backbone is cut out; the front, or belly, has no bones. After cleaning, the slabs are sprinkled with salt and put into the hogsheads in layers with a layer of salt between each two layers of fish. Some halibut is smoked, in which form it may be bought in almost any grocery store.

Herring, the halibut's favourite food, are found in nearly all the waters of Alaska. They move about in great schools, some of which cover several square miles. Twice a year, when they swim to the shores to spawn, they come in such large schools that they can be scooped up from the water right into the boats. One way of catching them is by driving nails into a board so that they stick out several inches. The boards are then dragged through the schools and the fish catch between the nails and are pulled by the boardful into the boats. In one year more than a million pounds of herring were caught at Prince Rupert alone and frozen by the cold storage plants to be sold for bait. A large proportion of the herring catch of Alaska is used for manufacture of fertilizer and oil, but at that statistics show an output of more than eight million pounds annually cured for food.

There are also large cod fisheries in Alaska, and the cod are said to be equal to those caught on the Banks of Newfoundland. Much of the cod fishing is about the Aleutian Islands, and there are many vessels and stations devoted to the industry. The amount of cod caught annually runs to more than twelve million pounds.

In addition to the ordinary cod there are black cod, a fish of about the same size as the ordinary cod, but darker in colour. The flesh, which is much richer in oil, may be prepared in such a way that it is delicious. It has been eaten for many years in Alaska, and has latterly been shipped to Seattle, where the restaurants make a special feature of barbecued black cod. This consists of the backs of the fish, which are kippered or smoked after being salted, served with drawn butter.

There is a prospect that an extensive industry will some time arise in the shellfish of Alaska. There are oysters on the southern coast as large as saucers, and there are many places among the Alaskan islands where you can catch crabs as big as dinner plates. There are clams large and small, delicious little butter clams and others good to eat the size of a man's hand.

I am told, however, that one has to be very careful as

to the source of his clam supply. Some of these bivalves feed in the water near the copper deposits, and the copper poisons their meat. The captain of one of our Coast Survey steamers, in speaking of this recently, told me how his life was saved by a pussy-cat. Said he:

"It was a narrow escape. I had bought a fine mess of clams and was just about to eat some of them raw when I decided I had better test their edibility by giving one of them to my cat. The pussy ate it, and a moment later she rolled over and went into convulsions. She kept on kicking until every one of her nine lives had departed."

CHAPTER V

COME with me for a walk through the old town of Sitka. It was founded in 1799 at about the time that George Washington was dying at Mount Vernon, and was a thriving manufacturing centre, building ships and making bells, plows, picks, and spades when the Indians were still hunting deer on the site of Chicago. For more than one hundred years it was the capital and commercial centre of Alaska. Situated here in the Panhandle one hundred and fifty miles northwest of Ketchikan and about as far north of Seattle as Minneapolis is north of New Orleans, it was selected by the Russians as the seat of their government and as the chief home of the officials and traders sent out by the Czar to what was then Russian America. Sitka was the capital of Alaska when we bought the territory, and it was here that the country was formally transferred to the United States. After that it remained the capital for almost forty years, until the seat of government was transferred to Juneau in 1912.

Looking at Sitka as it is to-day, one does not wonder that the Russians chose it as their chief place of residence. The town has a climate as mild as that of Baltimore or Richmond, and its surroundings are so beautiful that it must some time be a summer resort and place of permanent residence for retired capitalists. It is situated on

Baranof Island within a short distance of the open Pacific.
It lies on a little bay at the mouth of a fast-flowing river in
the arena of an amphitheatre of snow-clad mountains.
The waters in front of it have scores of small wooded
islands, while all about the hills rise to the clouds. One
of the mountains is known as the Holy Cross from a figure
of the cross in perpetual snow which gleams out near its
summit. This is Mt. Verstovia, which has a mantle of
white throughout the winter, but in the summer the snow
disappears, with the exception of this gigantic cross
painted by the hand of God upon a background of green.
Another mountain is Edgecombe, on the Island of Kruzof,
over the way. Mount Edgecombe is an extinct volcano
as regular and as beautiful in its outlines as Fujiyama in
Japan. It was one of the first of the landmarks discovered
by Captain Cook when he sailed through these waters in
1776.

On the hill, at one side of the town, was the site of the
Baranof castle, where the Russian governor lived, and
there to-day is the headquarters of the agricultural experiment station. To the left of the cliffs at the entrance
of the harbour are the wharves with the main business
street, named after President Lincoln, running back from
them, and farther down the cove is a long row of two and
three story houses, with many flagstaffs rising above them.
That is the Indian settlement. The town has altogether
something like one thousand Indians, and we shall see
Indians everywhere as we move through the streets. It
has also about five hundred whites.

In Sitka modern residences of Americans and log buildings more than one hundred years old, put up in the days of
the Russians, stand side by side. There is one great ware-

house of logs so carefully fitted together that you could not put a knife blade between them. The logs are each two or three feet in diameter. That building, which was a warehouse when we took over the territory, frequently had a million dollars' worth of furs stored in it. At the time of the sale to the United States it contained thirty thousand sealskins which then sold for less than three dollars apiece.

A little farther up the street is a log building covered with the moss of many decades, and still farther away, near the Russian cemetery, is a Russian blockhouse bearing the scars of the wars with the Indians.

The Sitka of to-day has a number of fine churches and a large missionary school. There is an Episcopal church, built of stone, with the residence of the Bishop of Alaska behind it, and there are the half-dozen large buildings of the Sheldon Jackson School belonging to the Presbyterians. These buildings include industrial departments and dormitories for both Indian boys and girls. The children are clean and well dressed and the school has done a great work with its practical educational methods.

At Sitka is also the Old Pioneers' Home where aged and dependent men and women, who have spent their years assisting in the development of Alaska, are well cared for by the territorial government. The most prominent church building in the town is the Russian cathedral. It stands at the end of the main street coming up from the wharves on the site of a church that was built here more than a century ago, when Baranof was governor. The present building dates far back in the Russian occupation, but it was in use until the Bolshevik régime in Russia suspended the activities of the Russian Church in Alaska.

34

THE STORY OF "SEWARD'S ICE BOX"

The Russians did a great deal of mission work here. They had mission stations on many of the Aleutian Islands and others scattered over the territory even to the mouth of the Yukon. The Russian cathedral at Sitka is a museum of interesting pictures and jewels. Many of its paintings were brought around Cape Horn or across Siberia, and some of them are by famous artists. One is an icon bearing the face of the Lady of Kazan. It represents a madonna and child and is of great beauty. I am told that the church refused an offer of twenty-five thousand dollars from J. Pierpont Morgan for this single painting.

Of late years Sitka has lost its commercial importance. The removal of the capital to Juneau took away about all the United States offices, and there is now no more quiet town in the territory. The place is away from the main lines of travel and is reached only by a small steamer, or by the tourist boats in the summer, which bring sightseers here on account of Sitka's beauty and historic interest. It is well worth a visit.

The history of Alaska covers just about one hundred and fifty years, and, roughly speaking, it may be divided into three periods of fifty years each. The first fifty was the period of exploration and discovery. The next fifty was the time of the Russian occupation, and the last half century covers the time since we purchased the territory.

Alaska was discovered by the Russians during the eighteenth century but very little was known about it until almost the beginning of the nineteenth. It was in 1711 that Peter Popoff sailed from Siberia around through Bering Strait and brought back rumours that a continent existed on the other side of Asia. Seventeen years later Peter the Great of Russia, who had heard of these stories, sent Vitus Bering from Kamchatka to find out if they were true. Bering went through the strait which now bears his name, but it must have been foggy, for he did not see the American shore or even the Diomede Islands, which lie in the middle of the Strait. So he came back and reported that he had found nothing. He tried it again nine years later with a similar result, and it was not until 1741 that he saw the American continent and discovered the Shumagin Islands. At that time he anchored near the mouth of the Copper River and went on back through the Aleutians to the Island of Bering, a part of Siberia. He was wrecked on that island and died there of scurvy. Some of his sailors who made their way back to the mainland carried the story of the existence of Alaska and of the wonderful furs of the Aleutians.

From that time the Russians made many expeditions to the Aleutians. Their glowing reports attracted the attention of other navigators, especially Britons and Spaniards, who made many voyages of exploration along the Alaskan coasts. It was in 1774 and 1775 that Juan Perez was sent by the King of Spain from Mexico to the north. He reached Dixon Entrance, our international boundary, in 1774, and the year following came to Sitka Sound. Captain Cook sailed from Plymouth, England, at just about the time that Jefferson was writing the Declaration of Independence. It was he who established the fact that there was no land connection between America and Asia, and he surveyed a part of the coast, outlining the chief features through more than twelve degrees of latitude. He then went south to Hawaii, where he was killed by the natives.

Later still there were other explorations by the Russians,

Sitka, the old capital of Russian America, has a safe and commodious harbour. Its surroundings are so beautiful and its climate is so mild that it should become a favourite summer resort for people from the States.

Indians so dislike to have any one pass behind them that when they can they sit with their backs against a wall. When we bought Alaska this old Russian warehouse contained thirty thousand seal skins, which then sold for less than three dollars apiece.

The old blockhouse at Sitka still shows the scars of the wars which Baranoff, first Governor of Russian America, waged against the Indians. In one massacre all but five of the colonists at Sitka were killed.

who formed trading companies, and there were independent fur traders from England and from our Atlantic coast. Five ships from New England came to Alaska in the latter part of the eighteenth century to buy furs. One of these, commanded by Captain Gray, took his cargo of furs to Canton, China, where he got a cargo of tea, which he carried on around the Cape of Good Hope to Boston, making the first voyage of an American vessel around the world. He landed in Boston, August 10, 1790.

Meanwhile, the Russians had been gradually staking out their claims to Alaska, and about the beginning of the last century they made treaties with England which conceded to them the Alaskan coast down to fifty-four degrees forty minutes of north latitude. At that time it is said that Russia had a great ambition to control the Pacific, and that it was her aim to grab the whole of California and the Hawaiian Islands as well. Baranof, the Russian who founded Sitka, had fur trading stations as far south as where San Francisco now is, and actually owned the farm which later came into the hands of John Sutter, on which gold was first discovered in California.

Eight years before our national capital was moved from Philadelphia to Washington Baranof established at Kodiak the first Russian colony. Among the settlers were a number of convicts, of whom he made fur-traders and farmers, controlling them with an iron hand. He was small in stature, but he had the qualities of a Napoleon, and it was due to his management and organization that Russia got such a foothold on our continent. He had many fights not only with the Indians but also with his own people. At one time, when one of the colonists at-

37

tempted to assassinate him, he grabbed hold of the hand holding the weapon and then strangled the man to death with his own hands.

In 1799 he moved his headquarters to Sitka, and three years later, while he was absent, the Indians massacred the Russians, killing all of the officers and thirty men. Only five Russians escaped. The Indians built a fort of logs and defied the Russians, but Baranof came back with a gunboat and starved the Indians into submission.

Baranof then moved the site of Sitka eight miles, to where the town now is. About the time he came to Sitka there was formed the Russian Fur Company, a monopoly backed by the government, the Czar, and the Empress, and many of the nobility. Baranof continued to manage the territory until 1817, when, through political trickery, he was deposed. He left Sitka and died on his way home at Batavia, Java, in 1819.

During the time of Russia's ownership much of the Alaskan coast was explored. The Yukon River was opened up as far as the mouth of the Tanana by Lieutenant Zagoskin, and Kotzebue went through Bering Strait and discovered Kotzebue Sound on the Arctic Ocean north of the Seward Peninsula. The delta of the Kuskokwim became pretty well known, likewise the southern coast, including the Panhandle, the Gulf of Alaska, the Alaskan Peninsula, and the Aleutian Islands.

Complications, however, were arising with the British, who, under the Hudson's Bay Company, were pushing their trading stations from the Mackenzie River on to the Yukon. Russia became anxious lest her American holdings should fall into the hands of Great Britain. At the time of the Crimean War she offered to sell us Alaska, but President Pierce refused to become a party to the transfer. The matter was again taken up when Buchanan came in, at which time an offer of five million dollars was made by us and declined by the Russians. The negotiations were continued, but the Civil War was then brewing and the pro-slavery element would not agree to the purchase of any more territory that was likely to be non-slaveholding. The subject was dropped until after the close of the war.

It was in 1863 that the Western Union Telegraph Company planned to build a land line across North America to Asia, and a little later they sent exploration parties down the Yukon and over the Seward Peninsula to Bering Strait and into Siberia. They explored the Yukon Valley and brought forth much new information regarding Alaska. They were about ready to push their line through when the Atlantic cable proved successful. Meantime, an increased interest had sprung up regarding Alaska. The negotiations for its purchase were resumed, and, to cut short a most interesting story, Russia offered to sell the territory to us for about two cents an acre. The actual figure was seven million dollars, with an extra two hundred thousand to settle the claims of the Russian residents and to pay the cost of the transfer.

Late one night Baron Stoeckl, the Russian ambassador at Washington, came to the house of William H. Seward, our Secretary of State, and told him that he had just received dispatches from the Czar authorizing him to sell Alaska. Secretary Seward was playing whist at the time and the Ambassador said that he would come to the State Department on the morrow to make the treaty. Secretary Seward replied: "Why should we wait until tomorrow, Mr. Ambassador? Let us make the treaty to-night."

"But the department is closed," replied the Russian. "You have no clerks, and my secretaries are scattered about the town."

"Never mind that," said Secretary Seward. "I can easily get the necessary clerks, and if you can bring together your legation by midnight you will find us awaiting you at the department, and we will settle the business."

To this the ambassador consented. They met at twelve o'clock at the Department of State and by four in the morning the treaty was engrossed, signed and sealed, and ready for transmission to the Senate. Within a month it had been approved and Alaska was ours.

Up to that time the territory had been known as Russian America. It needed a new name, and all kinds of ridiculous titles were suggested. One was "The Zero Islands," another "Andy Johnson's Polar Bear Garden," another "Seward's Ice Box," and a fourth "Walrus-sia." The treaty was called the "Polar Bear Treaty" and the senators who favoured it were dubbed the Eskimo senators. The name "Alaska" was finally chosen at the instance of Charles Sumner, who said that it was the title which the natives used. Translated, it means "The Great Mainland."

The ceremony of taking possession of Alaska was performed here at Sitka on Friday, the 18th of October, 1867. Two hundred American soldiers under General Jefferson C. Davis took their position on the east side of the flag-staff near the castle, and an equal number of Russian soldiers were lined up opposite them. It was three thirty o'clock in the afternoon when the Russian captain ordered his men to haul down the Russian flag. The men tried to do so, but it had caught in the ropes and would not move. A Russian soldier climbed up to bring down the flag. He tried and failed. Another man tried and did not succeed. A third soldier climbed up and got it, but it slipped from his hands, was caught by the wind, and fell on the bayonets of the Russian soldiers. The incident was so affecting that the Princess Maksutoff, who was present with the Russians, wept, and the soldiers were visibly moved.

Following this, "Old Glory" was hoisted, and the American gunboats in the harbour and the Russian battery on shore fired salutes. Prince Maksutoff, the Russian commissioner, then stepped forward and said to General Rousseau, the American commissioner: "By the authority of His Imperial Majesty the Emperor of Russia, I transfer to the United States the territory of Alaska." Prince Maksutoff then handed over the insignia of his office as governor, and General Rousseau made a speech accepting the transfer. That was all. With less than two hundred words Alaska's allegiance was changed and a new empire was added to Uncle Sam's domain.

Let me tell you briefly what we got for that investment in land at two cents an acre. Alaska is a world in itself, an unknown world at that to most of us, though every man, woman, and child in the United States is a part owner. The territory, which has an area of nearly six hundred thousand square miles, contains more than one sixth of all the land under the American flag. If Alaska could be lifted up and dropped down upon the main body of our country, with its eastern end touching the Atlantic Ocean at Savannah, the westernmost end would be in the Pacific beyond Los Angeles. Beginning not far west of Los Angeles, the territory extends Uncle Sam's dominions almost to Japan. Nome is three thousand miles west of San Francisco; and the mainland of Alaska is less than forty miles from Siberia at Bering Strait. The Island of Attu, at the end of the Aleutian chain, is not far from Asia. From north to south, Alaska reaches almost as far as the distance from Canada to Mexico.

This mighty territory is a world in the variety of its lands, its resources, its climates, and its waters. It is a country of seas, lakes, and rivers and of almost as many islands as the empire of Japan. It has a vast continental mainland with mountains and valleys, rolling plateaus, and great lowland plains. The navigable waters of its rivers reach many thousands of miles.

Alaska has the highest mountains on the North American continent. It has some of the greatest glacial fields upon earth, and scores of its peaks never lose their snow. McKinley, which kisses the sky at over twenty thousand feet, is the tallest mountain north of the Isthmus of Panama. A little farther east is Mount St. Elias, which is eighteen thousand feet high, and about Mount Wrangell, in a territory not three fourths as big as Massachusetts, there are ten snow-clad peaks twice as high as Mount Washington and two which are higher than Mont Blanc. The Alaskan Range runs around the whole southern coast and has a width here and there approximating eighty miles. The Range has several low passes, and one of these, Broad Pass, is only twenty-seven hundred feet above the sea. It is from six to eight miles in width and it forms an easy way for Uncle Sam's new railroad into the great central valley.

THE STORY OF "SEWARD'S ICE BOX"

Like the senators who ridiculed Secretary Seward when he purchased Alaska, we are apt to think of it in terms of the North Pole—of mountains of ice and of perpetual snow. We have read of the terrible cold, where the thermometer falls to seventy degrees below zero; of the reindeer and dog teams flying over the snow, and of the Cimmerian darkness of the long winter nights. The truth is, Alaska is a world in its climates. Only one fourth of the country lies inside the Arctic Circle. Parts of it are as temperate as Tennessee or Kentucky, and Southeastern Alaska, a region larger than Maine, has a winter climate milder than that of Washington city. The great Yukon Valley, a land of rolling plains and plateaus, has winters like those of Montana and northern Dakota, and the summers of the whole territory are not far different from those of Ohio, Indiana, and Virginia. In midsummer I found the whole land covered with a dense vegetation, and it seemed to me that if any part of it could be set down into the main body of the United States the change would not be recognized.

There is such crass ignorance concerning the climate of Alaska that I shall say a little more about latitude. Take the city of Seward, the terminus of our new railroad. That town is no farther north than Petrograd, and it is not nearly so cold in winter. Juneau, the capital of Alaska, is in about the same latitude as Edinburgh, Scotland, and is, I venture, by far the warmer. The same is true of Sitka and Copenhagen. The whole Scandinavian peninsula is within the latitudes of Alaska, and some of the Aleutian Islands are farther south than Birmingham, England, Berlin, Dublin, or Warsaw. Ketchikan and Moscow are on about the same parallel.

43

CHAPTER VI

THE THLINGETS AND THE HYDAHS

THE Alaskan Indians are of half-a-dozen different stocks. Those I have seen most in my travels in Southeastern Alaska are the Thlingets, an Indian family scattered throughout the whole of this part of the country. There are four or five thousand of them divided among a dozen or more tribes, including the Auk, the Chilkat, the Kake, the Sitka, Stikine, Tongass, and Yakutat. The Klukwans are Thlingets and so are the Hunas. These people are semi-civilized, and nearly every tribe has its own church and school. And then there are the Hydahs, numbering five or six hundred, and the Tsimpseans of Metlakahtla. The Athapascans, who number about four thousand, are divided into twelve tribes and may be seen all along the Yukon and Tanana rivers. The Aleuts, of whom there are about fifteen hundred, are closely allied to the Eskimos. They live in the long island chain extending from southwestern Alaska almost to Asia, and are fishers and hunters. The finely woven baskets made by their women show that they have some artistic ability.

The Indians of Alaska look far more like the Chinese and Japanese than like the Red Men of the States. They have yellowish or light brown complexions. Their eyes are a trifle slanting, and their cheek bones are as high as those of the Mongols or the inhabitants of Thibet

44

The Russian cathedral at Sitka is famous for its chimes and its valuable
paintings, many of them embellished with precious stones. It refused
twenty-five thousand dollars for this Madonna and Child, called "The
Lady of Kazan."

The Chilkat blankets, originally made only for chiefs, are always of three colours—white for the wool from which they are woven, black for the Crow clan, and yellow for the beak of the patron bird of the Eagles.

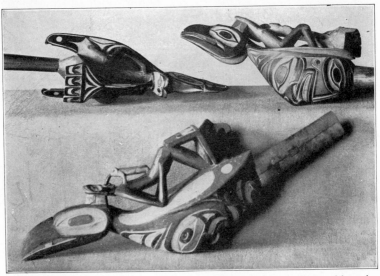

The Indians once thought that the evil spirits causing disease could not be exorcised without noise of rattles like these. Before beginning his work the witch doctor always took a drink of native paint.

THE THLINGETS AND THE HYDAHS

When they are dressed like white men it is difficult to tell them from the Japanese who come north to work in the fish canneries, and it is a question whether they did not originally come from Asia, crossing from Kamchatka in their canoes to the Aleutian Islands and making their way to the Alexander Archipelago. Bering Strait is only fifty or sixty miles wide, and there are two islands in the midst of it, so that it would have been easy for the Chukchi and other Mongolian tribes to cross over from Asia to the mainland of this continent.

Some of the Indian customs here are the same as those that prevailed in Japan before it adopted western civilization, and it is not hard to imagine that these customs may have come down from their Mongolian ancestors. For instance, when I first visited Japan, every widow shaved her head as smooth as a billiard ball to show that she was mourning for her husband. She also stained her teeth black to make herself unattractive. The widows of the Thlingets shaved their heads the same way until the missionaries taught them better, and they even painted their faces black as a sign of mourning. The black used was a water colour, and if this were streaked with tears it brought the widow respect because of her grief for her dead husband. Cremation is common in Japan. It was for years practised in Alaska. The Chinese will undergo any privation to have a good funeral. The Alaskan Indians do likewise.

In Southeastern Alaska I have seen many of the Thlingets. These Indians are found on the coast and in the islands of the Panhandle, their settlements extending as far north as Prince William Sound. They are the Indians best known to the tourists, and their totem poles or tribal

45

emblems and coats-of-arms, although gradually disappearing with the advance of civilization, are still to be seen in the villages. The Thlingets always build their villages near the shore; since nine tenths of their support comes from fishing, they like to live right on the beach. Nearly every family has its boats, while some families even own gasoline launches. Their houses are usually scattered about, without regard to any fixed plan. It is only lately that any of them have had gardens. In the past the buildings were made of rude slabs and bark thrown together over pole rafters. No house had a chimney or window and the smoke passed out through a hole in the roof. Now, most of the houses are shingle-roofed, comfortable frame dwellings with windows and chimneys. Some of them are ceiled, and some are papered and painted. The Indians have become good carpenters and use modern tools. The newer buildings show some regard for sanitary requirements, and a few of their towns have plank sidewalks and electric plants.

In Klukwan the Indians have piped the water from the mountains and established a municipal water system. Klukwan is a village of the Chilkats, on the Chilkat River not far from Skagway. The town is said to be three hundred years old and to have once had a population of a thousand souls. Its people were traders, exchanging dried fish and oil for furs with the Athapascans of the interior. The Chilkats are great trappers. They have divided their hunting grounds among the various families and the hunting rights descend from generation to generation. They have been noted for their skill in the various industries. They wove blankets a century ago. They also forged copper and did beautiful carving. Much of

46

this skill departed upon the advent of civilization, but they now make moccasins and cut out miniature totem poles and other things for the tourists.

The settlement of Klukwan has a flourishing coöperative store, which is so good that it gets much trade from the whites, and it is said that the Indians come a distance of a hundred miles to buy there. The town has its men's club, which holds meetings every week, when matters of town interest are discussed.

The Government is trying to induce these Indians to go into canning and some canning machinery has been sent there. The school teachers advise that a sawmill be installed. They say that the boys are quick to learn carpentry, and they are now making chairs, tables, and sleds in the school shops. Recently they began to work in sheet metal and to make airtight stoves.

The work of civilization among the Indians has been promoted by both missionaries and school teachers. The missionaries came first. They established schools, industrial and otherwise, and converted the Indians to Christianity. After the missionaries came the United States Bureau of Education, which has taken charge of the natives of Alaska. Beginning with the establishment of schools in all of the villages, it has added many other kinds of social service work to its activities. The teachers are now instructing the adult Indians in sanitation and civil government. They are inducing them to establish stores and to engage in all possible self-sustaining industries.

So far the most remarkable progress has been among the Hydahs, a tribe of five or six hundred Indians on Prince of Wales Island. On the government reservation there they have built a town called Hydaburg, which is perhaps the most advanced Indian community of the world. The natives have organized a coöperative trading company paying big dividends to the stockholders. In 1911, when the settlement was first organized, the par value of a share in the Hydaburg Trading Company was ten dollars. Ten years later the accumulation on each share, including the stock dividend and the purchase dividend each year, amounted to almost two hundred and fifty dollars. The company now owns, besides its store, a saw-mill, a cannery and dock, a moving picture outfit, an automobile truck, and equipment for electric lighting.

Nearly every family in Hydaburg has stock in this trading company, and the people are rapidly growing well-to-do. Many have gasoline launches and all have comfortable homes. The town elects its own officers. It has a mayor and councilmen and the business of the place is transacted in English.

One of the first coöperative works was the building of a sidewalk. There was no money in the village treasury, but the young men brought in the proceeds of their season's fishing, and the Indian girls had a basket social. Two hundred and ninety dollars were realized from the food sold. This bought the lumber, and the men gave their labour for nothing. That sidewalk is the best in Southeastern Alaska. It is ten feet wide and more than half a mile long.

Since then the citizens have erected a municipal dock four hundred and forty feet long, with a front of fifty-five feet. The coöperative store has created a hunger for business training, and business methods are taught in the school. The village has town meetings at which all

48

One of the government teachers reports that he has supervised the making of seventeen native school gardens inside the Arctic Circle. At a fair at Nulato two-pound potatoes were exhibited by proud child gardeners.

Under the leadership of the United States Bureau of Education the Indians now manage their own coöperative stores. They patronize the candy counter so much as to injure the teeth of the rising generation.

The tendency of the Alaska Indian is to dress more and more like the whites, but the native garb and regalia are still often seen. Indian women are by no means slaves and frequently control the family purse.

matters of public interest are discussed and the popular vote determines what shall be done.

The Hydahs are not Thlingets. They belong to a different Indian family, and for a long time their only home seems to have been on Queen Charlotte Island off the coast of British Columbia. Later some of them moved to the west coast and about two hundred years ago, according to their traditions, they drove the Thlingets out of a part of Prince of Wales Island and settled there. They have always been considered superior Indians and have had the reputation of being the best painters, carvers, and canoe builders of Southeastern Alaska. In the past they hollowed their canoes out of single logs of cedar, and built houses of cedar beams and planks, which were worked out with adzes of stone. At one time there were something like eight thousand of them, but during our possession of Alaska the number in the United States territory has never been more than six or eight hundred.

Among the other movements to better the Indians of Alaska is that of school farming. Both children and adults are shown how to make gardens, and some of the villages are growing vegetables and berries of various kinds. One of the teachers reports that he has supervised the making of seventeen native gardens inside the Arctic Circle.

The Government is doing all it can to improve the sanitary conditions among the Indians. The teachers are cleaning up the towns and the doctors and nurses of the Bureau of Education go from village to village and give directions for the care of the sick as well as instruction in how to keep the well healthy. It is estimated that thirty per cent. of the natives have consumption in some form or stage and that eight per cent. of the deaths are due to tuberculosis.

Of late a number of the squaws have taken to feeding their infants from the bottle. Since they know nothing about the preparation of this baby food, many of the children come out of the nursing stage feeble and scrawny. The school children are examined for trachoma, adenoids, and other diseases. They are taught to take care of their teeth and are warned against the use of tobacco and alcohol.

Alcohol has been the curse of the Indians of Alaska. It is said that before the coming of the Russians they knew nothing of liquor in any form. But they soon acquired the art of brewing and drinking, first the Russian *quass*, and later American whiskey. Its sale to the Indians has long been forbidden, but there have always been some whites willing to make money by supplying the natives with whiskey.

The Alaskan Indians try to imitate the whites in many ways. They are now dressing much the same, except that they delight in brighter colours. During my trip we have had a number of Indian men and women with us on the steamers. The other day a young squaw sat down at the table opposite two travelling salesmen from Seattle. As the meal went on they noticed that the girl's orders were the same as their own. She was pretending to study the menu, but they concluded that she could not read and that this was her first experience with the white man's victuals. Thereupon, one of them ordered for his dessert a slice of custard pie and winked at his friend to do the same. The squaw in her turn gave a similar order. When the pie came one of the travelling men seized the catsup bottle and sprinkled a liberal allowance of hot tomato sauce over his pie. His friend followed suit and then shoved the catsup across the table to the copper-skinned girl. She did the same, only more so. The men stopped eating to watch the agony of the Indian. The fair squaw, however, heroically finished her pie without winking, and, as far as any one could see, the joke was on the salesmen.

CHAPTER VII

TOTEM INDIANS AND THEIR CUSTOMS

IN SOUTHEASTERN Alaska a curious survival of the old Indian customs is seen in the totem poles which the natives used to put up before each house and often over the graves of the chiefs and heads of families. These totem poles are neither tombstones nor idols, and they were never regarded as such by the Indians. They are tribal crests or coats-of-arms, of which the natives are as proud as are the nobility of Europe of their emblems of heraldry. The Indian can read the story of a totem pole as easily as we read a newspaper. He knows just what each sign means, and where the tribal sign ends and the individual signs begin. The totem in front of a house tells him not only who lives there, but also the story of the owner's ancestors. Similar crests are used on baskets, on moccasins, and in carvings of wood, stone, and copper. If a native had a letterhead he would probably print some of these signs on the top of the sheet.

One of the former curators of the Sheldon Jackson Museum at Sitka says that the totem pole was invented by the Hydah Indians, and that it was of three different kinds. One kind was erected in front of a house. This had the figures of different animals, and represented the totems of a family and their relatives. Another was called the death totem. This was often a hollow mortuary post

Members of the Bear, the Whale, and the Frog families are buried under their respective totems in the native cemetery at Klukawn. Their memorials are carved of marble quarried near by.

The breast bone of the mallard duck furnishes the design, and totemic emblems the decorations, for the best Indian boats. This old canoe was adapted by the white man for mail delivery.

which contained the ashes of the dead and was sometimes erected over the grave. A third class of totem poles was put up by the Hydahs to memorialize remarkable events. These totems were historical records and their story was told by series of carved figures—a sort of picture-writing. The Hydahs were divided into three classes: the rich, the middle classes, and the slaves. The slaves were never allowed to erect poles in front of their dwellings, and the higher the pole, as a general rule, the richer and more aristocratic the owner.

The totem poles about the dwellings of the Indians range in height from that of a man to that of a four-story house. They are carved out of solid tree trunks, and some of the larger ones are valued at several thousand dollars apiece. Many of them are beautifully carved, their ugliness being that of design rather than execution. Most of the carvings are of animals and birds. The house poles indicate to which of the two great families of Southeastern Alaska the inmates belong. These are known as the Eagle and the Crow. Each has its subdivisions, which are shown by subtotems. To the Eagle family belong the subdivisions of the Bear, Wolf, Shark, Whale, and others; and to the Crow family belong the Seals, Frogs, Salmons, and Beavers. There are numerous other subdivisions, but they all belong either to the Eagles or the Crows.

According to the unwritten law of these Indians, a husband and wife cannot be of the same tribal family. A Miss Crow must always expect to marry a Mr. Eagle. It is perfectly proper for her to unite with a Shark, Whale, Wolf, or Bear, for they all go back to the Eagle family, but she cannot marry a Salmon, Seal, Frog, or Beaver, who descend from the Crow.

Some branches of the families so divided are much more aristocratic than others, and a woman who marries beneath her is considered to have disgraced her family. She is more despised than an English duchess who marries a shopkeeper, and at her death her relatives will not chip in for as costly a funeral as though she had married in her own class. A daughter of one of the Brown Bear divisions would be shamed by a marriage with a son of the Mouse or the Snail, while the Crows and Eagles at the top of the genealogical tree can marry only one another.

Another curious thing is the high position that woman has always held among these Indians. She rules the family. No bargain is made, no journey is undertaken, no important thing done without consulting her. On the totems the emblem of the wife is at the very top of the pedigree pole, and the totem of the husband comes lower down. Any Indian, on seeing the totem pole, can tell the family of the mother and knows that it rules the house. If he belongs to the same family he is sure to be welcome, but otherwise he thinks awhile before he risks stopping.

I am told that most of these Indian families were founded by women. The Bear family started with a chief's daughter, who, according to the legend, was out one day with some other girls picking strawberries. A great bear came up and all of the girls but the chief's daughter ran away. She put her hands on her hips and laughed at him. Thereupon the bear ran after the other maidens and killed them. He fell in love with the girl who had scorned him and made her his wife. The fruit of the union was a child half girl and half bear, who became the maternal ancestor of all the natives now belonging to the

Bear totem. Another story tells how a family originated with a female grizzly bear, and a third of how a woman founded the tribe of Woodworms.

The Indians love a fine funeral. They will take what they have and borrow more from their friends to spend in making a great show. They put the favourite possessions of the deceased with the body and clothing and bedding alongside the coffin. After the funeral is over they give a great feast in honour of the departed, eating the food which is supposed to nourish his spirit as it goes to the other world. In Southeastern Alaska it rains so much and the soil is so shallow that the Indians do not bury their dead in graves, but put them in little wooden vaults that look like tiny houses set upon poles. In the early days, before the coming of the missionaries, many of these Indians burned their dead, depositing their ashes in hollow poles. Among some of the tribes the ashes and bones left after the cremation of a body were put into a sack which was kept in the family dead house.

Indeed, these and other customs, myths, and folklore of the Alaskan Indians are so interesting that our Government should put its scientists to work gathering a record of them before it is too late. We need some such work in Alaska as Frank Cushing did among the Zunis and James Mooney among some of the Indian tribes of the West. What we have concerning the natives of Alaska comes largely from missionaries, and from Ivan Petroff, who wrote a great part of the census of 1880. Mr. Livingston F. Jones lived for twenty years among the Thlingets and got his information concerning them at first hand. His book, "A Study of the Thlingets of Alaska," gives legends of the Crow, Deer, and other families, and includes traditions of many of the tribes. The Whale family, for example, is said to have originated from an Indian boy who amused himself by carving images of whales out of cedar and sailing them upon the waters. One day one of his cedar whales expanded before his eyes and turned into a real live whale, which swam away. From this fact his parents knew he would become a great chief, and he did not disappoint them, for he founded the Whale tribe, branches of which are scattered throughout Southeastern Alaska.

The Thlingets have legends concerning the origin of man and telling how the sun, the moon, and the stars came to be. According to their story of the flood, all the men and animals were destroyed with the exception of a raven. This raven was a sort of witch bird. He could change himself at will and put his feathers off or on like a garment. When the flood had gone down, he looked about for a mate of his own kind, but could find none. At last he took a cockle-shell from the beach and called it his wife. By and by he heard a faint cry from the shell like that of a baby. The noise grew louder and louder, and at last a little female child came out. This child married the raven and from the two came all of the Indians of this part of the world, and so the country was peopled.

The raven is held sacred among the Thlingets, who in the past considered him a god. He was known as Yehl, the creator of the world. He was the benefactor of mankind and enjoyed the greatest respect. His power was unlimited. He put sun, moon, and stars in their places, and from him came man, animals, and plants. Before he was born the world was dark; but with him came light.

TOTEM INDIANS AND THEIR CUSTOMS

Few people realize the change that has been brought about among these Indians through the work of the missionaries and the bringing in of our civilization. Cannibalism was common along the coast of British Columbia when Father Duncan came. Slavery existed among the Thlingets at the time we took possession of the territory, and Ivan Petroff in his report for the Government on the condition of these Indians in 1880 said that able-bodied slaves were slaughtered on festive occasions, and that it was not uncommon for a rich man or chief to have slaves killed and buried with him, in order that he might have servants in the spirit land. There are Indians living in Alaska to-day who were slaves in their youth, and it is said their children are looked down upon by the families which have always been free. The slaves were of two classes—those captured in warfare and those born into bondage. The children of slaves became slaves in turn, waited upon their masters, did all sorts of menial work, and were cruelly treated. Not infrequently they were sacrificed to emphasize the power and wealth of an owner, who thus showed that he could afford to destroy such valuable property.

Before the missionaries came polygamy prevailed. To-day marriages are usually held in the churches. Monogamy is common, and even the chiefs seldom have more than one wife. In the past some of the heads of the tribes had as many as twenty wives. A Russian authority speaks of a man on the Nass River who had forty. In such cases the first wife ruled the harem. Child marriages used to be common, and even now marriages take place at an early age. One of the old Thlinget customs was to pen up the girls in some out-of-the-way place as they reached the marriageable age. A wooden coop or jail was made for the maiden where she was kept for from four months to a year. There was no light in the coop except what filtered through the cracks, so that when the door was opened the girl came out pale and wan and supposedly humble and ready for marriage. The marriages were usually arranged by the relatives, and the girls were carefully restrained from making any advances to the men.

Mr. Livingston Jones says that infanticide was not uncommon. Twins were considered bad luck and were often killed at birth. The usual method of killing babies was to stuff their mouths with moss or grass, and they were usually carried into the woods to be put to death. This was done by the women, generally the relatives of the mother.

Mr. Jones tells some queer stories of how the natives received the white man's civilization. When they first saw a steamboat they thought it was a demon and took to the woods. They called it a fire canoe and thought it might bring some terrible disease, such as smallpox. To ward off the danger they pulled up certain native vegetables, which they held below their eyes as they looked at the steamboat. They went wild over the phonograph when it came and paid a quarter to hear a single tune. When the first negro came north they advanced all kinds of theories as to what made him black, and when they saw a man with a wooden leg they regarded him with great wonder. Another curiosity was a man who had a wig, which he put on and off, and a still greater marvel was a store keeper who had a set of false teeth. The Indians flocked to the store, and their amazement knew

58

no bounds when they saw him take out of his mouth a set of uppers, gums and all, and then replace them. The natives came in from many miles around to see the wonderful sight, aud the storekeeper found his "set" an excellent business getter.

CHAPTER VIII

FARM LANDS OF THE FUTURE

I HAVE just had my first view of the practical possibilities of Alaskan farming. Our Agricultural Department's experimental station at Sitka is the headquarters from which the four other experiment stations are managed. One of these is at Rampart, on the Yukon River, near the Arctic Circle. Another is near Fairbanks, in the rich valley of the Tanana, in the heart of Alaska; a third is on the Island of Kodiak, not far from Seward; and the fourth is in the Matanuska Valley, which is being opened up by the government railroad. Kodiak is bigger than Porto Rico. Its specialty is stock raising and dairying. The Fairbanks station, which is in the centre of a great agricultural region, is devoted to all-round farming. Rampart is so far north that it forms the best place for experiments in raising oats, barley, and wheat for planting in cold lands. At Matanuska grain, hogs, cattle, and potatoes are raised. The government farm at Sitka lies under the shadow of Mount Verstovia, about a quarter of a mile from the town. The experiments here are chiefly in raising vegetables, berries, and small fruits. This is because of the character of Southeastern Alaska, which, though a region of rich vegetation, is better adapted to small farms and truck gardens than to large-scale farm operations.

I wish I could show you the vegetation of Southeastern

50

Small fruits and vegetables in southeastern Alaska grow to twice the size usual in the States. It is believed, however, that Alaska farmers' truck gardens will be limited to supplying local markets.

On the way to Mendenhall Glacier cows pasture on rich grass in the shadow of snow-capped mountains. This section of Alaska should some day have many small farms.

Pea crops like this raised on a farm near Sitka prove conclusively that Alaska lands are ready to yield bountiful harvests, needing only cultivation to make them wonderfully productive.

Alaska. For the last month I have been travelling along the coast and in and out among the islands, and the flowers and trees are a series of surprises. The topography of the country is much like that of the Alleghanies or the Blue Ridge, but the forests are thicker and the growth is denser. Nearly everywhere the bushes are so thick that it would be impossible to make a way through them without an axe or a knife. Beginning at the water's edge, the forest runs to the snow line about a thousand feet above the sea. For that distance the trees are choked with undergrowth; but above it the heavy vegetation disappears, and a carpet of grass or moss stretches up to the edge of perpetual snow.

Everywhere in the forest there is spongy, ankle-deep moss. Many of the trees are hung with mosses, and the bushes beyond the tree line seem to bend over and cling to the ground, bowed down, I suppose, by the heavy snow which lies upon them during the winter. The chief trees are evergreens. There are many spruce, and red and yellow cedars, including a vast deal of timber which would make wood pulp and which in the future will probably supply the newspaper demands of the States. The Indians use the cedar bark to make rope, and they tear out the inner part of it and weave it into baskets and cloaks.

And then the wild flowers! They grow everywhere. There are Alpine geraniums, goldenrod, and buttercups, and bluebells with cups an inch long. There are yellow violets and red daisies and lilies as black as ink. There are rosy laurel and pink bryanthus and little blue forget-me-nots such as we have at home. Southeastern Alaska has three varieties of orchids and other air plants as well.

This is a land of berries. The salmonberry, which is ripe throughout the summer, is twice as large as the largest raspberry, and tastes much the same. There are also raspberries that grow on the ground and cranberries of several varieties. There are wild strawberries and blueberries and red huckleberries. Strawberries are raised commercially at Haines and are shipped to Juneau and other towns.

As to the cultivated parts of Southeastern Alaska, they are so few at this writing that they are hardly worth mentioning. Coming up from Seattle the tourist does not see a dozen farms bigger than a bedspread; and in most places the land is so steep that it reminds me of West Virginia, where it is said the corn is planted with shotguns from the opposite hills. Nevertheless, back in the valleys are little cultivated patches where the pioneers have cleared off the dense timber and set up their homes. Professor C. C. Georgeson, who is at the head of the government agricultural experiments in the territory, tells me that there will eventually be many small farms scattered throughout this part of Alaska. He says that they will grow up to supply the mining centres with vegetables and fruits. He does not expect them to come soon, believing that it will be the task of a generation or so to clear the forests and take off the moss. He thinks the coast region is best adapted to gardening, chicken raising, and dairying, while the natural-grass meadows may be utilized for stock raising.

Small farms are already growing up about many of the fishing stations. One of the best of these is that of C. A. Burckhardt, the president of the Alaska Pacific Fisheries at Yess Bay, just north of Ketchikan. He tells me that he raises rhubarb with leaves as big as a parasol and stems the length of a baseball bat and quite as thick. He grows strawberries four inches in circumference.

Mr. Burckhardt, who spends only his summers in Alaska, takes his Jersey cow, Daisy, back and forth with him each season. She was first brought up on account of Mr. Burckhardt's baby daughter, and the experiment worked so well that Daisy has spent her summers in the North ever since. She seems to know when the time has come to flit southward. She goes on board the ship without urging and thrives under these changes.

At the Sitka experiment station there are acres of strawberries and raspberries and orchards of apples, cherries, and apricots. The strawberries are finer than I have seen in any part of the United States or Europe. The plants are vigorous and are loaded with fruit. I saw some berries almost as big as hen's eggs and many over an inch in diameter. These big berries have been produced by cross-breeding the wild native plants with other strawberries brought here from all parts of the world. There are now several thousand different kinds of strawberries growing at the station, but nearly all of them have more or less Alaskan blood in their veins. I wish you could taste them. They are strawberry all through. Only a few have a tart flavour, and most of them are so delicious that they fairly melt in your mouth. The plants are much hardier than our strawberries and bear for about two months, yielding fruit as late as September.

Among the other experiments going on at this station is the crossing of salmonberries with the raspberry. The salmonberry, which is as big as the largest blackberry, is red or pale yellow. It is delicious to taste, and is used in great quantities all over Alaska. Raspberries also will grow well almost anywhere, and the crossing is successful, although the new fruit partakes more of the flavour of the salmonberry.

The station is also breeding apple and cherry trees that will grow in parts of the territory, and is making experiments with filberts and other nuts of the hardier varieties. The most surprising things on the farm are its pansies, poppies, roses, and other beautiful flowers. Among the pansies now growing are many as big around as the bottom of a tumbler, and some are as black as ink and as soft as silk plush. There are also roses of exquisite perfume and poppies of the most brilliant red and as big around as a tea plate. These poppies, which come from Asia and are perennial, are among the new wonders of Alaska.

I went over the experiment farm with Director Georgeson. There is no man better fitted by ability and experience for his position. When I met him in Japan years ago on my first newspaper trip around the world, Mr. Georgeson, then a professor in the Imperial College of Agriculture at Tokio, was introducing modern farming into the land of Japan. Born in Denmark, he had been trained in farming on some of the large estates of that country before he came to the United States.

For more than twenty years Professor Georgeson has been in charge of Uncle Sam's farming interests in Alaska. He has travelled all over the territory, studying its soils, its climate, plant life, and farming possibilities. He has been the manager of a half-dozen different experiment stations and has combed the world for grasses and plants suited to this part of the United States.

We were loking at some alfalfa grown from seed im-

The mills and forests of the United States cannot supply the demand for newsprint. Yet in southern Alaska there are billions of feet of spruce and other woods suitable for paper making growing on slopes accessible to tidewater.

A large part of our northernmost territory still remains unexplored, so that one may have the thrill of starting off with packhorse and supplies on a trip into the uncharted wilds.

ported from Siberia, when I asked Professor Georgeson to give me his idea of the future of Alaskan farming. He replied:

"There is no doubt that Alaska will some day support a large farming population. I see no reason why the territory should not eventually have a stable population of three millions or more. We are discovering new plants and grains every season. This alfalfa, for example, will grow all along the Yukon, and we have made successful experiments with it north of that river. I estimate that Alaska has about one hundred thousand square miles that can be used for agricultural purposes. That means that it has sixty-four million acres, or an agricultural area as large as the states of Pennsylvania, Maryland, Delaware, New Jersey, Connecticut, Massachusetts, Vermont, and New Hampshire. It must not be understood that all this land is available for cultivation, however, for the estimate includes about fifty thousand square miles which will have little value except for grazing purposes.

"Of this territory about fifty-seven million acres lie in the interior beyond the coast range of mountains. The other seven million acres are in the coast region and on the islands near by. Each section will have its own crops based on its soil and climate. Some of the islands will be devoted to grazing and dairying, while from the gardens of Southeastern Alaska vegetables will be shipped to Seattle and command a higher price than the Puget Sound produce on account of their superior quality. Indeed, such shipments are even now being made."

In answer to my question whether Alaska would ever raise dairy products for the United States, Professor Georgeson replied:

"There is no reason why it should not. The climate of the Aleutian Islands is so mild that in many years hardy cattle and sheep can stay out all winter or be kept over with a small amount of hay and fodder. We can also raise cattle in the Yukon Valley, though there they have to be fed during nearly eight months of the year. In the interior grass grows as high as my head, and our experiments have shown that it is possible to raise many varieties of hardy grains."

"Tell me something about the soil of Alaska. How does it compare with that of the best parts of the United States?"

"The best soil of our Middle West," replied Professor Georgeson, "can be duplicated in very few places on earth. I doubt whether Alaska has any agricultural area equal to that. The country has no prairie lands, and there are no extensive bodies of uniform quality. Still, some parts are excellent for farming. The silt loam of the Tanana Valley will compare in productiveness with some of the best soil to be found elsewhere, and we have at the Fairbanks station land excelled only by the rich prairie soils of the Middle West. There are good lands in the Matanuska and Susitna valleys, and, in fact, there are millions of acres that can be made into farms."

"Where will be the farming centre of Alaska?"

"There will be many such centres," said Professor Georgeson. "Farms will spring up about every important mining settlement. Fairbanks is the largest of the gold camps to-day and that region has the most and best farmers. Since the Government decided to build the railroad two or three hundred families have located homesteads in the Matanuska Valley with a view to supplying

the demands of the coal mines of that region. There are
a number of successful farms in the neighbourhood of
Seward and many small ones about Juneau, which is
another mining centre of great importance. There are
little places scattered throughout this part of the territory
and, indeed, wherever there is a local market you will find
a farm centre. These will grow, and as new settlements
are established other farms will be opened up."

"Would you advise Americans to come to Alaska to
engage in farming?" I asked.

"Yes, if they understand the conditions and know what
they are going to find when they reach here and are ready
to stay and grow up with the country. I would not
advise people to rush in pell-mell and take up homesteads wherever they can be found simply because Uncle
Sam will give them a farm for nothing. The would-be
speculators will stand a slim chance of making money by
a rise in land values. There is no land for sale, and
Uncle Sam is the sole owner. He will give his real estate
only to bona-fide settlers who will keep on the job. The
farmers most likely to succeed are the men who know the
climate and what crops can be grown. Norwegians and
Swedes and Finns have been brought up under conditions
such as we have here. They are used to long winters and
short summers; they understand the methods of culture
necessary, and they are, I believe, best suited to the
country."

"How much money should a young man have who
wishes to take up a homestead? Give me some idea of the
cost of clearing the land."

"The right young man might come to Alaska without
any money and make a success," said Professor Georgeson.

"But in that case he would have to work for wages for other farmers or in the mining camps to get sufficient to live on until his farm paid. His path would not be an easy one. On the other hand, if he had a thousand dollars or so he could buy a team of horses or yoke of oxen and some farm tools. He could put up a modest house and furnish it.

"He might still have to work out occasionally, but he could soon clear enough land and get a sufficient start in cattle, sheep, and poultry to make life on the farm practicable. Such a man should locate on land that is already surveyed by the Government, and he should investigate the cost of implements, furniture, and freight before starting. He will find the freight rates high. The average price from Puget Sound to Fairbanks has been about sixty dollars a ton, but the rate via the new government railway, in carload lots, will, it is thought, eventually be only half this much. If the man could have four or five thousand dollars it would be still better, but with that amount of money he could make a fair start almost anywhere in the States.

"There is one thing that should be well understood," continued Professor Georgeson, "and that is that the settler must have enough muscle and skill to do most of the work on his own farm. If he starts out paying wages for clearing land he will soon be bankrupt. The wages of Alaska are governed by those paid in the mines of the interior, most of which are usually much higher than wages in the States. Sometimes it has cost us as much as one hundred and twenty-five dollars an acre to clear land on the experiment station farms."

Even oil is included in the mineral wealth of Alaska. The petroleum lake shown here is in the region of Point Barrow, the northernmost tip of our continent.

Clouds float down the mountain wall behind the city into the main street of Juneau, a centre of the mining and fishing industries, buzzing with politicians, lawyers, promoters, and tourists.

CHAPTER IX

LEAVING Alaska's old capital, I have come on to Juneau, the capital of to-day and the biggest city of the territory. It is a great mining and fishing centre and a live, up-to-date place. Here are the residences of the governor and the chief officials, whose offices are in an old frame structure not far from the governor's mansion, and here the territorial legislature meets every two years. Juneau has also a pretentious frame courthouse of two stories with a little dome on the top, and a city hall with a cupola that reminds one of the head of a pearl diver in his diving suit, ready to drop into the deep.

Most of the houses of Juneau are of frame. The country about is covered with timber, and there are great sawmills at the wharves that supply the building materials. Of late, however, concrete structures have been going up.

The Juneau of to-day has only three thousand inhabitants, but every man in the town is a hustler, and the place hums with politicians, lawyers, tourists, and miners. The crowd is of all classes and costumes. Some of the men wear clothes of the latest cut of Broadway or Fifth Avenue, while others wear slouch hats, mackinaws, and khaki trousers. Some have on boots that reach to the

69

knees, and now and then you meet one in white rubber pantaloons.

Drays, automobiles, and carriages move about through the city and a motor stage runs to the mining town of Thane three miles down the channel. At that place are the mills and reduction plant of the Alaska Gastineau gold properties. Near by are the Juneau gold mills, and on the other side of the channel, in plain view, are the Tread-well mines, with the towns of Treadwell and Douglas around them.

Juneau is beautifully situated on the mainland, at the head of the Gastineau Channel, a narrow strait which separates it from Douglas Island. The channel connects Stephens Passage with the Lynn Canal, at the northern end of which is Skagway. The harbour is so good that all of the ships that pass through Alaskan waters, excepting those plying between Seattle and Nome, call here. During the summer there are boats north or south every day and tens of thousands of tourists pass through.

The town is right on the water, with wooded mountains rising almost perpendicularly behind it to a height of perhaps two thousand feet. I have seen cliffs of this height in other parts of the world, but they were mostly straight walls of gray, red, and black rock, as bleak and bare as the Desert of Sahara. The walls behind Juneau are covered with a vegetation as green as that of the Valley of the Nile.

The city is cut out of the rocks or, rather, it is propped up by them. Most of the houses and streets stand upon stilts. The irregularities of the rocky foundation have been overcome by a trestlework of piles. The wharves are on piles, and from the channel as the tide falls they look like an army of centipedes tramping out to the ocean.

It is now planned to fill in the space between the piles with the waste rock dust from the gold mills, thus giving Juneau a substantial foundation. In the town of Douglas, over the way, a beach of such tailings was made along the edge of the channel and the baseball grounds are laid out upon them. Millions of dollars have come from the sand lying inside that diamond.

The streets of Juneau consist of more than ten miles of planked roadways running up hill and down. They give no spring to the feet, and your hips keep bobbing up to your waist and tire your anatomy. Both the central wooden roadways and sidewalks are so tipped that the water runs off into gutters of wood. As such streets are costly and need constant repair, the plan is gradually to replace them with a macadam of the gold-mine tailings.

The business section runs parallel with the channel. Close to the docks are sawmills, lumber yards, sheet-metal works, and machine shops, and farther back are long streets devoted to stores, banks, and shops of all kinds. The town with its department stores, cigar factories, daily newspapers, and thriving banks does a much larger volume of business than would be handled in a place several times its size in the United States.

Chicken Ridge, the Nob Hill of Juneau, is at the upper end of the city, well back from the water. The residents are not in love with the name and talk of changing it to Bellevue or Bon Air, or some other less plebeian title. The houses are pretty two-story frame structures built on patches cut out of the rocks. The richest man in the town has a lawn about as big as a parlour rug, which tourists are taken to see as one of the sights of the city. Other fine homes are still higher up and some of them cling to the green wall of the mountains. When I made a call last evening upon the editor of one of the Juneau papers I had to climb a pathway several times as high as that which leads to the Tea House of the One Hundred Steps above Yokohama, Japan.

These houses of Juneau have no double windows or other special arrangements for winter protection. Nevertheless, the people tell me they have no trouble in keeping warm. The thermometer seldom falls below zero, and the heavier water pipes are laid on the top of the ground. The chief complaint is of the long nights and the short days. In midwinter the electric lights have to be turned on two or three hours after noon, and it is not daylight until nine o'clock in the morning. In midsummer there are but few hours of real darkness. Up to ten o'clock at night one can go anywhere without lights, and the dawn comes between two and three o'clock in the morning.

The winter climate here suits even the Negroes, those children of the tropical sun. I had my shoes shined this morning by a coloured bootblack whose stand is on the main street. He charged me fifteen cents for the shine, and told me that in the interior I shall have to pay not less than a quarter. As he worked I asked him if the winter did not chill his African blood. He replied "no," adding that the winters here are quite as warm as those of Baltimore, where he was born, and that most of the time he does not need even an overcoat. He has lived four years in Alaska, and has worked as far north as Anchorage, the railroad town on Cook Inlet. He complains that Juneau is a poor place for bootblacks, except in the summer. The winters have so much rain that the people go about in oilskins and rubbers and no one wants a shine.

I am living at the Hotel Zynda, a concrete five-story building not far from the courthouse and the governor's residence. It has some rooms with baths and an elevator that runs now and then—usually then. Like most of the Alaska hotels it has no dining room, and I have to walk two or three blocks to the restaurants. The food is excellent and comparatively cheap. As these Alaskans have big appetites, the caterers make their portions generous. One order of chops or steak is sufficient for two people, and a single order of cracked crab is more than one man can eat. The crabs here are as big around as a dinner plate and delicious. The menu is *à la carte*, and as many of the dishes are given French names as the vocabulary of the restaurant keeper will permit. Among those on the bill of to-day, for instance, were "consommé en cup" and "beefsteak en platter." The waiters were good-natured girls from Sweden.

Many summer visitors, less informed than I was, bring to Alaska a great supply of unnecessary clothing. They load up with furs and overcoats only to find that the interior of the country is roasting and that the children are going about with bare feet. A party which went down the Yukon this season had nothing but heavy woollens along. Their steamer ran aground on one of the islands where they were stranded for five days with the thermometer at ninety degrees in the shade.

The same ignorance prevails as to the food of the country. The multimillionaire president of a gold-dredging company of the Klondike brought a load of fresh meats and vegetables with him to Dawson for fear he would suffer. When he got there, he found at the hotel everything he had on his ship.

They tell a story here of one of the merchants of Cordova, the ocean terminus of the Copper River Railroad, who ordered some woollen goods from a Minnesota mill through an agent in Seattle. The goods should have arrived within thirty days. Upon their failure to come, the agent wrote the Minnesota firm and received the reply that the order had not been filled, as navigation was already closed and there was no use in making any shipment to Alaska at that time of the year. The truth is that Cordova is right on the Pacific Ocean and ships call there every week the year round.

A Chicago man recently said to an Alaskan, who was telling stories about his country: "I can believe everything but what you say about the mosquitoes. There can be no mosquitoes in a land where there is so much ice and snow." Any one who has travelled in Alaska in summer knows that the country abounds in mosquitoes, and that at times it is impossible to go anywhere in the woods unless every bit of one's skin is protected.

Many of our people evidently think that the Klondike belongs to Alaska and that Dawson is one of its cities. This ignorance extends even to some of the government officials at Washington. Not long ago one of the big executives of our Post Office Department sent a letter of censure to the postmaster at Dawson because he had not been submitting his reports to the department at Washington. He told the postmaster that the Dawson office would be closed unless a report was submitted at once. The postmaster replied that Dawson was the capital and chief city of Yukon Territory, and that its reports went only to the Canadian Government at Ottawa. The incident occasioned great laughter in this part of the world and the Dawson agent thought so much of it that he had the letter framed and hung up in the post office.

To give another instance: One of the clerks of our Treasury Department once wrote to an official at Sitka, when that town was the capital, that the Treasury had very few blanks of the kind Sitka had asked for, but that the Alaska official might easily run across to Nome and get some, as Nome had a double supply. Now, Nome is as far from Sitka as New York is distant from Omaha. The only way is by sea, the voyage is as long as from New York to Liverpool, and the steamers go once a month.

Few people appreciate the distances in Alaska. By the ordinary summer routes it is from eighteen hundred to two thousand miles from Juneau to Fairbanks. Nevertheless, a merchant of the latter town told me that he had received a letter from a Boston firm, saying that they had drawn upon him through a banking establishment at Juneau.

Another citizen of Fairbanks ordered a well-known dictionary, consisting of ten or eleven volumes, which had been extensively advertised in the magazines. The man sent the money and asked that the books be delivered at Fairbanks. A month or more afterward he received a letter saying that the books had been shipped him from the publishers' Canadian branch, the company evidently thinking that Fairbanks was in Canada. The result was that the books were held at the international boundary for duty and have not yet been delivered.

Another amusing story belongs to the time of the boundary dispute between the United States and Canada.

75

When the subject came up in Congress a senator wanted to know "when the Lynn Canal was dug and who dug it." When it is remembered that the Lynn Canal is one of the great fiords of the North American continent and that it was ploughed out by Nature in the prehistoric past, the fund of information of the questioner can be appreciated.

A letter received at Juneau from a Philadelphia firm in response to an order for certain goods to be sent C. O. D. stated that the Philadelphia firm could not send goods C. O. D. to foreign countries.

Whatever the degree of ignorance about it "outside," Alaska is far from lacking in culture. I am surprised at the number of college men I run across in Southeastern Alaska. More than half of the professional men are graduates of colleges, and Juneau has a thriving university club. The majority are from western institutions, but Yale, Harvard, Princeton, and Cornell all have their representatives. The graduates of the University of Washington at Seattle came to dinner together on one occasion and thirty-five sat down to the table.

The public schools of Juneau are good. The high school has its business branches with courses in public speaking, mechanical drawing, sewing, and cooking. It gives its graduates certificates admitting them to the University of California and other Western colleges.

I came here expecting to find a population of men only. The sexes are almost equally divided. Many of the women have come as school teachers, or as clerks or stenographers, and have married. Some of the young men have gone back home for their wives, and the girls who are born here usually stay. The population is not transient, as is often supposed. I meet daily men who have

The Governor of Alaska has his official residence at Juneau where the Territorial legislature meets. Administration is seriously hampered by the leagues of red tape extending from a score of government bureaus at Washington four thousand miles away.

The streets consist of more than ten miles of planked roadways laid up hill and down. It is planned to replace them with macadam made from the tailings of the gold mines of Douglas and Treadwell.

The mills of the Gastineau mines are said to be the largest and most modern gold-crushing plants of the world. The machinery is designed to get the maximum of the gold specks from the rock with the minimum of labour and expense.

been in Alaska from fifteen to thirty years, and find young men and women who expect to spend their lives here.

There is much civic spirit in the town, which believes in municipal ownership. It owns and operates the principal wharf and it has a fuel depot where it supplies coal to the city. This municipal establishment has at times had a marked effect in keeping down the price of both coal and gasoline as sold by local dealers. The city has also aided in the building of a cold storage plant with a freezing capacity of eighteen thousand pounds a day and storage rooms for fifty thousand pounds of fish.

CHAPTER X

TREASURES UNDER THE SEA

MY TYPEWRITER is clicking away on the roof of the modern Cave of Aladdin. The rock underneath me has been cut up into tunnels, which wind about in a maze more complicated than the labyrinth of Rosamond's Bower. Some of the passageways go far out under the ocean and others have been cut for miles through the mountain. Out of them have come treasures far more valuable than those brought by the Slaves of the Lamp, and from them to-day a long procession of genii is continually marching, bringing out fresh gold from the caverns under the hills and the sea.

I am speaking of the Treadwell and Alaska-Gastineau mines situated on Douglas Island in the Gastineau Channel and on the mainland opposite. It is these properties which have given to Juneau the name of the Golden Belt City and made for her a place among the gold centres of the world. The rocks in these hills have yielded something like eighty millions of dollars, or more than eleven times what we paid for the entire territory.

There are in Alaska two kinds of gold mining—placer mining and quartz mining. In placer mining loose bits of gold, ranging in size from tiny grains to big nuggets, are washed out of gravel or sand, usually in or near the bed of a stream. The gold mining around Fairbanks and

Nome is of this character. In a quartz mine there are lodes, or veins of hard rock sprinkled with specks of gold, which must be ground to powder before the gold can be extracted by chemical process. Such ores are known as high or low grade, according to the amount of gold recovered from a ton of rock. The mines in the Juneau district, the most important quartz lodes yet found and worked in all Alaska, consist of low-grade ores. Nevertheless, they have produced more than four fifths of all the quartz gold mined in the territory.

These Juneau mines are among the most famous gold properties, being the first where paying quantities of gold were separated from such low-grade ore. Much of the ore in the Treadwell group contains less than two dollars' worth of gold to the ton, and of the millions of tons which have been mined the average has produced only two dollars and forty-two cents per ton. The Gastineau mines are an even lower-grade proposition, the average there being only one dollar and a half per ton.

Have you any idea of what gold ore carrying only one dollar and a half a ton means? Gold is worth twenty dollars an ounce, and at that rate a dollar and fifty cents' worth of gold would equal only about one thirteenth of an ounce. Divide a twenty-dollar gold piece into thirteen parts and no part will be as big as a pea. Nevertheless, that pea of gold is all that is to be found in one whole ton of this ore. A ton of ore is a cartload for two horses. Grind your pea into the finest powder and put one of the grains of that powder into every bit of rock in the cartload and you have some idea of how the gold is scattered through the rock and how difficult it is to get it all out.

Or suppose the gold to be salt, and the ore to be water. I went to a drug store to-day and weighed out enough salt to just equal the weight of the gold in a ton of this ore. The salt did not fill a teaspoon. But a ton of water would fill a two-hundred-and-fifty-gallon hogshead. Now, if you should drop your spoonful of salt into the hogshead and churn up the water until the salt is thoroughly mixed through it all, you would have just the proportion of gold and rock in some of the mines of which I am writing. Think of getting the pea made of gold powder out of the cartload of rock in such a way that half of it will more than pay all the costs, and you have the problem which the operators of the Gastineau mine successfully solved.

Obviously, in times of high prices for chemicals, supplies, and labour, these mines, like other low-grade properties, cannot be operated at a profit, and are forced to close down until prices drop and the buying power of gold goes up, or until cheaper ways of treating the ore are found.

But before I go further let me tell you something of the romance of these properties. Immediately back of me on the side of the mountain is the great Glory Hole, on the site where the first gold was discovered. It is several hundred feet above the Gastineau Channel, and far down the slope of the mountain, the upper portions of which are now covered with snow. The Glory Hole is a mighty ellipse eight hundred feet long, six hundred feet broad, and more than six hundred feet deep. The Washington Monument could be dropped down inside and its aluminum tip would still be fifty feet from the top. It could be laid lengthwise within it and the ends would not touch the sides. The walls of the Glory Hole are of black rock streaked with drab and gray, while here and there is a string of white quartz from which comes the gold.

As I looked down on it, a great rock slid off the top and went crashing down to the bottom. It was from such rocks that the mine got the name of Glory Hole. Miners were often killed by them and thus transported to Glory. Strange to say, many of the deaths were due to crows, which made the neighbourhood of the Glory Hole their favourite roosting and feeding place. They were so numerous that trumpeters were stationed about the hole to warn the miners of danger in case a flock should light on the edges. The first blast of the trumpet meant, "The crows are now lighting," and the second warned the miners that the rocks were loosening and would soon be down upon them. A slight pecking of the gravel overhead was liable to start an avalanche that would carry tons of rock down the sides.

Even now the Glory Hole is by no means safe. The earth and the rock about it have not yet reached their equilibrium, and slides like those in the Panama Canal sometimes occur.

The richest ore of the Treadwell mines was found at the top. Like cream, it seemed to have risen from the low-grade gold-bearing rock underneath. This ore was discovered by a Canadian whose nickname was French Pete and whose real name was Pierre Erussard. When Juneau and Harris were making their gold finds on the opposite side of the Gastineau Channel, and beginning to prospect Douglas Island, French Pete came along with some Indians. He washed the sands on the beach and found colour. A little later he climbed up the hills to where the Glory Hole is and there discovered an outcrop of gold-bearing quartz upon which he located two claims. He named one claim Paris where he expected to spend the great treasures he had discovered, and called the other Bear's Nest, because it was in a little cave occupied by a bear and two cubs. French Pete then started mining, but had nothing more than rockers and sluice pots and could crush and wash only the softer parts of the lode. He did not get enough to pay well, and a little later on sold the mine to John Treadwell for the sum of five hundred and five dollars to pay a pressing debt.

John Treadwell, who had come to Alaska at the instance of some California capitalists, had been prospecting in the Silver Bow basin, back of Juneau, and had found quartz gold in the belt where the Ebner mine now is. But the gold was poor, and he was about to give up in despair and go back to San Francisco when he met Pete and learned of his discovery on Douglas Island. He went to see the claims, but did not think much of them, as the ore seemed to be of too low a grade to pay for the mining. He suggested, however, that Pete should give him a quit-claim deed for the two properties for five hundred dollars, and he would try to sell them to the capitalists of San Francisco. Pete had a store, and the understanding was that if the mines were opened the miners would trade at his store. This was an additional consideration, and so for five hundred dollars was sold this property from which have already come more than sixty millions of dollars.

The stock was floated in San Francisco and Treadwell got one third of it. The other owners were large capitalists, among them D. O. Mills, much of whose fortune came from this source. Later on the Rothschilds of London bought into the property, and to-day the mine is owned by the Mills estate, the Rothschilds, and other rich men.

From the start the mines were operated with large capital. The first excavations were in the Glory Hole, out of which five million tons of gold-bearing rock have been taken. About fifteen years ago the first underground stoping was done, and then began the tunnelling of the earth and the work altogether underground. I cannot tell you just how many miles of underground works there now are, but the mining goes on for a long distance up and down the Gastineau Channel and far out under the ocean. The ore is lifted into great shafthouses, from which it descends by gravity to the mills. The ore bodies dip toward the channel, and some of the tunnels have hundreds of feet of salt water overhead.

There are four mines in the Treadwell group—the Treadwell, the Mexican, the Seven Hundred, and the Ready Bullion. The first three suspended operations in 1917 when a cave-in flooded the workings.

One month after French Pete made his discovery a handful of prospectors landed on Douglas Island. One of them scooped up a pan of gravel from the foot of what seemed to be an outcropping of a quartz lode and washed it out. When he saw what a find he had made, he exclaimed, "We have it, boys, almost the ready bullion!" And so was christened the mine which I went through yesterday with Mr. Russell G. Wayland, assistant manager of the Treadwell properties.

We climbed into a five-ton steel bucket as big as a hogshead and held on to the rim. Then an electric signal was given and we shot down into the darkness. The great bucket wobbled this way and that as we fell. Our descent was at an angle of about fifty degrees. We continued at that angle for something like two thousand feet, after which the fall was even more precipitous. At last we stepped out far under the sea. With acetylene lamps we picked our way through the tunnels and stopes. The tunnels were lighted by electricity and each of them had its railroad. We walked between the tracks, stepping now and then to the side, and squeezing ourselves to the wall to let the ore trains pass. These trains were of cars drawn by mules. At one place we passed a mule stable, and I was told the mules were kept down in the mines for several years at a time. Those I saw were fat and not at all vicious. The darkness does not affect their eyesight, as is generally supposed.

I stopped now and then in the stopes, or great caverns, where the miners were blasting the ore. They use drills operated by compressed air to sink the holes for the dynamite, and thus blast out great rooms away down under the water. These stopes are several hundred feet high, and of almost an acre in area. Some of them are filled with gold ore nearly to the roof. Nevertheless, only a slab of rock lies between them and the ocean.

Leaving the mines, I went through the mills, where they were crushing the mighty masses of rock to powder and saving the small quantities of gold. The red buildings may be seen from the ship's deck as one rides up the channel. They wall the sides of the hills and as one comes near them a noise like so many blasts of artillery fills the air. Inside the din is furious. You may shout into the ear of the man at your side but you cannot make yourself heard. You cannot even hear your own words. "Niagara is a soft hum beside Treadwell," said John Burroughs.

A few miles back from the coast of southeastern Alaska are countless lakes and waterfalls, most of them of glacial origin, which will some day be put to work to furnish power for paper or other mills.

Many of the icebergs are the size of a New York office building. Such baby fellows as these on the beach of Taku Inlet are lassoed by steamers for their ice chests.

The noise is from the hundreds of stamps, which are always falling upon the ore to pulverize it. As the ore comes in, it is of all sizes from that of the broken stone of a macadamized road to masses as big as a flour barrel. The larger chunks are broken until fit for the stamps. These reduce everything to a powder as fine as the finest flour dust.

As one of the mills was not working, I was able to examine the stamps. Each consists of a long steel beam as big around as the arm of a man fitted into a mighty steel shoe eight inches in diameter and perhaps a foot long. This shoe is fastened to the end of the stamp, and the stem and shoe together weigh about half a ton. In crushing the ore, the stem is raised and dropped on the ore one hundred times every minute. Think of dropping a half ton upon rock every time your watch ticks and you have a slight idea of the power that grinds this ore. There are hundreds of these stamps working at once, and as you look at them you do not wonder at the racket. This smashing goes on day and night, Sundays and week days, all the year through.

The wear and tear on the machinery is enormous. The shoes are of solid steel. Each of them is twice as big as a loaf of bread, but it is worn to the thinness of a knife blade after it has crushed three tons of ore. The iron block upon which the ore lies is soon ground away and has to be replaced for every five tons.

The process of getting the ore out of the gold dust after the crushing is simple. In front of the stamps is an apron of netting made of wires put together in a mesh finer than that of any kitchen sieve. As the ore is crushed a stream of water carries the flour dust through the mesh and it falls on to inclined tables of copper coated with quicksilver. Now, quicksilver has an affinity for gold, and as the powdered ore flows over it it swallows the free gold and the rock sand passes on. After a time the quicksilver becomes loaded with gold. It is then scraped off and put into a furnace, where the heat vaporizes the mercury and the pure gold only is left.

In addition to this free gold there is some in the baser minerals found in the rock. These minerals are taken out on shaking tables and then treated to a cyanide bath, which sucks up the gold just as water takes up any salt dropped into it. The cyanide water is then put through a process which makes it give up the gold.

CHAPTER XI

THE WORLD'S GREATEST GLACIERS

ETWEEN Lynn Canal and Seward there are
more than five thousand glaciers. Hundreds
of them come down to the sea and twenty-
five are now dropping icebergs into the tide-
waters.

With the exception of Greenland and Antarctica
Alaska is the greatest glacier region of the world. It has
many glaciers in the southeastern part of the territory,
some of the biggest of which can be seen in a ride of four
or five days from Seattle on a comfortable steamer. I
am now in the Lynn Canal on my way from Juneau to
Skagway. My ship has been moving in and out among
icebergs of crystal sapphire right up to the precipitous
ends of these ice rivers that are slowly flowing down the
sides of the mountains. Now and then the tide leaves
icebergs on the shores, and the tall pines bend over and
sweep them with their branches.

Looking through my stateroom window, I can see a
wall of snow-capped mountains green almost to their
tops. Just opposite me is a great field of ice upheld
between two lofty peaks. That field is miles in width
and slopes upward into the clouds. It is a glacier.

The true glacial region of Alaska begins a little beyond
the international boundary and runs from there along
the coast as far as from New York to Chicago. It skirts

the ocean and extends for a hundred miles or so back into the interior.

Most of the glaciers are north and west of Skagway within an area about one hundred miles wide and five hundred miles long, a region perhaps as large as New York State. This does not comprise one tenth of Alaska, but it is that part of the country most frequented by tourists, whose stories have given the idea that the territory is nothing but mountains of ice.

The interior of Alaska is comparatively low; the coast glacial region is rugged and high. Many of the mountains are lost in the clouds and some of them kiss the skies at an altitude higher than any other part of the continent. They are so high, so steep, and so cold that they precipitate the moisture rising from the warm ocean currents that wash southern Alaska, and give the snowfall that has built up the glaciers and keeps them alive.

Let me show you some of these big ice masses. Taku Inlet is a fiord eighteen miles long walled with steep mountains and guarded by islands. In steaming up it one can count forty-five glaciers. At the end is the Taku, the front of which, where it enters the sea, is a mile wide and more than two hundred feet high. At a little distance from the sea the glacier is two miles wide and it continues to broaden for about eight miles, until it is lost in a great ice field close to the boundary of British Columbia.

The Taku Glacier is a live glacier—that is, it is moving down to the ocean and dropping great bergs into the sea. It is travelling at the rate of eight or ten feet a day and some of the masses which fall from it are as large as a city skyscraper. Close by, so near that it can be photographed by a swing of the camera, a dead glacier shows out gray and dusty on the other side of the hill at the west. This is about a mile wide but it seems to end at the shore.

It was at five o'clock in the morning that I had my first sight of the Taku Glacier. The sun was already two hours high, and its rays catching the icebergs floating about in the inlet turned them to enormous sapphires. There were hundreds of these blue masses through which our steamer pushed its way to the face of the ice wall. It took us right up to the glacier, so that we were within six hundred feet of the ice when we stopped.

At that moment the sun came out of the clouds and shone full on the glacier, which became one vast expanse of silver frosted with diamonds and sparkling with sapphires. A moment later, with a deafening report, a great fragment of ice broke off and the face of the glacier looked like a mighty cutting of the whitest ice cream, while the berg fell into the water and rose up a gigantic floating mass of aquamarine.

As we anchored the wind came to us over the glacier. It had been warm in the inlet, but here the icy breath of Jack Frost sent a chill to our bones. It was so cold that I could hardly write.

The face of the glacier is ragged. Its top has hundreds, I might say thousands, of peaks, some of them as sharp as spires and others broken and shattered. It reminds one of the relief map of a rugged mountain range. The ice is melting and now and then, with a noise like thunder, a great mass plunges off into the water. The shooting of a cannon would bring down hundreds of icebergs, and the vibration of the air caused by the blowing of our steam whistle never failed to send an avalanche of ice into the water.

The captain of the *Humboldt* gave a number of salutes to show the effect of the sound. As the shriek of the whistle tore the air, immense blocks began to drop from the glacier. As the whistle continued to blow there was crash after crash, and at one time a mass as big as a New York office building broke away and splashed down into the ocean. It buried itself in the water, throwing a mighty spray almost to the top of the glacier, and causing great billows to roll out to the steamer. A moment later it rose to the height of a hundred feet above the sea and moved up and down on the surface of the water.

As the mountain of ice fell I said to the captain of the *Humboldt*, a giant of a man, "You remind me of Joshua who commanded the trumpets to blow and the walls of Jericho fell."

The scenery of the glacier was so beautiful as to be awe-inspiring. It brought out expressions of wonder from the tourists. I remember especially the words of one woman who stood at my elbow. She said:

"My, ain't that grand! It reminds me of the drop curtain at our opery house. But there ain't no polar bear here."

As the great ice mass fell into the water a man—he may have been a restaurant keeper—remarked:

"Gee, what a lot of ice cream a man could make out of that bunch!"

The ice as it comes from the glaciers seems pure enough for ice cream or even lemonade. The ships sometimes fill their ice chests by lassoing the smaller bergs and hoisting them on board. For a long time considerable business was done in picking up this ice and selling it to the mining camps and towns. About fifty years ago glacier ice was shipped from southern Alaska to San Francisco at seventy-five dollars a ton, and a little later contracts were made at thirty-five dollars.

Not far from the glacier we saw a large deer swimming about in the water. Our steamer passed within two hundred feet of him, and a Texan on board said he could have lassoed him from the deck. The deer had magnificent antlers. Its horns and head rose above the water and its body could be seen close to the surface. It was still swimming as we moved onward and we saw some hunters near the shore start out to catch it. They chased the animal this way and that, and finally dragged it into their boat.

From Juneau I rode out in an automobile to see the Mendenhall Glacier. The moraine of this mighty ice mass lies within nine miles of the city. One can leave the liveliest section of the liveliest town in Alaska, surrounded by mines and mills, by stores and banks and the other activities of business men, and within less than an hour be in the heart of the wilds and in the shadow of one of the most famous glaciers of this wonderful territory.

Think of going to a glacier by automobile! I have climbed Vesuvius by a wire cable and have crawled up the Rigi by the famous cog-railway, but this was my first experience in shooting a moraine in a gasoline car. I went as the guest of Mr. B. H. Behrends, the banker of Juneau, a man who, as they say down South, is the very "spi't an' image" of James Whitcomb Riley, and in good fellowship quite the equal of the Hoosier poet.

We rode from Juneau right into the woods. Trees from fifty to one hundred feet high climbed the steep walls about us, and elderberry bushes with trunks as big around as my arm brushed our wheels as we passed. The sides of the road were lined with ferns of a dozen varieties and wild flowers blue, red, and yellow. We passed through great beds of crimson fire-weed, and rode through thousands of lupins the hue of the sky. There were also wild carrots with their lace-like blossoms of white, and fuzzy yellow devil-clubs. In some places the grass was as high as my waist and the mountain slopes on both sides of the road were the greenest of green. The vegetation was more like that of the mountains of Java than I had expected to find in Alaska.

Our way was over the path of the glacier. The valley through which we went was once filled with its ice, but this has slowly receded, leaving the earth covered with cobbles and great boulders ground smooth and round in their long glacial ride. Nevertheless, flowers grow among the stones and their red and blue blossoms dot the landscape.

As we came nearer the glacier the size of the boulders increased. Some of them weighed many tons. They were of white and black granite with here and there some slate. In the windings of the valley we turned to the right and all at once came in sight of the glacier. The mountains on each side are as high as the crest of the Alleghanies and the glacier half fills the valley between. It juts out in a precipitous ice wall which runs back and gradually rises to the skyline until it seems to fill the whole space between the hills and to merge into the clouds.

Coming closer, we rode almost to the foot of the glacier. There we left the car and climbed over the rocks of the moraine to the edge of the glacial stream which flows along the foot of the ice wall.

Where Taku Glacier enters the sea its front wall is two hundred feet high and over a mile wide. Icebergs are continually dropping off into the ocean and a blast from a steamer whistle will break loose great fragments.

Mendenhall has slowly receded, leaving the earth covered with stones ground smooth by its movement. Nevertheless, flowers grow among the stones almost up to the edge of the corrugated wall of blue and white ice.

Out of the mountains guarding the coast come the ice rivers that make Alaska the greatest glacial region in the world which is readily accessible to the traveller. Juneau is only one thousand miles from Seattle.

Think of going to a glacier by automobile! Trees from fifty to a hundred feet high climb the steep mountain sides, and ferns and wild flowers line the nine miles of road from Juneau to Mendenhall.

THE WORLD'S GREATEST GLACIERS

The Mendenhall Glacier, where it bursts forth from the mountain, is about a mile wide. It is a huge corrugated wall of blue and white ice sloping upward into ice mountains which, in the distance, seems to be of carved marble. Its face is ploughed by deep furrows and pitted with many small holes which the guides tell the credulous cheechako, or tenderfoot, have been made by the ice worms. They say there are certain worms that live in the ice and are often caught and eaten by the starving miners. Indeed, they prove the story by showing a photograph of a miner actually chewing the worms which he is sucking from the ice. The man is real, but the "worms" are strings of spaghetti.

From the Lynn Canal westward, for a distance of four or five hundred miles, are to be found the greatest glaciers of Alaska. General Greely catalogued the names and locations of more than two hundred of them and G. K. Gilbert of the Harriman Expedition says the ice covers from fifteen thousand to twenty thousand square miles. Most of these glaciers are within one hundred miles of the ocean, the largest being on the south side of the coast range. There are eleven wide glaciers on Prince William Sound and standing on the street corner in Seward one can see glaciers all about on the sides of the mountains.

Nearly every Alaskan river has its source in a glacier. The tributaries of the Yukon and Kuskokwim are fed by ice masses. The Tanana, upon which the town of Fairbanks is located, is formed by the Chisana and Nabesna rivers, both of which rise in glaciers in the Wrangell Mountains, and the Susitna springs forth from a glacier of the Alaskan range. The Copper River is fed by glaciers and the railway which goes through its valley, connecting the Kennecott Mines with the sea, passes between the Childs Glacier and the Miles Glacier on its way to Cordova.

Glacier Bay, only a short distance from the end of the Lynn Canal, is a body of water fifty miles long with more than half-a-dozen glaciers of enormous size sloping down to it. The biggest is the Muir Glacier, named after John Muir, who discovered it. It is three miles wide where it enters the water, and the height of the ice wall is almost one thousand feet, seven hundred feet being lost in the bay.

The Muir Glacier is very lively. It has been supposed by some to move as much as sixty feet a day, but a fair estimate would be about one sixth of that speed. Very few of the well-known glaciers move more than a foot a day, although there are some in Alaska that move from five to ten feet. There is one in northern Greenland that is said to travel over four feet every hour. The movement of a glacier may be measured by laying stones upon it or by driving posts into the surface. As the mass slips onward the space between these posts and fixed points on the landscape shows how fast it is travelling.

In addition to the valley glaciers, Alaska has great ice fields or caps, such as the Malaspina Glacier, a sheet of ice larger than the state of Rhode Island. It has a front of about fifty miles as it faces the sea and runs thirty miles inland to the St. Elias range. It is really a vast plain, or plateau, of ice with lakes and rivers, and with hills and mountains of gravel. It is the biggest ice field on the North American continent although it is only a patch in comparison with the ice caps of Greenland and Antarctica. The Greenland cap has an area of over four hundred thousand square miles, being two thirds as big as the whole of Alaska. The ice sheet of Antarctica is supposed to cover about three million square miles. It is as big as the United States.

Some years ago the Malaspina Glacier was shaken by an earthquake which changed its whole surface, twisting the bed-rock and uprooting the timber for miles about. In 1912 a lake in one of the crevasses of the Miles Glacier burst through the walls of ice and hurled blocks weighing thousands of tons down into the river. A wave thirty feet high spread over the flats, and icebergs weighing many tons were jammed against the bridge of the Copper River Railroad.

CHAPTER XII

SKAGWAY, THE GATE TO THE KLONDIKE

IN THE days of the Klondike gold rush Skagway here at the head of the Lynn Canal was one of the most talked-of towns in the world. It was the chief gate to the rich new gold fields, and miners came by the thousands to tramp their way over the passes to the headwaters of the Yukon and thence float down to Dawson. A little later it became the terminus of the White Pass Railway, which was built when the gold fever was at its height, and runs from here to White Horse, the head of the navigation of the Yukon; as if by magic it sprang from a village of tents to a bustling city of wood and stone of fifteen thousand population. Most of these people were transients moving back and forth from the gold mines. Then the mines began to play out, and the blood of Skagway grew weak. The cream had been skimmed from the Klondike and the bottle was empty. The miners grew fewer and fewer, and the city dwindled and pined until it now has all told, only five or six hundred.

The saloons and dance halls have all disappeared. The hotels and rooming shacks have rotted away and many of the better class houses are vacant. The town has changed from a booming, wide-open community of gamblers, fortune hunters, and miners, to a staid little settlement living on the travellers who pass through on their way to Yukon Territory and the interior of Alaska, and on the tourists who come north by the thousands every season to view the glaciers and other scenic wonders.

The usual "tour of Alaska" is confined to the islands of the southeastern part and ends at Skagway. Many travellers make the excursion by rail to the top of the White Pass and return during the stay of their steamer in port. So far, not a great many have gone on into Canadian territory to Dawson, while those who make the long trip down the Yukon and across Norton Sound to Nome, as I have set out to do, are fewer still.

Many of the tourists, who mean to go no farther than Skagway, do not return with the steamer that brought them, but stay on for several days or even weeks. The place is fast becoming a summer resort. It has a mild climate, with much less rain than other parts of the Panhandle. In addition, Skagway offers no end of excursions on horseback, on foot, or by motor boat. This tourist travel will increase as soon as our people awake to the wonders of Alaska and know they can be warm enough, comfortably housed, and well fed while they enjoy them.

I can well see how Skagway got its title of the "Flower City of Alaska." Flowers are everywhere. One of the gardens I visited was that of Mr. F. J. Weber, who is in charge of the shops of the White Pass Railway. He has more than forty varieties of dahlias of every colour and tint. Some are snow white, some blood red, others of a delicate salmon. He has even blue dahlias of the deep hue of the mountains far off in the distance.

And such dahlias! The stems of some of the plants reached to a height of nine feet, and their blossoms were as big around as dinner plates. I took my two-foot rule and found that this was so by actual measure. One gorgeous purple blossom was nine inches across. Another, the Geisha dahlia, with blossoms of old gold and fiery red, measured more than ten inches from side to side. Indeed, the size of the flowers was so great that I had myself photographed standing at the roots of one of the plants to make the camera testify to the truth of my story. The stem reached so high above me that I could just touch the blossom, and, as I looked up, the flower seemed as big as a pie pan. Nevertheless, it grew from a bulb planted in the open just about two months ago.

Most of Mr. Weber's dahlias are growing, not in hothouses, but in beds in a lawn, and their only protection is a windshield, a wire fence walled with glass which faces the channel to keep off the cold blasts from the sea and the mountains. Among the other flowers I saw in this garden were marigolds five inches wide and red geraniums equally large. There were also Japanese gold-banded lilies with flowers as long as your hand. I counted nineteen such lilies on a single plant.

Just now great beds of white clover grow on the sides of the streets, and the hills are covered with bushes and wild flowers. Many of the residents have garden patches where they grow all the vegetables used by the town. I saw one patch of raspberries this morning which had bushes as high as my head and berries as thick as my thumb. I saw rhubarb with leaves as big as two pages of a newspaper and stems that reached to my shoulders.

I am staying at the Pullen House, a place which, it is said, has entertained more distinguished guests than any other hotel in Alaska. It is run by Mrs. Harriet Pullen, who came to Skagway in the days of the gold fever, landing on the beach with four children and seven dollars.

Now she has this modern hotel of twenty rooms with many baths and several acres of grounds. Around the main building are bungalows which may be rented by families or parties of friends. The lawn is planted with trees and flowers. In the middle of the mountain stream flowing through it is a little island and there are rustic bridges here and there, giving a pleasing Japanese effect.

This morning when I came down to breakfast I found beside my plate a blue-enamelled pan full of rich milk from which I skimmed the cream for my coffee and cereal. This is one of the special features of the Pullen House. Mrs. Pullen gets her fruit, vegetables, and dairy products from her three-hundred-and-twenty-acre farm, which covers the site of the old town of Dyea. She tells me she has forty acres in oats, which she is raising for grain-hay, and that she has already put her rye-hay crop in the barn. The barn, by the way, is one of the deserted houses built during the mining boom, when Dyea had something like ten thousand people. Other of the houses have been torn away to make room for the crops, and practically nothing of the once-thriving mining centre is now to be seen.

When gold was first discovered in the Klondike there were two roads, or trails, from the head of the Lynn Canal over the mountains. One started here at Skagway and climbed up through the White Pass to Lake Bennett, then went on down the Yukon to Dawson. The other began at Dyea, four miles away, and went over the Chilkoot Pass to the Yukon. At first Dyea had the lead over Skagway. It built an aërial tramway, running on a cable, that carried freight up the pass, although the passengers had to walk, or, as they say here, "mush it" up the sheer thirty-five hundred feet of Chilkoot Pass. As the cars rose into the air, upheld by the wire rope, they swung this way and that, and now and then some of the freight was spilled out. Once a car carried ninety-four hogs. The motion made them dizzy and seasick and half of them jumped out and were crushed on the rocks far below.

The building of the White Pass Railway sounded the death knell of Dyea. The inhabitants rushed to Skagway, where the new road began. Many of them left their houses without trying to sell them, and some abandoned their furniture. One family departed, leaving a table half set for dinner. All were crazy to get to the gold mines or to share in the prosperity which it was thought Skagway would have. After a short while all had left with the exception of a man named Emil Klatt, who took up a homestead on the site of the abandoned city, ploughed the streets, and laid out his fields among the town lots. He farmed there for years and became generally known as the Mayor of Dyea, although his only constituents were cattle and sheep. I do not think he made any money. At all events, he finally sold the property, which now belongs, as I have said, to Mrs. Pullen.

It is interesting to hear the Skagwayans tell of the days when their town was at the height of its drunken prosperity. It was, to use a slang phrase, "wide-open," having sixty-one saloons, each with its dance hall adjoining. There were neither courts nor police. At that time there was no law in Alaska under which a municipal government could be organized and the only representative of Uncle Sam was a deputy marshal. He was a rough character and was supposed to be in league with the

Skagway is named from "Skag-waugh," the Indian word for "cruel wind." The natives feared the icy blasts that blew down the canyon from the White Pass. It was the chief gateway to the Klondike goldfields.

The Fourth of July, with its eighteen hours of sunlight, is a big day all over Alaska. One of the events at Skagway is a tug-of-war between members of two rival Indian tribes.

Skagway deserves its name of the "Flower City of Alaska." It is no unusual thing to find dahlias as big as dinner plates blooming on stalks nine feet high. Other flowers grow with equal luxuriance, and even the rudest houses are surrounded in summer by brilliantly coloured blossoms.

criminal element. At least he did nothing to control it, and bands of thugs held up the cheechako and even robbed the old miners as they came from the Klondike.

A little later the criminal element was combined by one Randolph Jefferson Smith, who has a traditional fame here something like that of Slade of Mark Twain's "Roughing It." Smith got the nickname of Soapy in Colorado because he peddled soap which to the purchaser seemed to be wrapped in ten- and twenty-dollar bills. The game is a swindle well known throughout the West.

Arriving in Skagway about the time the United States declared war on Spain, Soapy got together four hundred of the vicious element of the place and offered them to President McKinley as a band of rough riders, ready to fight the Spaniards. The President, who had been posted as to their character, declined their services. Soapy then armed and drilled them and used them to prey upon the community. They robbed strangers singly and in crowds. They committed a number of murders and it was almost sure death to oppose them. The people were intimidated and there began a reign of terror that lasted for months. The gang had all sorts of ways of fleecing the miners who passed through on their way to the Klondike, as well as getting the gold of those who came back.

The advance agents of Soapy's gang would go to Seattle and come back with the crowd on the steamer. The passengers were mostly gold-seekers, each of whom had an outfit that had cost about five hundred dollars, besides enough money to get him to Dawson. Some had more, some less. Soapy's agents, who pretended to be miners, would organize companies with a view to getting cheap freight and would take from each member of the company an order to the ship to release his goods to the packers, or men who carried the goods over the trail. Upon landing the men would run the miners into Soapy's gambling saloon, where, within an hour, they were sure to lose all their money at cards. They then had not enough to pay their freight bills and as a result their outfits would fall into the hands of the gang. Captain Baughman of the S. S. *Humboldt* told me that it would take only about forty or fifty minutes after the ship came to anchor for the prospectors to land and lose all their money, and come back weeping and begging for a steerage passage home.

As time went on the robbers grew bolder and matters became worse and worse. Miners coming out from Dawson had their bags of gold stolen from them, and it finally became unsafe for any stranger in Skagway. Stories of the outrages went to the outside and hurt the town. The climax was capped by the robbing of a young miner named Stewart, who had just come from Dawson with a poke containing twenty-seven hundred dollars in gold dust. The man made a fuss, and prominent business men went to Soapy and asked him to give back the money. When he refused, a vigilance committee was formed. Soapy threatened to shoot upon sight any man that dared to attack him, and when four attempted to make an arrest he put his cocked rifle against the stomach of their leader, Frank Reid. Reid grabbed the gun and drew his revolver, but Smith pulled the trigger and the ball passed through Reid's body. At the same time Reid fired two or three shots in rapid succession, and one of his bullets pierced Soapy Smith's heart, while another wounded him in the leg. Before falling, Smith fired a second shot, striking Reid in the leg. Then both men fell, Soapy Smith stone dead and Frank Reid mortally wounded.

News of Smith's death sent his gang scurrying for the hills like jack rabbits. In their panic not one of his men thought of him and his body lay on the spot where it had fallen until two o'clock in the morning, when some women took it away.

I asked Captain Baughman, who knew Soapy Smith, what became of his money. The Captain replied:

"He spent it as fast as it came, and when he was killed he had nothing to speak of except about six hundred dollars of the gold dust he had taken from Stewart. This was found in a poke in his trunk. Soapy gave a good deal to the men who were with him. In fact, he was one of the most open-handed men that ever came to Alaska. He paid the expenses of many who went broke and helped them out of the country. If a man died, Soapy was always ready to spend several hundred dollars on groceries for his widow and children. He was free also in his gifts of money, while his orders for provisions to be sent to the poor were so generous that his trade was worth hundreds of dollars a week to several of the Skagway stores. This was one reason why some of the citizens said nothing against him.

"A few days before his death he was actually marshal of the Fourth of July. Even preachers sometimes asked his aid. They tell a story here of a young cheechako 'sky pilot' who once got Soapy to help him get contributions for some church work. Smith turned in with a will on the understanding that the minister should handle all the cash. When the sum seemed satisfactory to the outlaw, he sent one of his gang to steal it from the confiding divine. Another reason why his career was not interrupted sooner was the fact that Soapy's enemies had a strange way of disappearing and being nevermore heard from."

The Skagway of to-day is an orderly community with good schools, waterworks and sewers, electric lights and telephones, a daily newspaper and several churches. The chief business of the town seems to be the selling of curios to the tourists. There are a half-dozen stores that sell jewellery, carvings, moccasins, and baskets. The jewellery is made by the Indians, who pound it out of silver dollars. The carvings are of walrus tusks cut by the Eskimos, and the moccasins and baskets are manufactured by the natives about Skagway and in other parts of Alaska. None of these things is cheap. The best baskets, little ones that will not hold more than a quart, bring from fifty to one hundred dollars, while cigarette cases of the same character sell for fifteen dollars apiece. No basket of fine workmanship can be bought for less than eight or ten dollars. The best are made under water. They are of straw woven finer than the finest Panama hat, and so delicate and intricate that it takes several months to make a basket as big as the head of a baby. The best ones come from the Aleutian Islands. They are woven by the older of the Indian women, for the art is dying out and will probably pass away with this generation.

Most of the carvings come from the Nome Eskimos and the Indian settlements about the mouth of the Yukon, although some very good carvings are done by the Indians about Skagway and Sitka. The Indians make their own

Skagway's eloquent query as to the whereabouts of "Soapy" Smith in the hereafter was painted on a mountain boulder above the town. The rock later rolled down the steep slope, landing near the spot where the famous "bad man" was killed.

Mrs. Pullen landed at Skagway in the Klondike gold rush, a widow with three children and seven dollars. More distinguished men have been entertained at Pullen House than at any other hotel in all Alaska.

carving tools, grinding them out of old razor blades. In working they pull the instrument toward them, digging out the ivory after the style of the Japanese. This is just opposite to the way our carvers work.

The commercial photographer also reaps a rich harvest in Alaska with its wonderful scenery and its picturesque natives. I know of one photograph that has netted its owner five hundred dollars, and there are many steady sellers which bring in a good income every season.

CHAPTER XIII

OVER THE GOLD-SEEKERS' TRAIL

I HAVE just taken a trip over the first railway line ever built in Alaska. This is the "White Pass," which runs from Skagway over the coast range to White Horse, at the headwaters of the Yukon. The road was built at the height of the Klondike stampede to carry passengers over the mountains to where they could get ship for Dawson. The work was begun in 1898 and finished less than two years later when the first passenger train, a string of flat cars, brought out gold dust worth two million dollars.

The White Pass Railway is only one hundred and eleven miles long and, although not as expensive as the Copper River road of the Guggenheims, it cost millions to build. The first twenty miles cost on the average more than one hundred thousand dollars per mile, and there are sections which cost half as much more. During the construction three thousand five hundred men were employed, less than thirty of whom died or were killed on the job. The work went on right through the winter, and within eighteen months after the first pick was raised the trains were carrying thousands of passengers and millions of dollars' worth of freight down to the sea coast.

Beginning at Skagway at the head of the Lynn Canal, the White Pass Railway runs through the rocks along the winding valley of the Skagway River and up the steep slope of the coast mountains. Here and there the track hangs to the sides of cliffs so steep that the workmen had to be lowered in slings from above to drill and blast out the ledges for the road-bed.

After reaching the top of the pass the track runs for twenty-seven miles along the winding shores of Lake Bennett, crosses a canyon two hundred and fifteen feet deep upon a great bridge of steel, skirts the White Horse Rapids, famous in the days of the Klondike, and finally ends at White Horse, three hundred and fifty miles from Dawson by the overland trail and over one hundred miles more by the river. The bridge over the canyon is the farthest north cantilever bridge in the world.

The road was well planned and well built, and has been well managed from the start. Notwithstanding the heavy snowfalls, it has most of the time been kept open throughout the winter. It has rotary snow ploughs which will cut a path twelve feet deep through the drifts.

There were few accidents during the construction work. At one place an engine jumped over the cliffs, but the men raised it with block and tackle. At another place, now marked by an iron cross perhaps two feet high, a rock weighing more than one hundred tons fell from the side of the mountain and crushed two men who were blasting the way for the track. The rock was so heavy that it could not be moved, and the monument was sunk in its centre.

The endurance of the workmen was almost incredible. At one of the construction camps at the top of the pass the festoons of ice that formed in the dining-tent in winter from the steam of the cooking had to be swept down before each meal. But the icicles would form again before the meal was over. Everyone ate muffled up in coat, hat, and gloves.

Enormous quantities of supplies were needed and the base was a thousand miles away. Not only must they be brought to Skagway by steamer from Vancouver or Seattle, but after they arrived they had to be packed up the steep trail to where the building was going forward. Many of the workers were gold seekers glad of the chance to make expenses while they waited for the spring to open up the way into the interior. They were high-class labour but not always dependable. When news came of the gold strike at Atlin, some twenty-five miles east of the White Pass, fifteen hundred of them dropped their picks and started helter-skelter for the new fields.

The man who built the White Pass road was Michael J. Heney, who afterward constructed the Copper River railway for the Guggenheim syndicate. Heney was an expert engineer, had an iron nerve, and was a master in handling men. He would not allow liquor or gambling inside his camp. At one time a desperado belonging to Soapy Smith's gang set up a gambling saloon in a tent close to the route. When Heney ordered him to go away he refused. Heney then turned to his camp foreman and, pointing to a rock half as big as a house that hung over the tent of the saloonkeeper, told him in the hearing of the gambler to blast that rock out of the way by five o'clock the next morning. The gambler, thinking that this was only a bluff to make him move, did nothing about it. At five minutes to five o'clock the next morning the foreman came and told him that he must get up and leave or he

The prospectors, having found a promising site, are "staking" out their mining claim by squaring and marking the stump of a tree, according to the Alaska mining law.

The Indians of the interior are Athapascans, tall, strong people, some of whom have Russian blood. With education they are proving themselves intelligent, reliable, and useful.

would be killed by the rock. The gambler replied that the foreman might go to Hades, wherepon the latter said:

"I am too busy to go there this morning, but if you are not out of this tent within two minutes by this watch you will find yourself there. I shall order my men to touch off the time fuse within sixty seconds. The fuse will burn one minute only, and at the end of that time the rock will fall and crush you to death in this tent."

Then the foreman ordered "fire" and sought the shelter of a rock. Ten seconds later the gambler rushed after him with his shirt flapping against his bare legs. He continued to go, and when last seen was on a dead run down the trail.

But come with me for a ride over this first railroad of Alaska. The cars are comfortable and we shall have moving pictures of magnificent scenery all the way up the mountains. We shoot out of Skagway into a canyon through which flows a rushing glacial river. We follow this for a mile before climbing the hills, and pass on the way some log cabins which the old-timers tell us belonged to a town nicknamed Liarsville, because no one who lived there could tell the truth. A little beyond we can see where the river breaks through, and farther up the mountains we find it tumbling down over the rocks, splashing like the Falls of Lodore.

Great beds of red flowers line the track all the way to the top of the pass. There are trees on the lowland and everything is green. Passing onward, the engine toils up the steep sides of the cliffs, winding about in horseshoe curves until it reaches the top twenty-nine hundred feet up from the sea. The White Pass makes this great climb within twenty miles and has only one tunnel along its whole route.

As we go up the mountains the climate rapidly changes. Now and then we get a breeze from a glacier, and Jack Frost, travelling on the wings of the wind over the perpetual ice, chills us to the marrow. This is perceptible as we cross the canyon and catch the cold air of the Muir Glacier not far away. We see one glacier with a silver thread falling down the green slope below it. A little lower the thread swells to a rope. Lower still it has become a great cable, and it ends in the foaming Skagway River, dashing down over the rocks to the sea.

Passing over the mountains of the coastal range, we come into a new and different country. Skagway is as moist as Puget Sound, while White Horse in Yukon Territory is as dry as Denver. In Southeastern Alaska it rains almost every day, and the soil is like a wet sponge. Once over the pass we are in a region which is as dry as a bone and in midsummer as hot as the Sahara. It suffers from many forest fires.

There is plenty of soil on the northern slope of the range, and at first sight the country would seem excellent for farming. I am told that it is not. The soil is sand on a bed of gravel and the rain sinks through and is lost. Farther north the soil changes, but the air grows dryer, and the climate is like that of our Rocky Mountain Plateau.

All the way up the mountains runs the trail the gold hunters climbed before the iron track was constructed. They made their way through the ice and snow, and many died, never reaching the top of the pass. One part of the trail, known as the Dead Horse Canyon, was so named for the horses that, unable to bear the toil of the journey, gave up their equine ghosts at that point. The year before the road was built more than five thousand dead horses were counted on the trail. Some had lost their footing and were dashed to death on the rocks below. Others had sunk under their burdens in utter exhaustion and had to be thrown over the rocks, while still others lost heart and actually committed suicide by throwing themselves over the cliffs. One miner driving a mule team got the animals at last to the top, when the leader, who had been twice over the trail, jumped over the precipice, dragging the others with him.

Not far from Dead Horse Canyon are traces of the old road built by George A. Brackett before the steam line was constructed. Brackett came from Minneapolis to Skagway and built a road up the mountains. He had tollgates here and there, and the charges ranged from fifty cents each for foot passengers to two dollars for a four-horse team. It is said that when the White Pass Railway put him out of business, he sold his route for forty thousand dollars, cash.

During the winter of 1897–98, thirty-three thousand men and women came up over the trails on their way to Dawson. Most of them carried packs on their backs, some making numerous trips with loads of from fifty to one hundred pounds at a time. Some had sleds, which they pulled up the mountains, carrying perhaps two hundred pounds on a sled. The average outfit of the Klondiker weighed about one ton, or two thousand pounds, and the cost of getting this over the trail was enormous. Mules and horses were used, and Indians were hired at the rate of seven cents and upward a pound for taking an outfit fifty miles. The natives worked in families. A man would pack from one hundred to one hundred and forty pounds, a squaw from eighty to one hundred pounds, and girls and boys from twenty-five to fifty pounds apiece. Some of the white men went into packing and teaming as a business. One man is said to have made three hundred thousand dollars by transporting the baggage and supplies of the gold-seekers. Another threw a log across a stream and charged fifty cents, toll for the use of his bridge.

During my trip over the White Pass route I had as a seat-mate Elmer J. White, long our American consul at White Horse. His stories of the queer sights of the trail are interesting. Said he:

"The men carried goods of every description. I remember one prospector who packed a grindstone up the hills on his back. Everyone wondered what under the sun he was going to do with it. He brought it to White Horse and finally to Dawson. There he had a carpenter make him a frame for the stone. When this was completed he let the miners sharpen their axes and picks at twenty-five cents apiece. They did the work while he sat back and took in a dollar or more an hour for the rent of the grindstone.

"Another man was loaded with seven-by-nine-inch glass window panes. When he got to Dawson he sold them for two dollars a pane. Glass was so scarce at that time that beer bottles brought a price as window panes for log cabins. They were piled up lengthwise or set endwise into the windows and chinked round with mud."

The town of White Pass in those days consisted of thousands of tents occupied by men and women waiting for rafts and boats to carry them down by the lakes and river to Dawson. In the spring of 1898 there were twenty thousand persons camped at the head of Lake Bennett awaiting the ice break, and on the shores of the lake you can still see the remains of Mike King's sawmill, which cut lumber at the rate of eighty dollars per thousand and upward for the making of boats to cross the lake.

"All of these settlements," said Mr. White, "had their saloons and dance halls and games of chance of one kind or another. The men, who were crazy for amusement, did all sorts of strange things. I remember one night coming into a saloon at White Pass where a dozen miners stood around the bar gambling for drinks. Their goddess of fortune was the wee insect that Bobby Burns immortalized in one of his poems when he saw it creeping on a young lady's bonnet. As this kind of "wee beastie" was very common in those days, the miners had no trouble in finding one for their sport. The louse was placed on the bar and the gamblers laid their right hands about it at equal distances away. Then they waited to see upon whose hand it would crawl first. That unfortunate man paid for the drinks."

As the crow flies, the distance from Skagway to the summit of the White Pass is only fourteen miles, but the railroad track is six miles longer on account of the grades. Our train stopped at Carcross on the crest of the pass, where the waters flowing into the two oceans divide, and where side by side float the flags of America and Canada. Here, within a few feet of each other, are two streams. One flows toward the west, through United States territory, and after a course of twenty-odd miles tumbles into the Pacific at Skagway. The other winds its way on down into the Yukon and has over two thousand miles to go before it reaches Bering Sea. I threw a couple of chips into the streams. One has long since been lost in the Pacific Ocean, and I am in hopes that the other will in time reach the same body of water not far from the Arctic.

CHAPTER XIV

IN THE YUKON FLATS

I AM right under the Arctic Circle at Fort Yukon. For days past I have been steaming slowly down the Yukon River through the wilds of Alaska. This mighty stream rises only twenty-five miles from the Pacific Ocean in the headwaters of the Lewes and the Pelly rivers. It flows far into the interior of Canada's Yukon Territory, then bends toward the Bering Sea, where it ends its two-thousand-mile course. The Yukon is one of the world's largest rivers. Only four on the North American continent—the Mississippi-Missouri, the Winnipeg-Nelson, the Mackenzie, and the St. Lawrence—surpass it in length and the area of the basin drained.

Here in what are called the Yukon flats the stream is from ten to twenty miles wide, and the channel winds sluggishly in and out among islands of all shapes and sizes. Some are circular, some oval, and some are perfect crescents of vegetation and sand. The waters are like glass, putty-coloured during the daytime and with all the hues of the rainbow when the sun rises or sets. Just now it is about midnight and the river is one sheet of molten gold, or the hue of flowing copper as the metal pours forth from the furnace.

At White Horse, the northern terminus of the White Pass Railway, I took the steamer which brought me on through the Canadian Yukon Territory and past Dawson.

About nine hours after leaving Dawson I crossed the international boundary and was once more on United States soil, which I had left at Carcross on the railroad.

The course of the Yukon from White Horse to Dawson is as picturesque as any part of the Rhine or the Danube, and the whole of the journey has all of the wildness and charm of a virgin country.

In coming down the Upper Yukon we steamed by mountains rising to the clouds, passed by rocks like lofty castles, and wound our way among hills blanketed with pink flowers recalling the heather-clad hills of old Scotland. Just inside the Canadian boundary I saw two rocks facing each other on opposite sides of the river. One bore the almost perfect face of a man, whereas the profile of the other was that of a woman. The rocks are known as "The Old Man" and "The Old Woman."

A little farther down stream is a place where the Yukon cuts its way through towering cliffs banded with a dozen different colours, white, gold, black, brown, green, and red. The strata lie in undulating folds, like the stripes of a waving flag. They look rough enough to have been gnawed out by the snaggy teeth of old Father Time. In Europe this rock formation would have some romantic title. Here it is called "The Calico Bluff." As we went by it in the steamer one of the passengers who had a revolver amused himself by sending bullets into the strata, declaring in advance just which coloured ribbon he expected to hit.

Leaving the bluffs, we struck a patch of green forest and frightened two moose that had come to the river to drink. We saw a lynx swimming the river, and a mile farther on passed a fishing wheel which, turned by the

The strata of these cliffs are brilliantly coloured, red, gold, white, brown, and green. If in Europe they would undoubtedly bear a romantic name but to travellers along the Yukon they are simply the "Calico Bluffs."

The Alaska-Yukon boundary is the longest straight international border line ever surveyed. Where it crosses the Yukon River it is marked by a cleared strip through the forest.

For hundreds of miles through the Yukon flats no signs of human habitation are to be seen except the shack of an occasional woodchopper or the fish-wheels set in the stream.

current, was scooping up pink salmon and throwing them into a wooden box at the end. Behind the wheel on the shore were the tents of the Athapascan Indians, who were thus laying in winter food for themselves and their dogs.

I have been interested in the homes of the Athapascans on this part of the Yukon. They live in substantial log cabins painted in all the colours of the rainbow. Many of their houses have frame doors and glass windows. Some of these Indians are now planting gardens, and not a few use cook stoves and other furniture like that of the whites. Most of them have become Christians, although they retain many of their old superstitions and customs. The Government has established public schools in all of the large villages, where the younger generation is learning to speak English.

The Canadian boundary line is so marked that it can be easily seen. It is a wide strip cut through the woods up hill and down dale, from south to north, from where our line ends near the Pacific Ocean to the Arctic Ocean. It starts within thirty miles of the Pacific and goes straight toward the North Pole for a distance of eight hundred and seventy-five miles. It is the longest continuous straight boundary line ever surveyed. We could see it from the steamer coming down the slopes on the south side of the river and climbing straight up to the hills at the north.

At the international boundary the Yukon is comparatively narrow. Its width varies, according to the level of the river, from twelve hundred to thirteen hundred feet. It has two channels at that point, one of which is six hundred feet wide and twenty feet deep, and the other four hundred feet wide and twenty-six feet deep.

The river widens as it leaves the boundary, and keeps on its winding way through the hills for two hundred or three hundred miles, until it reaches Circle, where the great inland sea of the Yukon flats begins.

Here in the flats the land is low and built up by the silt of the river. The flats, which have an area almost as large as that of South Carolina, lie between the two ranges of mountains bordering Alaska at the north and the south. The Yukon corkscrews for two hundred miles through these lowlands in a network of sloughs, great inland lakes, and ox-bows made by the islands. The river stretches on and on as though it would drop into space, and the low wooded banks seem fences over which, if one climbed, one would fall into nothingness. Standing on the bridge of the steamer, one can almost look over the trees. The earth as far as one can see is flat.

Everywhere the Yukon is at its work of earth-building. Its waters are melting the prehistoric ice that begins two or three feet under the moss and muck covering; and great blankets of earth, studded with trees, fall down into the river. Sandbars rise in a season, and islands are created or swept away with the floods of one spring. There are no rocks anywhere. The bed of the river is silt, which goes down to great depths. There are so many channels among the islands that a man without a compass and sailing directions would surely get lost. Indeed, in the early days the cheechakos, or tenderfeet, coming here to get gold, were facetiously warned to beware of the Yukon flats, as they might wander into channels that would lead them into the Arctic Ocean instead of the main course of the river. Our steamer had spars at the side which could be dropped into the sand so that the engine could pry itself off in case it grounded on a newly made or uncharted shoal.

The river is wonderfully quiet. Sometimes we sailed a hundred miles or more without seeing a town or any sign of habitation. The few men living along its course within the flats chop wood to sell to the steamers. The captain asked one of them the other day the price of the wood.

The man replied: "Dave Drollette has been telling around the neighbourhood that I have been selling wood at five dollars a cord, but it ain't so."

"Neighbourhood," indeed! The man's nearest neighbour is forty miles off and Dave Drollette lives one hundred miles up the river.

This absence of man made the wilderness impressive. The mighty stream and the great dome of the sky with its low-hung clouds, which seemed always stationary, made me feel but an atom in God's mighty world. Most of the time the only living things visible were those on our boat, and the only noises the splashing of the paddle wheel at the stern, the voices of the people on deck, and the howls of the dogs we were carrying to the roadhouses down stream.

The first settlement over the international boundary is an Indian village above which, on a pole erected beside a log church, floats the American flag. Near by may be seen the black mast of the wireless station of Boundary, the first outpost of the Signal Corps of our army, whose telegraph system covers the greater part of the territory. Still farther on is Eagle, the first American town on the Yukon. Eagle prides itself on its Americanism. It has a poem, celebrating the advantages of Alaska over Canada, which was prepared as a greeting for the tourist on crossing the boundary. I give you a part of one verse:

> You may here forget there are crowns and kings,
> Ladies-in-waiting and such like things;
> For now you are under the Eagle's wings.

We could see the American flags of Eagle even before we caught sight of the houses. Every cabin had a tall flagstaff attached to its roof, and from the Yukon I counted a dozen flags floating in the breeze.

The Eagle of to-day is a "has been." It is like the deserted mining camps of the West which were abandoned when the gold played out. In its palmy days it was known as Eagle City, and had hundreds of inhabitants and all the riotous life that came from the successful diggings close by. It still has about one hundred one-story log cabins, but half of them are deserted and some are falling to ruins.

Many of the cabins have gardens about them in which are large crops of potatoes and carrots. The streets are grass grown, and grass and flowers grow luxuriantly on the dirt roofs of the cabins. As our boat came to anchor I heard a rooster crowing, and as I walked up the banks I could hear the bells of the cows pasturing near the town pump.

The town pump is one of the features of Eagle. It stands over a well and is worked by a windmill. There is a tall white tower beside the windmill and a drinking place at the front. In the days before prohibition Eagle had a first-class saloon but no public school. I asked one of the women why this was. She replied: "The only revenue the town had was the one-thousand-dollar license paid by the saloon, and it took all that to keep up the town pump."

Leaving Eagle, we stopped next at Circle, another half-deserted village living on the memories of its past. It sprang up in 1892, when gold was discovered on Birch Creek near by, and a little later it had a population of one thousand miners. It boasted that it was the largest log-cabin town in the world. Then the gold began to give out and most of the men left in the stampede to the Klondike. It has now many abandoned homes made of logs, a store or so, and a restaurant. The population altogether is two or three hundred.

While the steamer was tied up there, I called at the restaurant, and its owner, Fred Brentlinger, showed me a pair of Arctic ox horns which he had dug from the ice thirty feet under the ground. These horns measure three feet from tip to tip and are well preserved. He told me the price was five hundred dollars. The whole country has the remains of prehistoric animals locked up in vaults of perpetual ice. In the Klondike there have been dug up the bones of mastodons and other giant animals of the past; and nearly every town has a great ivory tusk or skeleton of an animal that lived in Alaska before the Ice Age began. Curios made of such ivory are for sale in many of the stores, and if one wants a tusk or tooth some hundred thousand years old it is easy to get it.

Brentlinger has two bear cubs, each of which lives in a ten-gallon keg back of the restaurant. They are as black as ink and as lively as kittens.

It is wonderful how tame these Alaskan bears become when caught as cubs and treated as pets. I find some in every mining settlement. There are two here at Fort Yukon within a stone's throw of where the steamer lands. They watch for the stranger and will eat and drink out of his hand. I have amused myself feeding them pop out of a bottle. I buy the pop at Jim Haley's roadhouse, and the bears will drink it out of a bottle while I hold it in my hand; or I can give the bottle to Bruin and he will sit down and drink it all by himself.

Fort Yukon is just inside the Arctic Circle, and at this time of the year it is light for twenty-four hours. It is the most northerly point on the Yukon River and a fine place to see the midnight sun. I have experimented here with taking photographs at midnight. My snapshots are fairly good, and with a gentle squeeze of the bulb I got the best of results.

Fort Yukon has been of great importance as a mining centre but is to-day better known as a fur-trading post. The Hudson's Bay Company used to come here to buy furs, and boat loads are now brought down the Porcupine River by the Indians and other fur traders. The Porcupine is navigable for two hundred and twenty-five miles, or as far as Rampart House on the other side of the international boundary. One of our passengers was Dan Cadzo, the trader, who lives there. He left us here to go up the Porcupine to his trading station.

Everyone in Alaska has heard of Dan Cadzo. He is one of the biggest traders of the Far North. Cadzo is content to live almost all alone in the wilds two hundred miles from the nearest settlement. His home is about one hundred and fifty miles south of the Arctic Ocean, a little farther from Ft. McPherson on a branch of the Mackenzie, and two hundred and twenty-five miles from Fort Yukon.

Nevertheless, he likes it. He said to me to-day: "I am mighty glad to get back from outside. I am tired of the crowd, and want to be where it is quiet again."

I asked him to tell me about his home in the wilderness. He replied:

"My house is about sixteen by forty, with wings at the side. It is made of logs and lined with the best beaver board. We have double windows, and our wood stoves keep us as warm as toast, though the thermometer sometimes goes down to seventy degrees below zero."

"Tell me something about your store."

"It is just over the boundary in Canada, and I take my goods there in my own steamer up the Porcupine River. Most of the freight on this ship belongs to me. My stock is worth about twenty thousand dollars. I use it to trade with the Indians, Eskimos, and white trappers who hunt there for furs. We have the best of goods, get high prices, and pay cash for furs. We buy thousands of dollars' worth of furs every season. Most of them come from the Indians, for there are not a half-dozen white men in the whole country. We are so far away that we did not know there was a war in 1914 until we came out with our furs in 1915. You see our nearest mail station is here at Fort Yukon, and we have to go four hundred and fifty miles every time we call at the post office."

CHAPTER XV

WINTER TALES OF TANANA

TANANA claims to be the hub of Alaska. It is a little town lying on the right bank of the Yukon just about half way between the Pacific and the Arctic oceans and half way down the Yukon on its course from the Canadian line at Eagle. I have come eight hundred miles down the river from Canada on my way to this point, and I have eight hundred miles more to go before I can get the little steamer that will take me over Bering Sea to Nome. Just opposite where my boat is anchored is the mouth of the Tanana River, a wide sluggish stream having a course of something like six hundred miles from the Wrangell Mountains to where it flows into the Yukon. It will take me two days to go up it to Fairbanks.

There is no doubt that Tanana can offer room for all the population she may have in the future. The corporate limits at present are large enough to give an acre to every man, woman, and child of the population of less than three hundred and leave some to spare. The log and frame buildings of the town are strung out along the waterfront for more than a mile. At the lower end of it begins the army post of Fort Gibbon, which extends three miles farther, and which has a government reservation of sixty square miles.

The people of Tanana are enthusiastic Alaskans. They

Steamers on the upper Yukon have to make frequent stops at the choppers' stations to take on fuel. The nearest neighbours to these woodcutters are often over one hundred miles away.

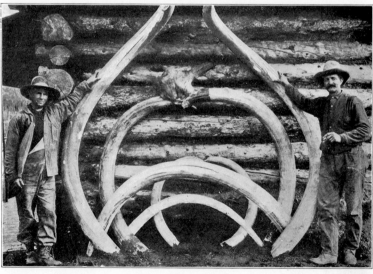

Nearly every Alaskan town has collections of mastodons and other prehistoric animals dug up out of the bed of perpetual ice that lies beneath the layer of top soil. Curios carved from these ancient bones are sold everywhere.

Alaskan bears, caught as cubs, make wonderfully tame pets. They watch for the stranger and will eat out of his hand. A bottle of pop is especially welcome to "Brer B'ar's" sweet tooth.

have a live chamber of commerce, a camp of the Arctic Brotherhood, and a lodge of the Loyal Order of the Moose. Talk to them about their village and they will make you think it a paradise as beautiful as the Vale of Kashmir and as salubrious as Los Angeles. I asked Judge Dehn, the United States Commissioner, who has been here a number of years, what he thought of the climate. He replied:

"I like it and I keep healthy and happy summer and winter. Our summers, which last from May until the middle of September, are more delightful than those anywhere in the States. The thermometer ranges from forty-five to ninety degrees above zero, and for most of the time there is scarcely an hour that you cannot read within doors without artificial light. From June 15th to the 10th of July there is no real darkness, even at midnight."

"How about your winters?" I asked.

"The man who went away from here and said that we have nine months of hard winter and after that three months of bad sleighing is a liar. Our winter starts in about October 1st, when the thermometer drops to fifteen degrees above zero. At that time the ground freezes and remains solid all winter. The frost goes down to the bed of glacial ice that lies under a great part of Alaska, and, as far as we know, we live on a solid ice block for seven months of the year. The glacial ice does not melt in summer. The frost gets only through the moss and muck which is ten inches or more deep, and where you pull up the muck you find the ground below frozen solid. If you clear off the moss and the muck it will thaw down to eight or ten feet, but in the winter such ground seems to freeze from the top and the bottom both until it is all hard as rock. The frost begins to go out of the ground about May 1st when the hot sun thaws the ice. It is then that summer begins."

"But your winter weather must be terribly cold."

"Not so bad. Not so bad," said Judge Dehn. "The weather keeps growing colder and colder from October on until it gets down to fifteen degrees below zero. It holds that average throughout the winter although it now and then falls to forty and even sixty degrees below. I have seen it down to seventy-three below. Zero is warm winter weather and we do not consider fifteen degrees below that point uncomfortable. At such times we wear our ordinary winter clothing and take off our top coats if we are at hard manual labour. I came here from Canton, Ohio. Fifteen degrees below zero on the Yukon does not seem as cold as fifteen above in Ohio. Our air is dry and we do not feel the cold.

"Besides," continued the judge, "our houses keep out the cold. They are made of logs, chinked with Arctic moss. The warmest building I have is my log chicken house which is lined and ceiled with a framework, the space between being filled with shavings. I keep an air-tight stove going in it, and my hens lay all winter."

I went out with the judge to see his chickens. He has one hundred and fifty, mostly Rhode Island Reds and Plymouth Rocks. He sells his pure-bred fowls at five dollars apiece, and he gets a dollar and a half a dozen for eggs in summer and two dollars and a half in winter.

Speaking of chickens, I have been greatly interested in how they are handled in these cold regions of the Far North. We brought eight hundred brooded fowls on our ship down the Yukon. They had come from Seattle and were consigned to a man in Fairbanks. They are still on the boat and will go up the Tanana River to-morrow. At Dawson I met Chicken Billy, who at one time had nine hundred chickens and who has sold eggs in the winter for as much as five dollars a dozen.

The chickens imported from the States will not lay unless there is the same proportion of light and darkness in their days as they were used to at home. I heard of a man at Circle who imported a lot of fowls from the States with the idea of starting a chicken farm. After a week or so they grew droopy. They lost flesh and he got no eggs whatever. He was then told the chickens were suffering from lack of sleep. It was midsummer when the light is bright throughout the twenty-four hours. The chickens had no sunset to mark their bedtime, and they kept on scratching gravel all night. The man decided to put them in darkened coops at 8 P. M. and keep them there until morning. The hens at once regained their old vigour and began to drop "ranch eggs" which sold at top prices. I am told also that the coops must be lighted during the long dark days of the winter in order to make the hens lay.

In the past few years there has been a craze in Alaska in favour of the "helpful hen." Most of the residents have been keeping chickens and raising their own eggs. At first many kept them throughout the summer and sold them as cold weather came on to save the expense of warming and lighting the coops during the long winter nights. They would import a second flock for the following summer. To-day it is the custom to keep your chickens in summer and put them out to board in winter. In several of the largest towns there are a number of chicken boarding houses, where fowls are cared for in well-warmed, well-lighted coops at a regular rate. The eggs laid during the winter go to the landlord. As soon as the warm weather comes on, the owner takes back his chickens and is thus able to raise broilers and pullets and at the same time have plenty of eggs.

All winter the whole country is a cold storage plant, so that it is easy to keep meat. Each householder, having decided how many chickens she will put out to board, kills the rest. She cleans and dresses them and hangs them out of doors or in an unheated building. They freeze solid the first night and can then be laid away in a cold place and used as needed.

A teacher told me how they managed to have fresh meat all winter long. Said he:

"We bring our beef and mutton in on the hoof before navigation closes. About the middle of October, when we are sure of a steady cold until spring, we kill and dress them and hang them up out of doors. We then lay them away and thaw them out as the market demands. We freeze caribou and moose the same way. Last year one of the butchers froze a caribou with the skin and horns on, just as it looked when alive. He stood the carcass out in front of his shop and used it for a sign."

Betting on the ice in the river is a regular sport in this part of the world and many are the speculations on when it will form, how deep it will freeze, and when it will go out in the spring. One of the river captains tells me he has measured the ice of the Yukon and found it at times five feet thick. In the ordinary season the ice on the main part of the stream is only two and one half or three feet deep. The ice forms the great highway of travel in winter weather.

I asked this captain to tell me more about the ice on the Yukon. He said:

"Navigation opens at Dawson between the 6th and 16th of May, and it usually closes about the 25th of October. Long before the centre of the river is frozen, there is a continuous strip of ice along the shores, and cakes of it float in the channel. As the cold weather continues, the ice extends farther and farther out, until the channel grows so narrow that the steamers cannot make their way through. The floating cakes increase in number, and pile up until at last they make gorges at the narrow places and form solid ice there. As winter settles down into a steady cold, the whole river is frozen from bank to bank, so solidly that a train of cars could be run over it.

"The most interesting time on the Yukon," continued the captain, "is when the ice breaks up in the spring. That on the upper part of the river breaks first and pushes its way down the stream, breaking the other ice as it goes. The boats start in behind the ice and move along as fast as they can, and sometimes small boats start in the ice. The water never freezes again after it once melts, for we then have the long days and the sunshiny nights of the summer."

I asked the captain to tell me about the betting on the ice-break.

"That is most exciting," was his reply. "All along the Yukon the people bet when the great ice-break will occur. They organize pools at Dawson and Fairbanks, where large sums are lost and won at the whim of Jack Frost. At Dawson they cut a hole in the ice in the middle of the Yukon and erect a pole about four inches thick and twenty feet high. This freezes solid. They then fasten one end of a wire cable to the top of the pole and the other end to an electric stop clock on the shore set to standard time. The moment the ice moves the pole the clock stops, and that moment marks the record of the beginning of the ice-break and decides all bets. As soon as the clock stops a steam whistle is blown, and everyone knows the hour and the minute of the running. The usual date is about May 10th, the time when corn is planted in the Middle States.

"Generally the betting pool at Dawson has about sixty subscribers," the captain went on, "and the total amount may be as much as six thousand dollars. After a pool has been formed, sixty slips of paper, bearing the numbers from one to sixty, are put in a hat. Each number represents a minute of the hour, and the man who gets the minute shown by the stop clock as the flood reaches Dawson is given the purse. Bets are also made on the day of the month and week and upon the hour of the day at which the whistle will blow. One year the engineer on the steamship *Sarah* invested one dollar in a five-hundred-dollar pool, and won it all. That was a day, hour, and minute pool. He guessed the right time to a minute. There are also many individual bets. The crowds gather on the banks of the river as the ice shows signs of breaking and watch the pole. When the whistle blows the city goes mad.

"The same betting goes on at Fairbanks. The time there is the exact minute the ice tears away the bridge across the Chena River, in the heart of the town. It does that every spring, breaking the posts as though they were matches."

I find there is a difference of opinion as to Alaska winters. All are not as enthusiastic about the delights of the cold and darkness as those I have quoted.

"I tell you the winters are awful," said one of the women I met here. "These people say they enjoy life when the thermometer is twenty or thirty degrees below zero, and that it is not cold. I tell you it *is* cold, although the still air does not make it so bitter.

"When it is more than twenty below we women stay in the house and so do the men as much as they can. We work by artificial light for most of the day, and when spring comes everyone is peaked and deathlike. With the coming of the long days our colour returns, and in summer we are as healthy and rosy as can be.

"But the long, dark days rack your nerves almost to breaking! You get tired of yourself and your friends and want something new in the way of amusement. You sleep as long as you can and pay but little attention to hours. All parties are held late and they often last far into the night. And then the trouble of entertaining! Everyone has the same supplies, and the same canned stuffs to select from. You go to your pantry and look at the shelves in despair. It is hard to know what to serve."

When people go out into temperatures of sixty or seventy below they avoid violent exercise. I am told that a quick, deep breath of the freezing air makes the lungs feel as if they had taken in burning steel. Horses are seldom allowed to go out of their warmed stables when the thermometer is around fifty below, as the icy air kills them by "burning out" their lungs, as they say up here.

Another Alaskan, talking to me about funerals, said:

"It is difficult to bury your dead in a land where the

prehistoric ice lies only two feet under the moss, and where you have to build fires to thaw the ice-frozen gravel beneath. In winter you sometimes have to chop the graves out of the ice. There is no need of brick walls or cement. The coffin is laid in its ice tomb, the earth shovelled back, and soon all is frozen solid again. The dead buried in the winter remain frozen for an indefinite period, and when taken up years later look just as in life. The ice has turned them, as it were, to statues of marble."

In the long, dark months the only contact with the outside is the mail brought over hundreds of frozen miles by dog team. It takes little imagination to realize what it means to the interior towns to have a poor mail service and we can readily sympathize with the complaints and pleas for delivery of letters, papers, and magazines that bombard the Government.

The people complain that a large part of their newspapers and magazines which should arrive during the winter are held over until spring when they are delivered in bulk. For instance, one postmaster received in June six hundred sacks of such mail, much of which was dated as far back as September, October, and November of the previous year. Think of getting all the copies of your pet newspaper published this winter in one big package in the coming May!

Moreover, the people of Alaska say that the long winter is their time for reading, and they want their newspapers and magazines delivered as they come out. They especially resent the fact that in Dawson, situated far inland, the Canadians get all their mail regularly in spite of transportation difficulties as great as those to be overcome in reaching Alaska towns.

Interior Alaska in winter time is a natural cold storage plant, and dried salmon, meat, and furs are kept in outdoor caches, built high above the ground to protect them from prowling dogs and deep snows.

The inland rivers freeze up in October, sometimes to a depth of five feet or more, and become the main highways. Floods often accompany the spring thaws, filling the streets of towns with tons of ice.

"Stooping down on the narrow fork between the two streams, I put one hand in hot water and the other in an ice-cold brook—both from near-by springs."

Alaska offers opportunity for unusual "stunts" in photography. This picture of Mt. McKinley was made at night near Fairbanks, over seventy-five miles away, with two hours' exposure when the moon was shining.

CHAPTER XVI

HOT SPRINGS IN COLD LANDS

HOT springs in Alaska! Boiling water bubbling out of the beds of glaciers! Steam rising from the earth on the edge of ages-old ice several hundreds of feet deep! Scalding baths in hot water from Mother Earth's own tank almost in the shadow of the North Pole! These are some of the wonders of our great territory whose shores are washed by the chill Bering Sea and the icy Arctic.

I have heard of hot springs ever since I came to Alaska. They are to be found from the islands of the Panhandle to the very edge of the Arctic. Fifty miles north of Ketchikan are the Belle Island Hot Springs, where the water is 164 degrees Fahrenheit, or hot enough to cook eggs. A little farther north are the Sitka Hot Springs, whose waters register 156 degrees above zero, and on Chichagof Island, between Sitka and Juneau, are the Tenakee Hot Springs which have been made a flourishing resort for both the summer and the winter seasons. In fact, the Geological Survey has discovered hot springs in many different parts of the territory.

The Baker Hot Springs, which I have just visited, are on the Tanana River about twelve hours by steamer from Tanana and Fort Gibbon, and one hundred miles from Fairbanks. They lie about three miles back from the Tanana River, and upon landing I got a hay wagon to carry me across to the town near the springs. A fairly good corduroy road covered with sawdust and muck crosses the lowlands and goes up to the springs. This land is now covered with patches of bushes and grass as high as my knee. Some of the grass is in tassel, and the land is sprinkled with wild flowers, white, yellow, and red, whose names I know not.

Nearing the town, we drove over a corduroy bridge, crossing a creek that flows into the Tanana River, and stopped at the post office, which is a wire cage inside the galvanized iron store building of the Northern Commercial Company. American flags, floating from high poles above three of the log houses, showed the patriotism of their owners. Not far from the post office were the burned ruins of a hotel, which was once a winter and summer resort. The hotel had great bathing and swimming tanks. It was built of logs and cost, it is said, more than forty thousand dollars. To-day there is only one bathing tank left. A cabin is built over it and the water is piped from the springs about a half mile away. I tested the bath with a thermometer and it was just 114 degrees Fahrenheit. It was hot enough to paint my skin scarlet when I jumped in.

Leaving the ruins, I walked over the hills to visit the springs, passing through a farm of three hundred acres on the way. The road is through an oatfield where there were perhaps thirty acres ready for cutting. In the centre of this field I saw the large glass hothouse built to supply the hotel and mines with cucumbers, tomatoes, and other vegetables.

Coming to the steaming brook that flows from the spring, we passed a chicken and hog shed about four hundred feet in length. When business was booming its owner kept there six hundred and fifty hens, fifty ducks, and seventy pigs, as well as horses and cows. The sheds were built into the hill from whence the spring comes. The ground is so hot that it kept the poultry and other stock in comfort throughout the winter, and that without the stoves necessary to other parts of Alaska.

The water moderates the temperature of the land of almost the whole farm. The adjacent hill slopes are a natural hotbed. Snow falling on the warm ground thaws so rapidly that the surface is seldom white for more than a couple of days at a time, and the frost goes down only an inch or so. On the edge of the warm land young parsnips have been dug in March from under the snow, and all other crops are much in advance of those planted elsewhere.

At the springs the warm water flows out at the rate of one hundred and fifty gallons a minute. It is as clear as a crystal, but it is steaming at a temperature of 125 degrees Fahrenheit. I watched Mr. Waring, the hot springs' expert of the Geological Survey, as he tested the heat and measured the flow. He says the water is hot enough to soft-boil eggs in ten minutes.

Walking down the stream thirty or forty feet, I found another brook flowing into it, and supposed this would be of about the same temperature as the one we had tested. I put in my hand. The water was icy cold. Stooping down on the narrow fork between the two streams, I put one hand in hot water and the other in cold.

Bouncing back in the hay wagon over the corduroy road to the river, I sat beside Tom Davis, a farmer who does teaming from the Tanana to the gold mines north of here. He told me that the hay they are now unloading from our steamer is worth ninety dollars a ton at the river and one hundred and forty dollars a ton when it gets to the mines. I remarked that the price seemed an extravagant one. Said Mr. Davis:

"It is not high for Alaska. I have known hay to sell as high as eight hundred dollars a ton or at forty cents per pound. That was in the Klondike when the gold fever was raging. I once sold one thousand pounds of hay to the freighters for fifty cents a pound, and weighed it out on the grocery scales."

During my stay in Alaska I met G. D. Schofield of Seattle, the owner of some of the largest hot springs on the Seward Peninsula. These are even more wonderful than the Baker Springs. They are situated about seventy miles north of Nome, at the foot of the Saw-Tooth Mountains, fifty feet above sea level. A number of them boil out of the ground at a temperature of 160 degrees Fahrenheit, maintaining the same heat winter and summer. The springs form a stream called Hot Creek that runs through a farm of three hundred and twenty acres. I asked Mr. Schofield about this farm. He replied:

"We have forty acres under cultivation and sixty more that could be put into crops. The whole of this hundred acres is kept warm by the springs and the hot water under the ground. If you dig down anywhere inside this tract you will find hot earth, and the lower you go the hotter it gets. At a depth of six feet you cannot hold the earth in your hands. There seems to be a stratum of hot water under the whole hundred acres. On the other hand, the land outside that area is frozen solid to no one knows what depth. Our farm is like the crust of a hot pie fresh from the oven, set on the ice but never getting cold.

"We have a glass greenhouse, thirty-six feet long and sixteen feet wide, built above one of the springs. The hot water furnishes the heat, and no matter if the temperature goes to thirty degrees below zero outside it never goes to freezing within. The plants grow in the hothouse all winter and in the summer we have cantaloupes, cucumbers, mushrooms, tomatoes, and watermelons. We also raise lettuce, young onions, and other green stuff. We have a tree onion that grows well. It does not lie in the ground but grows on the branches of a tree twelve or fourteen inches high."

I asked Mr. Schofield whether many people came to visit the springs.

"Yes," he said, "we have a hotel accommodating thirty and the people come in from Nome and all parts of the Seward Peninsula. Our best season is in the winter. The guests come on dog sleds and you can sometimes see as many as four hundred dogs there at once. It usually takes two days to make the trip from Nome in winter, but it can be done in one day in the summer by going over the railway track with the Pup-mobile, a car drawn by dogs, which takes you within six miles of the springs."

In coming from Tanana to Hot Springs Landing I was all day on the Tanana River. It carries down such a vast deal of silt that the water is as thick as bean soup. There are frequent sand bars and we passed islands in every stage of formation from the bare brown patch of silt to forest-clad areas washed by the waves. Now and then there were floating islands, great beds of green, with bushes and trees upon them moving down the stream. In places the river is from five to ten miles wide and quite shallow.

I saw soil and trees, bushes and the earth fall down into the current before my eyes. The river banks are lined with trees still living and still green, which have fallen this way into the current. At times the water so melts the frozen strata that caves are formed under the matted moss, and where there is an open space and no trees this green mat slopes down into the stream like a great green carpet laid from the bed of the river up to the shore.

At the wood camps, where the trees had been cut away to furnish fuel for the steamers, were great beds of pink fireweed rising out of high grass. Coming up the river we saw here and there pioneers chopping little farms out of the forests. They first cut the trees and a year later pull out the stumps. The ice is so close to the surface that the roots cannot go down deep, so the stumps come up rather easily. After clearing, they plant patches of vegetables or fields of oat-hay. None of the farms is large, and I believe it will be a long time before the local market will be big enough to pay the farmers of the United States to leave their good homes to try their luck here.

CHAPTER XVII

FAIRBANKS, the northern terminus of Uncle Sam's new railway, and the point where the river and rail navigation centre and join, might be called the hub of Alaska. It is in the heart of the territory almost equidistant from Bering Sea and the Canadian border, and about half way between the Pacific and the Arctic oceans.

The business of Fairbanks is all the more astonishing when one realizes how inaccessible the town was before the government railroad opened quick passage to the sea.

It took me two days to come up the Tanana River from Fort Gibbon to Fairbanks. The Tanana is navigable for some distance above Fairbanks and its valley has millions of acres of agricultural land.

Fairbanks has a delightful individuality. It is a combination of the picturesque and the plain, of the shabby and the sumptuous, of the old and the new. Altogether, it is different from any other town I have ever seen.

Take a look at the main business street. It is a wide dirt road with plank sidewalks from which rise frame buildings of one and two stories. The front walls of the stores extend high above the roofs and are cut off horizontally, making the buildings look taller, and giving a jagged skyline. The shops carry a wide assortment, for Fairbanks is the trading centre of interior Alaska, and goods from here go to the gold-mining camps of the Tanana, the Yukon, the Koyukuk, and the Innoka rivers. Some of its wholesale firms do a business that runs into the millions, and steamers are always lying at anchor just off the principal street. There are establishments filled with mining machinery, and stores carrying all sorts of goods for miners, including mackinaws and khaki suits for rough wear. They sell high boots of white rubber and hob-nailed shoes for tramping over the rocks and through the brush. They have also silks and broadcloths and shoes of fashionable makes. They have moccasins beautifully beaded. Entering the banks you will see them taking in gold dust at one window and handing out bank notes at another. Every bank buys gold and all have their assaying and melting establishments where the metal is tested and made into bricks to be shipped outside.

The crowds on the streets are a mixture. They include men and women as well dressed as those of any city east of the Alleghanies and miners clad in blue jeans or khaki. On the street corners are groups of shirt-sleeved men in soft hats or sombreros.

Now turn your eyes to the roadways. There are scores of motor vehicles away up here in the heart of Alaska and jitney buses go regularly each day to the gold creeks. There is an overland stage that makes the trip over the beautiful road from Fairbanks to Chitina, the terminus of the Copper River Railroad. By it one can motor more than three hundred miles through the wilds, and then have a two-hundred-mile railroad ride down to the sea.

Fairbanks has several hotels. I am stopping with Tony Nordale, on Front Street, where I have a sitting

Fairbanks has its women's club and its library. Everywhere one meets college men and women. Before the railroad came the citizens complained bitterly of the winter mail service which made their books and magazines months late.

The log cabin residences are snug in winter, when the mercury gets down to 30° below zero, and in summer the people raise in their gardens three-pound tomatoes and pea plants six feet high.

Betting on the hour and minute of the spring icebreak provides intense excitement in Alaska river towns. In Fairbanks the official time of the break is when this winter bridge begins to move down stream.

room and bedroom at about three dollars per day. I get my meals at a restaurant kept by a young lady whose rosy cheeks and tow hair have won her the nickname, "The Little Pink Swede." Her charge is from fifty cents to seventy-five cents a meal and the food is delicious. Like many of the restaurants, hers has a pet brown bear, a cub fastened to a chain outside the front door. It does tricks for sugar plums or sweet cakes.

When I had my hair cut to-day it cost me twice what barbers charge in the States. As I left the barber shop I stepped into the chair of a bootblack outside and the shine cost me a quarter. The day was hot, so when a miner asked me in the camp parlance if I would "wash my neck," I knew what he meant and said yes. He treated me to a glass of lemonade at a cost of twenty-five cents. A little farther on a newsboy offered me the Alaska *Citizen*, for which I handed him a quarter, the regular price for the paper. A quarter is the smallest coin in circulation here and means about the same as a nickel at home.

Fairbanks is an incorporated town with a mayor and council and claims to be the livest city in Alaska. It has much civic spirit and practically all the community organizations and activities of a town many times its size in the States. Its Women's Club is affiliated with the Federation of Women's Clubs. There are two dailies and an attractive public library built of logs, besides a fire department and telephone exchange. More than half a dozen denominations have churches here.

The most picturesque feature of Fairbanks is the homes of the people. The residences are chiefly log cabins, ranging in size from two-room huts to some mansions of a dozen or more rooms. The cabins are built of cypress and birch logs, with the bark on or off at the taste of the builder. The logs are chinked with Arctic moss, and their corners are joined, now in notched shape, now dovetailed, and now with the logs sticking out like a doll house built of corn cobs. Nearly every home has its porch and on the smaller ones the low ridge roofs extend far out at the front to shade the lounging place of the family during the hot summer days. Some of the houses are half log and half frame. Some are roofed with boards, some with galvanized iron painted green, and others with poles covered with earth. The latter have grass and flowers growing upon them. Most of the houses have cellars and all have their walls set deep in the ground and banked up for warmth. In the larger houses there are big living rooms with wide windows artistically set.

Most of the log cabins have pretty green lawns with beds of beautiful flowers. All have gardens and nearly every one has its patch of potatoes and turnips. Hedges of sweet peas the height of a man may wall one side of a garden and great beds of poppies line the walks through the centre. I have never seen anywhere flowers so large, so fresh, and of such a velvety texture; and I may add that I have never visited any town where the people seemed to love flowers so much and where they have so many for themselves and their friends.

There is a friendly strife between families as to which shall have the best and earliest vegetables. I called upon a lady last night who showed me one of her hothouse tomatoes weighing three pounds, and a cauliflower from her garden with a head as big around as the largest dinner plate. She had lettuce as fine as any raised in the South and rows of peas six feet high, with pods as big around as a man's thumb. This woman has the earliest potatoes in Fairbanks by starting them in boxes of earth in her kitchen a week or so before the frost goes out of the ground.

To get some idea of the business of Fairbanks and interior Alaska, I visited to-day the headquarters of the Northern Commercial Company at Fairbanks. This company is the offspring of the Alaska Commercial Company, which leased the seal islands about a year after we bought the territory and established a general fur-trading business something like that of the Hudson's Bay Company. It made such vast sums dealing in sealskins that the royalties paid to our Government were soon more than the first cost of the territory. The Alaska company originated and developed the transportation of Alaska, and had its stores and trading posts not only in the islands of the Southeast, the Aleutians, the southern coast of the mainland, and in Bering Sea, but also at St. Michael, at the mouth of the Yukon, and all along that river to the boundary of Canada.

When the Alaska Commercial Company dissolved, the Northern Commercial Company took over its business in interior Alaska and now has a number of stores in the basins of the Yukon and the Kuskokwim, serving the mining camps and fur-trading stations. It supplies many of the roadhouses, and does a wholesale and retail business over a territory perhaps one tenth as large as the United States. The company has a capital of three million five hundred thousand dollars, the stock being owned mostly in San Francisco and England.

There are firms outside the Northern Commercial Company that do a large business, but none that covers such a great area and handles everything needed by the people. Their establishment here at Fairbanks, for instance, consists of stores, warehouses, and cellars, with a floor space of six or eight acres, machine shops and foundries, cold storage and warm storage plants, branches devoted to wholesale and retail, as well as waterworks, steam heat and electric plants.

The mercantile department has now on hand more than a million dollars' worth of groceries, provisions, and other supplies, and its retail section is like a small department store in the States.

Goods have to be bought in large quantities, for the country is locked in ice for seven months of the year. With the use of the new railway these stocks will not need to be so large. Less capital will be tied up in goods and merchants should be able to sell at somewhat lower prices. In one of the cellars I saw ten thousand cans of condensed milk, condensed cream, and other canned goods, including egg powder, from which camp cooks, I was told, make up omelettes quite as good as from ranch eggs. I saw thousands of eggs in the shell which had been packed in the States, carried one thousand miles to Skagway, and after crossing the mountains, had come down the Yukon. I saw canned potatoes and canned corn. The potatoes are cooked whole and put up in cans, in which shape they realize as much as forty or fifty dollars a bushel. Some of the corn is canned in the ear, and had only to be warmed to give the Alaskan miner corn on the cob in the heart of the winter.

Goods have to be carefully packed for the Alaskan trade. They must stand the changes of climate, the heat of the summer, and the cold of the winter. Perishable provisions are coated with gelatine. Hams, for instance, must be so protected that they will not be ruined if dropped in the snow or into a river. Each ham is sewed up in canvas, which is dipped in a gelatine to give it a gluelike coating and make it airtight. Cheese is packed the same way.

The company keeps billiard and pool tables ready for shipment. It has wagons and sleds, some of the latter with a capacity for a ten-ton load. It has also dog sleds, and dog harness with tugs, collars, and back straps. The average dog sled is ten dollars. Another article of merchandise is dog feed, a great deal of which is tallow. The huskies are fed once a day when on the trail, and that at nightfall. Their usual meal is dried salmon and rice cooked with tallow. The Northern Commercial Company will sell about a hundred thousand pounds of tallow next winter.

In the hardware department are all kinds of machinery and parts. There are great bales of wire cable for hoisting the earth from the mines, steam engines, air compressors, and steam points for thawing the ground. There are bales of wire for chicken yards and fox farms. There is wire netting for fish wheels and some of fine mesh for the gold reduction plants. There are all sorts of farm machinery, ploughs, reapers, and mowers, as well as plumbing supplies, window sashes, and porcelain bathtubs.

The Northern Commercial Company runs a steam plant which heats the business section of Fairbanks. It has a central station with pipes to all the buildings, including many private homes in an area of several blocks. The plant furnishes heat to its customers at so much a month throughout the year. It keeps the stores and the houses warm even when the thermometer registers sixty or seventy below zero. The steam pipes run side by side with the water pipes, so that the latter are kept from freezing in the winter.

Some of the smaller merchants denounce the company as a monopoly. There is probably considerable truth in the statement; but any one can import goods and there are several firms here doing a very large business for this part of the world. One is E. R. Peoples, Incorporated, and another is the Dominion Commercial Company, both of which have their headquarters at Fairbanks and sell to the mining camps within a radius of a hundred miles or so.

Goods are sent by small steamers far up the tributaries of the Yukon. One of the Far North trading stations is at Bettles, the head of steamship navigation on the Koyukuk River. From Bettles supplies are carried something like fifty miles across country to placer mines.

Another trading station is Wiseman, about ninety miles from Bettles. It is also on the Koyukuk, but the stream is so shallow that the goods are hauled there on barges drawn by horses. As the freight rate is a dollar and forty cents a ton, the prices at Wiseman are very high. Most of the merchandise is paid for in gold dust, the store-keeper weighing out the right amount from a miner's poke.

Most of the business of Alaska is done upon credit and any one who would sell much has to give time. The people here tell me that the merchants are liberal in their advances to miners. I talked last night with a commercial traveller who started to Fairbanks with six horses freighting goods in over the trail. A cold snap caught him on the way and his horses died. He arrived in Fairbanks with only enough for a mining outfit, but the storekeeper gave him credit and in company with a partner he leased a claim on one of the creeks for twenty-five per cent. of the profits. At the end of the year he was two thousand dollars in debt. The next winter he and his partner had no money to pay wages, but by their own work they got out three thousand dollars' worth of pay dirt. They then paid up their debts and within the next year or so cleaned up thirty thousand dollars out of the claim.

Indeed, few people realize the extent and possibilities of our Alaskan trade. The commerce in this territory in a typical year was one hundred and ten million dollars. It was nearly as great as our trade with Spain or Sweden, and was one fifth as large as our total trade with all South America. The exports were twice the value of the imports. In proportion to the white population, the trade was greater than that of any other country of the world. The per-capita commerce was about twenty-two hundred dollars, while that of Great Britain was only two hundred and seventy-nine dollars. This means that the trade of Alaska was, on the average, for every man, woman, and child, almost eight times as great as that for every man, woman, and child in Great Britain.

If this is true when the land is a wild waste, so covered with moss and other vegetation that only about one third of it has had even a general survey, and not one acre in a thousand has been brought into cultivation, what may we not expect of the country with the railroad and with the developments of the future?

CHAPTER XVIII

HOMESTEADING UNDER THE ARCTIC CIRCLE

THE Tanana valley has the largest body of good soil in Alaska. Much of the land is in what is known as the Tanana bottom, a tract about two hundred miles long and, in places, seventy miles wide. Altogether it is about as big as the state of New Jersey, and its cultivable area is one fifth as large as Ohio. I motored to-day through a rolling region as beautiful as the foothills of the Alleghanies. It was difficult to realize that we were just below the Arctic Circle. The thermometer was at ninety degrees in the shade. There was no snow on the tops of the mountains, and the hills and valleys were covered with green. At times we passed through plains thick with wild flowers. In some places the ground was covered with blueberry bushes, their fruit as large as cherries and loaded with juice. Now we passed through forests of birch, spruce, and cottonwood. Where the woods had been cut or burned away there were vast expanses of flaming pink flowers as high as the wheels of the car, and everywhere the roadside was hedged with grass and red-top that reached to the hubs. Now and then we bumped over corduroy, our automobile bouncing high under the fast driving of the Jehu of this northern frontier.

We passed many small farms cut out of the woods, with oat-hay and potatoes in blossom. We saw cattle grazing,

148

The homesteader along the Tanana River must literally chop his farm out of the woods. Pulling stumps is easier than in the States, as the glacial ice-bed prevents tree roots from going very deep.

Pitching hay in the interior farm lands of Alaska is just as hot work as in the fields of Virginia. Alfalfa is successfully grown, even where the ice-bed is not far below the surface.

and by and by came to the Government's experiment farm in the heart of the Tanana valley, about four miles from Fairbanks. The farm covers twelve hundred and eighty acres of gently sloping hillsides and bottom land. At one end of the farm stands the new Alaska Agricultural College, commanding magnificent views for fifty miles up and down the Tanana valley, taking in Fairbanks and the blue mountains far off in the distance. On a bright day Mount McKinley, the tallest peak on the North American continent, is visible. The campus includes a forest of silvery birch trees as straight as arrows.

As we rode by the farm we could see men cutting trees and burning brush. A little farther on we came to grain fields, not little patches, but fields that would be large on any Virginia farm. We passed tracts of oats ready for reaping and rode through barley four feet high. Above these on the hillside were long strips of Siberian wheat ripening side by side with strips of experimental grains of one kind and another.

The work of these experiment stations is not like that of the ordinary farm. Crops are not raised to be sold, although enough is produced to feed the stock and there is sometimes a surplus. The business of Uncle Sam's agricultural experts here in Alaska is to test out grains and plants and find those best adapted to the country. The old patriarch's agents have scoured northern China, the Desert of Gobi, and the highlands of Pamir, and have ransacked the Frigid Zone, looking for seeds adapted to the territory. They have seeds from Abyssinia and samples of grains from the Atlas Mountains of North Africa and there are no end of plants that have come from Finland and Norway, as well as from northern United States and Canada.

It has been found that potatoes do well in this part of Alaska. Two hundred bushels per acre have been grown, and the valley is now raising about all that is needed for the towns and the camps. One year the station sold the yield of five acres for three thousand five hundred dollars, and it has records of three acres which have produced a value of from five hundred dollars to six hundred dollars per acre for years in succession. Some claim the tubers lack the mealiness of those of the Rocky Mountains, but those I have had have been dry and delicious.

The home of the station farmer is a one-story cottage surrounded by beautiful flowers. Near the cottage is a hothouse where tomatoes and cucumbers are grown, and across the way are barns and outhouses where grain-hay is stored for the winter. There is also a root cellar in the side of a hill not far from the barn, where the potatoes and other root crops are stored as soon as they are dug, which is some time in August. Just opposite the root cellar and a little below it is a large turnip patch. I climbed the fence and pulled up a turnip which was eight inches thick; by actual measurement the leaves were seventeen inches long.

The crops at the Fairbanks farm are similar to those grown at the Government's experiment station at Rampart right under the Arctic Circle where I stopped for awhile on my way down the Yukon to Tanana. One of the things that interested me there was the way potatoes are sprouted. They are often started in greenhouses or cold frames. About four weeks before planting they are put in trays and lightly covered with soil. Sprouts come out to the length of from a half inch to three inches. When they are planted outdoors they are so set that the sprouts just reach the surface. The tubers given such a start indoors more than double the yield of potatoes planted in the ordinary way.

Another crop which has turned out well at Rampart is a yellow-flowered alfalfa imported from Siberia. In the United States alfalfa roots sometimes go down many feet into the soil. Here in Alaska when the alfalfa roots strike the glacial ice bed the ends freeze off but the roots keep spreading out above the ice stratum.

Speaking of Rampart, I am reminded that I saw there Rex Beach's deserted cabin. Once it was in the midst of the seething excitement of a log cabin metropolis of the gold fields. Then the placer deposits played out and to-day the place is practically deserted. Many of its houses have been cut up for firewood and others are falling in ruins. Beach's hut is a one-story shack made of slabs and boards. Over the rude door hangs a pair of white caribou horns from a beast that may have been shot by the novelist. There is a pile of wood outside the cabin, lying just as it was when the last occupant left.

I am told that Rex Beach came here to mine gold. He failed to find the precious metal but he unearthed the lode of human-interest stories and tales of adventure that have delighted us all. The history of his stay at Rampart is prosaic. The only story I picked up relates to an Indian woman who, according to the custom of the country, had three straight blue lines tattooed in ink on her chin. Rex Beach had bought some fish of the squaw and wanted to find her to get another supply. Asked to describe her, he said:

"I don't know her name, but she carried her head in the air. She is short and dirty and has her house number marked on her chin. It is III."

But to return to Fairbanks. We left the experiment farm and visited some of the homesteads near by. The first was owned by a man named Young, who came to Alaska some ten or twelve years ago. He took up three hundred and twenty acres of government land, a large part of which is now under cultivation. He is raising oat-hay and potatoes; he has also a big greenhouse where he grows tomatoes and other vegetables for the mining camps and the town. Mr. Young was not at home when we called, but Mrs. Young showed us about. As we looked over the farm I asked her how she liked living in this far-off Alaska. She replied that she had been a little dissatisfied until she had gone "outside" last summer, but that since she returned she had had no desire to go out again.

"This country is my home," she said, "and a mighty good home it is. You can see what the summer is like. We are perfectly comfortable during the winter. We always have plenty to eat, we get high prices for all that we sell, and we are farther ahead every year."

At that moment we were looking over the stock in the barnyard, which included two big sows, each of which had eight or ten little month-old pigs running with her. Mrs. Young pointed to them, saying, "We sold a pair of those pigs yesterday for twenty dollars. That will give you some idea of what things will bring in this country."

Our next visit was to the dairy farm belonging to a Mr. Hinckley, which supplies much of the milk and cream consumed in Fairbanks. Mr. Hinckley also sells butter, buttermilk, and cottage cheese. He has twenty cows which average three or four gallons of milk each twenty-four hours. They are what we would call in the States good ordinary stock.

The dairyman has not bought any hay for several years, but relies on the native grass and his oat-hay for his stock. He says the oat-hay is quite as good as timothy, and very much crisper.

Before leaving I pulled up a handful of the young oats growing outside the barn and measured the stalks. They were eighteen inches long, though the oats had been planted only three weeks before.

We went on to visit a three-hundred-and-twenty-acre truck farm on the very edge of Fairbanks. This is a homestead taken up fifteen years ago by Stacia Rickert, the wife of a business man of Fairbanks. Mr. Rickert has built here a very pretty cabin surrounded by flowers, and his home is as well furnished and as comfortable as that of any well-to-do farmer of the States. He has cleared about one fourth of the land, and the farm is one of the show places of Alaska. The ground is as flat as a floor and as green as the valley of the Nile. He is now cutting oat-hay, of which he has many acres. He has also great fields of barley and potatoes, the latter in full blossom.

The Rickert farm supplies a great part of Fairbanks and ships vegetables to the towns and the mining camps for miles around. It sends green stuff to Hot Springs and Fort Gibbon as well as to the gold mines of the Iditarod and Ruby.

The gardens of this farm cover twenty or thirty acres. As we walked through them I asked about the crops, and was told that there were in the ground twenty thousand cabbages, thirty thousand stalks of celery, and some acres of head lettuce. The celery, which is especially fine, grows to a height of four feet. Some of it was sent to Montana a few years ago to show what Alaska could do, and President Taft sampled it during his trip through that state. He declared it the finest he had ever tasted. As we went through one of the fields I pulled up a cabbage and put it on the scales in the greenhouse. It weighed twenty-six pounds.

There are several hothouses each devoted to a different crop. There is one which is one hundred and twenty feet long that grows melons only, including watermelons, casabas, and cantaloupes. The cantaloupes sell for a dollar a pound, and some of them bring four or five dollars. The vines are trained upon wires running along under the glass and from the beds up to the roof. From these wires the melons hang down, the heavier ones being supported by slings to prevent their breaking the vines. In other hothouses tomatoes, peppers, and cucumbers are grown.

Farming conditions are altogether different from those of most parts of the United States. Fairbanks is only about one hundred miles south of the Arctic Circle, and the growing season is short, ranging from three to four months, and extending in favourable seasons perhaps a half month longer. The last spring frosts occur about the middle of May, and frosts begin again during the latter part of August or the first of September. The long summer sunlight makes the crops grow very fast, however.

This part of Alaska is a region of scanty rainfall. Heavy showers are almost unknown; but it drizzles often in summer and much of the rain is during the growing season. The yearly average is about ten or twelve inches of water, including the snow of the winter. Besides the rainfall, there is the moisture from the layer of perpetual ice below the surface of the ground.

CHAPTER XIX

THAWING FORTUNES OUT OF THE ICE

THE country surrounding Fairbanks is the richest of the gold-bearing regions of Alaska. Since gold mining began there in 1886 the Yukon Basin has produced over one hundred and thirty millions of dollars' worth of gold, about eighty millions of which came from the Fairbanks district. This is one fourth of the value of all the gold taken out of Alaska. When one considers the seven million the United States paid for the territory, three hundred and twenty million dollars in gold output in something like forty years seems a pretty fair return on our investment.

All the gold of the Fairbanks district has been washed from creeks and their valleys. The valleys are streaked with a bed rock which lies far down under the surface. The gold-bearing stratum is five or six feet in thickness and has an average value of more than five dollars per cubic yard. Imagine a strip of land from New York to Philadelphia, five times as wide as the ordinary road, and worth one and one third million dollars per mile, and you will have some idea of the gold-bearing earth of this land of wealth.

The miners are still working on the oldest of the creeks, although in places these are almost deserted. When I visited the creeks yesterday I went by log hotels and dance halls, now empty and silent; and passed great masses

The chinked log roadhouse is still a feature of travel in the Fairbanks district, but many of the rude hotels are deserted and the "dance hall ladies" are gone.

The prospector's supplies and equipment may weigh a ton, and though a dog can pull more than a man can over the snow, the "musher" must sometimes help out even the stoutest-hearted team.

Rex Beach failed to find the gold he sought in Alaska, but he unearthed the lode of human interest stories that have delighted so many. His cabin at Rampart is deserted and falling in ruins.

This "sourdough" miner is coming to town for grub. Another summer service the dog renders is to help pull his master's boat over the gravel bars of shallow streams.

of gravel, the monuments of the work of the past. Leaving Fairbanks, we motored up one stream and down another, passing pile after pile of these tailings. We went through villages, which were once almost cities, now going to ruin, and after traversing the valleys of Fox Creek, Pedro Creek, Engineer Creek, Queenie Creek, Esther Creek, and other creeks named after the "dance ladies" of early days, stopped for the night at Chatanika on Cleary, one of the richest creeks of the Fairbanks district.

I am told there are places along Cleary where every foot of ground is worth twenty-five hundred dollars. Cleary has produced about twenty-four million dollars, worth of gold, and it is estimated that there is more gold in the ground than has yet been taken out. They are now working over some of the claims for a second time and, with cheap coal, better transportation, and modern dredging machinery, most of it will be handled again. I heard one miner discussing the possibilities of his men's striking for higher wages. "They can strike if they want to," said he, "but I can make a living working over my dump heap. I can take a rocker and wash out fifteen dollars any day in the week."

Nearly all of the gold taken out of the ground about Fairbanks has been placer gold. This means it is made up of gold dust and nuggets scattered through the earth and gravel, so that it has only to be washed to get the gold out. Of quartz gold, this region has as yet produced little, although several quartz mines are now working, and more will be opened with the coming of cheaper fuel from the Nenana coalfields.

Placer mining in Alaska is far different from that of the

States. In California and in the Rockies all that a miner needed to start business was a pick, a shovel, and a pan to wash out the gold. He might add a rocker or some other rude pieces of machinery, but, all told, the outfit cost little. The free gold lay on the top of the ground, or on the banks and in the beds of the creeks, and it was comparatively easy to find and wash it out. Here about Fairbanks more than eighty per cent. of the productive deposits lie at from forty to two hundred and sixty feet under ground, and most of them are in valley bottoms which are solidly frozen and have to be thawed out before the gold can be got at.

The whole country is covered with moss, which must be stripped off to find what lies beneath. To test the ground the prospector must go down to bed rock. The result is that his outfit is much more costly than in the Rockies. It should include a small boiler and pipe for steam thawing, rubber hose, steam points, and steam fittings. He needs a windlass, a cable, and wooden buckets to get the earth out after it is thawed, and if he expects to prospect in deep ground he should have a steam engine as well. There is sold here a prospecting outfit which costs about six hundred dollars. It consists of a four-horsepower boiler, a hoisting engine, steam points, pipe and fittings, and buckets and cable. The outfit is compact and can be carried on a dog sled. One of the best methods of prospecting is with drills, but the freight rates have been so high that few have come in. Of course the new railway should mean lower prices for the best drills, which were formerly around two thousand dollars.

It will be seen that it costs something to grub-stake a man in Alaska. Still, much grub-staking is done. Outsiders will furnish the provisions and the outfit and the miners will agree to prospect and work for half what they find. Stock in some of the mines is held largely in the States, and there are many little claims scattered here and there over the country that are kept going that way. Most of these are honestly managed. Now and then one is not. They tell a story here in Fairbanks about a miner who was working away in good spirits notwithstanding his output, which was practically nothing. He had plenty of money and seemed happy. Asked how he was doing, he replied:

"Fine! Fine!"

"Then you have reached the paystreak, I suppose?"

"Yes, I struck that at the start."

"But where is it? I don't see any gold."

"Oh," was the reply, "the paystreak is not here; the paystreak's in Chicago."

While I was at Chatanika I went into some of the mines. In the Nolan mine we got into a bucket and were dropped down a well eighty-four feet deep. Leaving the bucket, we walked through tunnels, stopping now and then to watch the miners thaw out the ice layer. The work is done with steam points or pipes through which steam is driven into the ice. The boilers with which the pipes are connected force the steam through rubber hose into the steel pipes. These end in points in which are small holes to let out the steam. The pipes are driven into the frozen walls with hammers, working their way on inch by inch as the steam thaws out the ice. It melts the gravel for several feet about the pipe. The thawed stuff can then be dug down and thrown into wheelbarrows, which carry it to the shaft and the hoists.

We saw the gold-bearing earth going out of the mine in the same bucket in which we came down. An engine raised the bucket by a steel cable high above the shaft, whence it slid on a pulley to the dump over the sluice box. The work of getting out the ore goes on winter and summer, but sluicing, or washing out the gold, can be done only when the weather is warm.

We were fortunate in being at the Nolan mine during one of its weekly clean-ups. The gold is washed in a trough perhaps a yard wide, a yard high, and several hundred feet long. This sluice box is made of rough plank and is set up at an angle of fifteen or twenty degrees so that it extends to the ground from the high crib containing the dump. When the time for the clean-up comes, a door is opened in the dump and the gold-bearing gravel pours down into the sluice box. A stream of water flows over it, forcing it onward and washing the dirt and gravel away. In the bottom of the sluice box are riffles or grates of steel which catch the gold. As the gold is heavier than the rock, sand, and earth, it falls into the riffles while the stream washes out the débris.

At first the water came in a flood, carrying down the stone, gravel, and sand with a rush. Five miners, clad in rough clothing with rubber boots to their thighs, stood in the current and stirred the mass as the water poured down. They threw out the big boulders and pitchforked over the mortar and sand. They stopped it here and there with their shovels, so that every bit of gold-dust might be washed out. After a time bits of the bottom of the sluice box were visible. In some places the box had turned yellow; the gold dust had piled up and coated the boards. The riffles became filled with black sand mixed with the yellow and now and then a small nugget was to be seen. The riffles were lifted out and the black sand containing the gold was carefully washed over.

The water now flowed slowly and the men agitated it with brushes of seaweed about the size of a whisk-broom. With these they separated most of the sand from the dust and the yellow flour and grains were caught in a scoop and thrown into a pan. It covered the bottom of the pan like a coarse yellow cornmeal.

After getting the gold out of the box we took some of it into the office cabin near by and dried it over a fire. It was then tossed up by the miners to blow out the bits of sand that were left. They threw the gold into the air much as you throw screenings to chickens, blowing the black sand away and catching every bit of the gold in the pan. The clean-up of this week amounted to about three quarts of gold. It was worth over four thousand dollars and the gold contents averaged seventeen dollars per ounce. This was the clean-up of a small mine. Larger clean-ups sometimes run into the tens of thousands of dollars.

CHAPTER XX

STORIES OF GOLD AND GOLD MINERS

HOW would you like to stub your toe on a gold mine? That is how the Rhoads-Hall quartz mine in Bedrock Creek valley near Fairbanks was discovered.

The mine has now more than a mile of underground workings, and has netted its owners over two hundred thousand dollars. The discoverer was L. B. Rhoads, a prospector who was mushing over the trail. He had made some money placer mining, but fortune had gone against him and he turned his attention to quartz. On his way down the hill to the Bedrock Creek valley he stubbed his toe and fell headlong. As he got up he looked for the cause of his stumbling, and found it was a rock speckled with coarse yellow bits of gold. He marked the spot, got an outfit, and dug down until he discovered a rich vein of quartz. He staked out a claim and thawed a shaft to the fifty-foot level, melting his way through with wood fires. Every week he crushed enough of the best rock to give him gold for his supplies for the week to come. In the winter he worked underground. The next spring he tunnelled in on the vein; and, to make a long story short, he finally established a mill of five stamps, out of which he and his brother-in-law, Hall, have already cleared almost a quarter of a million dollars.

Travelling through a gold country like this makes one

covetous. Everyone thinks gold, talks gold, and, considering the prices at the restaurants, I might almost say eats and drinks gold. One sees so much gold in the mines and the banks that he feels like the beggar boy with his nose flattened against the glass window of the candy store. There is plenty to be had were it not for the barrier between him and the taking. At the clean-ups of the camps I have handled gold nuggets as one handles shelled corn, and at the assay offices I have held up ten thousand dollars' worth of pure gold in one brick. At Dawson I saw two hundred thousand dollars' worth of bricks wheeled about on a truck such as you find at a country railroad station. The gold bricks were heavy and worth from fifteen thousand dollars to thirty thousand dollars apiece. At the same place I saw a ton of amalgam, consisting of quicksilver mixed with gold, ready to be shipped out to be reduced to gold bullion.

I have met at Fairbanks a man who has melted more than fifty million dollars' worth of gold dust and nuggets. This is Mr. G. E. Beraud, the assayer of the First National Bank. He is a chemist and metallurgist of note, and was the government assayer at Dawson when the Klondike rush was on.

All of the banks at Fairbanks have melting pots where the dust and nuggets are turned into bricks for shipment outside. You see these gold bricks on the bank counters. Some are as small as a cake of sweet chocolate and others are so large that if one fell on your toes it would crush them.

The assaying and melting is usually done outside the bank. Mr. Beraud's shop is a rude zinc shed like a portable garage. It contains a little furnace and the various implements of the assayer, including moulds and bone-ash, and scales so delicate that they will weigh a pencil mark on a single sheet of fine tissue paper or a single silky hair of a baby.

The gold dust is brought in to the banks by the miners in pokes, or bags of buckskin as big around as your arm and about a foot long. The banker takes the poke and pours the metal out on the scales, and then either pays cash outright for the gold according to weight or gives the miner a credit slip which entitles him to its actual value after it has been turned into bullion. The gold dust is of different values. Some is mixed with silver and is not worth more than thirteen dollars an ounce. Other gold dust may be worth twenty dollars an ounce. When the dust comes to Mr. Beraud, it is assayed—that is, it is melted and its gold content tested.

The assay is made after the gold is cast into bricks. From each brick a corner about the size of a marrowfat pea is chiselled off. This is hammered out on an anvil and run through rollers until it is as thin as a sheet of paper. A little strip of this gold leaf is taken off and weighed on the fine scales. It is so treated by melting in a furnace that the impurities are extracted and a little button of pure gold is left. This button is weighed and its weight is subtracted from that of the strip before it was melted. The result shows the proportion of pure gold in the brick; and there are tables giving its value in dollars and cents.

I asked the assayer whether he did not covet the metal he handled. He replied:

"I never think of the value. I have been working in gold so long that the stuff seems to me just like corn or oats in the hands of a farmer. When I first began to assay at Dawson I had never seen gold dust and nuggets in

Pipes filled with live steam are forced into the frozen ground to thaw it so that it can be removed and the gold-bearing gravel taken out. This is one of the reasons why cheap fuel means so much to Alaska.

Gold worth $4,000 was taken out of this Chatanika sluice-box in a single clean-up. Mines of the Fairbanks district have produced one fourth of all the gold from Alaska.

quantity before and I almost went crazy. I liked the looks of the gold and I bought nuggets and gold pins and chains made of them. I wore a nugget as a scarf pin and had nugget cuff buttons. After a time I grew tired of them and gave them away."

I asked Mr. Beraud about his early experiences in Dawson, when fortunes were made in a week. Said he: "The gold came so easily that they almost threw it about. The miners would go from saloon to saloon treating the crowd and throwing their pokes to the bartender to weigh out the amount of each treat. They were so careless that a man might take out double the quantity and not be detected. A miner might have a thousand dollars' worth of gold in his bag, and spend it all in an evening. Now and then one would come into a dance hall, and taking his seat in the gallery, call one of the girls to stand under him while he poured gold dust into her hair. A dance hall girl might thus clean up fifty dollars in a single shampoo. I remember a miner named Hauser, who fell in love with a girl and got her to marry him by paying her what she weighed in gold dust. As she stepped on the scales and tipped the beam at one hundred and thirty-five pounds avoirdupois, she weighed more than twenty-one hundred ounces troy weight, which, at eighteen dollars an ounce, made his wife cost him over thirty-eight thousand dollars."

Similar extravagances prevailed here at Fairbanks when the camp was in the height of its glory. Miners are always generous and communities like this are far more charitable than those in a long-settled country. Said Mr. L. T. Erwin, the United States Marshal at Fairbanks, to me the other day:

"The people here are the most generous on earth. It is no trick to raise five hundred dollars to send a sick man or woman outside. Only a few months ago a man was taken outside with a trained nurse and enough money was sent along to pay his hospital expenses in Seattle. I have lived in Alaska eighteen years and in all that time I have not seen one person obliged to go begging.

"We have, you know, many unsuccessful men," the marshal continued. "Mining is to a large extent a gamble, and where one man succeeds there are hundreds who fail. I remember an instance of a man who came to Fairbanks to make his fortune, leaving his wife and family outside. He found no gold and finally fell sick and died in a cabin on one of the creeks. When the miners looked over his papers they found a letter that had just come from his wife in a little town in Massachusetts. The letter was full of news about the baby that had been born since the father had left and inside it was one of the baby's stockings. The miners stood around the dead body in the cabin as the letter was read, and when the stocking was shown the tears ran down their faces. One of them reached out and took it. He pulled forth his poke and poured in enough gold dust and nuggets to fill up the toe. Another miner poured in more dust, and this kept on, the stocking passing from hand to hand until it was filled. But all had not yet contributed. The gold was then poured on to the table, the miner who did so saying: 'We'll dump this and start over again.' In the end it was passed around the whole camp, with the result that five thousand dollars' worth of gold dust was collected and the money therefor sent to the widow."

United States Marshal Erwin has the unique distinction

of being the only man who has ever driven a flock of turkeys from the Pacific Ocean across the mountains into the Klondike gold region. We had been talking about old times when he told me this story:

"My father then lived near Danville, Kentucky, in one of the chief turkey and goose raising sections of the United States. When I was a boy turkey raising was a regular business there, and we sometimes drove our turkeys and geese as far as sixty miles to the markets. We had to put shoes on the geese before starting out."

I laughed. "You need not smile," said the marshal; "that is the truth. We made the shoes by driving the geese through melted pitch and then through sand. The sand and pitch stuck to their feet and gave them a pair of hard shoes.

"Well, when I came to the Klondike and saw the high prices they were getting for poultry I concluded I'd make a fortune by bringing live stock from outside. I left the camp and went to Seattle, where I bought six hundred chickens and eighty-four turkeys. I took them on a steamer a thousand miles northward to Dyea, and from there sent the chickens by wagon over the White Pass. The turkeys I drove. It was no trouble except they would persist in stopping at night. You cannot prevent a turkey from going to roost when the sun sets. I tried it, but the turkeys would jump up on the rocks. You might push them off but they would go on a few steps and then get up again. However, I finally got them over the range and down to Lake Lebarge, whence I took them by boat into Dawson."

"How did you succeed in the sale?"

"Very well. But I had to learn how to sell them.

There was a great competition for fresh fowl among the provision men and everyone wanted to corner the market and crowd out the others. When I entered the first store and told them I had eighty turkeys and six hundred chickens the dealer's face fell, for he saw that he could not monopolize such an enormous proposition as that. I changed my plan, kept my mouth shut about the supply, and began to peddle them out in small numbers. I got twenty dollars apiece for the turkeys and from eight to ten dollars for the chickens. Altogether I got three thousand dollars out of my chickens and two thousand from the turkeys, so that my gross receipts for the trip were five thousand dollars."

CHAPTER XXI

AMONG THE OLD TIMERS

THE winter is coming and Monte Terrill will have to go to jail so we can take care of him." This remark, which one hears as the summer ends in Fairbanks, gives in a nutshell one of the strange conditions obtaining in the heart of Alaska. This country has no accommodations for vagrants and no laws for the needy poor. There is the Pioneer's Home, it is true, but that is at Sitka about two thousand miles from where Monte lives.

Monte Terrill is a character. His whole life has been a fight against misfortune, and still, although blind and lame, he is not willing to give up the battle. I do not know his age, but he has long passed three score and ten. Years ago, when he first came to the Klondike, he was one of the most ambitious, determined, and industrious of the sourdoughs, as hardened Alaskans are called. One day when out trapping he sank through the ice to his waist. The thermometer was twenty-five degrees below zero and his legs were so badly frozen that one had to be amputated at the ankle and the other taken off half way to the knee. Equipped with an artificial leg and feet, he again took up the battle of life. He got about so well on his wooden pins that but few knew of his infirmity, and he obtained a job with a gang working on the Copper River Railroad. He did not want his condition known to his mates in the construction camp for fear he would be fired. But one night, when he had taken off his false feet and laid them beside him in his bunk, the string attached to one of them hung down and tickled the man in the bunk below. The man gave the string a jerk and the wooden foot came down and kicked him in the face. Monte's lameness was reported to the boss, who discharged him at once.

After that, Monte went about working at anything he could get and drifting from camp to camp. Finally, he settled in a cabin on the River Cheena not far from Fairbanks, where for several years he earned a living cutting wood for the steamers. Then his eyesight failed. It was pitiful to see how he tried to keep people from knowing his misfortune. When he heard a man coming he would straighten up and start to walk about boldly, often running into a tree or a fence. He was offered assistance but would not take it. At last he was known to be on the verge of starvation and was arrested on a charge of vagrancy and sentenced to jail for the winter, so that the citizens might have a legal right to take care of him. Even then he complained, saying that he wanted to go back to his cabin, and that he knew he could in some way earn enough to care for himself.

This story was told me by Mr. L. T. Erwin, Chief of Police as well as United States Marshal at Fairbanks. "Judge" Erwin has the job of keeping order in a district half again as large as either Germany or France. The district has only twenty thousand population, but these are so scattered that fifteen deputies are stationed at posts over the whole country from the Canadian boundary near Eagle to the Russian mission on the Lower Yukon and from the Arctic Circle to the edge of the Kuskokwim region.

AMONG THE OLD TIMERS

Here in Alaska marshals and their deputies have to refer almost everything to Washington before they can act. When a crime is committed, not a cent can be spent to detect the criminal without authority from the Attorney General five or six thousand miles away. Not long ago a terrible murder was committed just outside the city. No one knew who was the murderer and it was important to scour the neighbourhood and begin the work of investigation at once. Before he could proceed the marshal had to send this cable to Washington:

ATTORNEY GENERAL, Washington, D. C.
Woman foully murdered last night along the railroad track within five miles of Fairbanks. Authority requested to pay expense of office deputies and make investigations in the surrounding country.
(Signed)   UNITED STATES MARSHAL.

It was days before authority was granted. In the Yukon Territory the Canadian mounted police would have been on the job before the murdered woman grew cold, and the arrest would have been made almost immediately.

"Judge" Erwin has had considerable experience in Canada, having mined gold in the Klondike before he came here. I asked him whether they did not do these things better there. His reply was characteristic:

"Yes, they skin us a mile. When the mounted police have no law, they make one, settling small offences out of court. It is said that no murderer of the Yukon Territory has ever escaped."

The wheels of justice are badly clogged by Washington red tape. I have before me a copy of the Alaska *Dispatch*, giving a list of twenty-five murders which have occurred within the last decade, whose perpetrators were not hung, shot, or brought to judgment. The paper says that the criminals in every case could have been convicted if the marshals had been allowed sufficient funds for securing the evidence. It gives the details in a number of cases, and among other stories, tells of two prospectors murdered in the Chandlar. The body of one of them, a man named Smith, was unearthed and brought to Fairbanks by the marshal on a dog sled. The Government at Washington objected to paying the expenses of the dog team and refused to allow any funds with which to make a search for the body of the partner or to investigate the murder.

I asked the marshal about crime in this part of Alaska. He replied:

"The territory is supposed to be full of bad men, but that is a mistake. The order here is much better than in the Southern States, where I was reared. You cannot pick up a Georgia newspaper even now without finding in it a report of one or more shooting affrays. In the last eleven years I know of only one man killed in Alaska with a pistol. There are but few people in the country who carry weapons. The murders that have been committed have been perpetrated with guns, clubs, or knives.

"Our people are as law-abiding as any people of the world. Burglary is almost unknown. I lived in Fairbanks eight years before I locked my door. The people will not stand for robberies. We have our strikes but there is no bloodshed and no destruction of property.

"Our people are charitable. As an instance of the generosity of Fairbanks," continued Marshal Erwin, "take the San Francisco earthquake. The news of it was telegraphed here one Saturday. There was a meeting

172

Many thousands of dollars' worth of gold have been handled in such cabins as this in Alaska, where locks on the doors are almost unknown, yet fortunes in nuggets and dust are safe.

The miners remove the black sand often mixed with the gold dust and nuggets by blowing it out, or sometimes by tossing the contents of the gold pan again and again into the air.

The coal of the Nenana fields, not far from Fairbanks, is a lignite, excellently suited to domestic use and very clean. The first coal mined by the railroad, chiefly for its own use, cut in half the price of $18.00 a ton.

that night at Eagle Hall and by noon the next day twenty thousand dollars had been collected and started on its way to the sufferers. A month later there was a fire in Fairbanks which destroyed almost the whole town. The people outside remembered what we had done for San Francisco, and offers of help poured in. They were all refused, the mayor sending this message: 'We thank you all, but we can carry our own skillet and don't need any help.'"

It is surprising that there is not more crime in Fairbanks. The city is in the heart of the wilds and surrounded by mining camps that have produced millions in gold dust and nuggets. At times the banks have been crammed with gold and in the camps are the bags of gold washed out at every clean-up. Gold is often kept in cans and other common receptacles in the log cabins, and I have not yet seen a house that could not easily be broken into and robbed. Millions of dollars' worth of gold is annually carried out on the steamers going down the Tanana and up the Yukon to White Horse. The present method of transporting this treasure is in an old-fashioned iron safe with handles on each side. The safe is left out in the open under the decks, merely chained to the mast.

In the past the gold was kept in a strong room, and now and then thefts were attempted. One day a sailor unscrewed the bars of the room and got out a box of dust and nuggets worth thirteen thousand dollars. He and his partner in the crime tied a life preserver to the box and threw it overboard, thinking the life preserver would act as a float and enable them to find the box when they came back later on. At the next stop one of the men dropped into the water, swam to the bank, and went back up the river to look for the gold, but could not find it. A little later the officers of the steamer found that the strong room had been tampered with and that one of the boxes was missing. They caught the criminals, who were tried and sent to the penitentiary. The life preserver was afterward found by an Indian, but the box of gold is still in the Yukon.

On another steamer a man named Miller came all the way from the "outside" to steal a big shipment of gold. He got a job as night watchman, and one night, when the boat was tied up at the wharf, he succeeded in getting forty thousand dollars in dust from the strong box, putting buckshot in its place. Before he could return the treasure chest two half-drunken men came aboard and stumbled over the little safe which Miller had brought out on deck. Realizing what it was, they dropped it over the side in the darkness and then buried it in the woods on shore. Next morning one of them, frightened over his share in the robbery, told the steamship people what he had done, and helped them recover the strong box. But when it was opened it was found to contain, of course, only the buckshot Miller had substituted for the gold. Miller was convicted of the original theft through his purchase of the buckshot and served a sentence in the penitentiary, but the gold was never recovered and it is supposed he succeeded in getting it safely to the outside.

Though Fairbanks has long since become a settled community without much of the lawlessness usually associated with mining camps, many of the picturesque features of the earlier days are still to be found here. One is the habit of nicknames. Everyone calls his fellow by his first name or a nickname, and "mister" is almost unknown.

One character here is generally known as "the man who talked the crow to death." This is a miner who talks so much that his fellows have time and again left him in disgust. One day they left a raven sitting on the fence outside his cabin. As the story goes, the man addressed his conversation to the raven and talked to it until at last the bird dropped dead.

Another man is known as "Short and Dirty," others are "Skookum Bill," and "Sourdough Bill," and "the Malamute Kid," noted for his fine malamute dogs.

The "Bear Kid" is a husky fellow who got the title by wrestling with a tame black bear before an admiring crowd, while the "Hungry Kid" is said to be able to eat at any and all times and never to refuse a meal. One very thin man is called "the Evaporated Kid." His friends say that he is a human string bean with the bean left out. "Eat-em-up Frank" owns a cabin on the Tanana River between Fort Gibbon and Fairbanks, where he has a little potato farm. He is called "Eat-'em-up" because when he gets drunk, which is often, he shouts that he can eat up any man in the crowd. He weighs only one hundred pounds. "Step-and-a-half Johnson" has one leg shorter than the other. Nevertheless, he is fond of racing and can get over the ground faster than the average sprinter. He is said to insist that the race track be along the side of a hill, where the slope gives his short leg the advantage.

Another striking character is "Two-step Louie," who got his title during the gold rush at Dawson. He was a successful miner and a nightly frequenter of the dance halls. The usual charge was a dollar a dance, the man being expected to treat his partner at the end. The story is told how "Two-step Louie" once sold a claim for five thousand dollars with the understanding that fifteen hundred dollars was to be paid in Alamander Left chips, each chip being good for one dance. It is said he would sometimes come into the dance halls and pin a one-hundred-dollar note to the curtain over the orchestra telling the men to give the crowd a century's worth of "Turkey in the Straw." The musicians would play two or three dances and then take down the note.

These tales are vouched for by the people of Fairbanks, but I am beginning to doubt whether all the stories I hear in Alaska are true. I have just been told about a miner at White River who had his toes frozen so that his feet sloughed off to the instep. The man had his toes amputated and was able to walk on the stubs with the aid of a pair of bear's feet made into moccasins, the bear's claws taking the place of his toes. The man who told me this showed me a photograph of the miner with his bear feet tied on.

The people here say that Alaska is as free of snakes as was Ireland after the advent of St. Patrick. They claim that the only snake that ever came into the territory was one brought from the outside several years ago in a bale of timothy hay. The snake arrived on the edge of winter, crawled out of the bale when the thermometer was about forty degrees below zero and immediately froze solid. It was a long snake and in freezing the head bent over so that it looked like a cane. An Indian chief picked it up and used it for a walking stick all that winter. He is even said to be using it still. He buries it in the ice under the moss as the spring comes on, and when the thermometer falls brings it out as a prop for his declining years.

And then the fish stories! Judge Wickersham of Fairbanks tells me of a lake near the headwaters of the Tanana River where he often goes for sport in the summer. The water is as clear as crystal, and looking down over the side of the boat he can see hundreds of fish swimming about. He picks out those he wishes to catch, dropping his bait in front of only the best, and pulling it away when a small fish or one of the wrong variety might swallow it. As I remember, he could catch a boat load in an hour, but on account of this careful selection and his desire for sport he takes rather longer.

It is said also that when the women of Fairbanks go fishing, instead of dropping the flies on the water, they hold them at the edge of the line, some distance above it, and wager as to who can make the trout jump the highest. The loser has to treat the crowd to a luncheon.

CHAPTER XXII

FROM FORT GIBBON TO THE SEA

TO-DAY, after steaming down the Tanana River for two hundred and seventy-five miles from Fairbanks, I am once more on the mighty Yukon, this time on my way to Bering Sea and Nome. For the last two months I have been travelling on this great river and its tributaries. The section where I now am is known as the Lower Yukon and is about eight hundred miles long, or about one third the length of the main stream.

Though it drains thousands of square miles, the Lower Yukon basin numbers its population, I venture, by the hundreds. Going down river, we have now and then passed an Indian village and stopped at several towns which form the river ports for gold mines. One of the chief of these latter is Ruby, one hundred and seventy-five miles below Fort Gibbon. Ten years ago this was the scene of a stampede when gold was discovered on Ruby Creek. It is still the most important settlement on this part of the river, with its log and sheet-iron buildings so jumbled together that they look as if they had been pitched out of the sky and allowed to lie as they fell.

The people are supported by the gold mines. About some of the houses are gardens and there are two hot-houses noted for their fine vegetables. The proprietor of one of these, who boarded our steamer for Nome, had

178

as a sample of his products a cucumber eighteen inches long. He said that was only a small one.

A little below Ruby we passed the mouth of the Koyukuk River, which is navigable for more than five hundred miles north of where it flows into the Yukon. Its rich mining camps are reached by small steamers.

A few miles beyond the mouth of the Koyukuk we stopped at Nulato. This is an Indian village, one of the oldest trading posts on the Yukon. It was established by the Russians when Van Buren was President and at about the time that Tyler entered the White House it was taken over by the Russian-American Company and became the chief market for the furs of this part of Alaska.

The Nulato of to-day is interesting chiefly because of its Indian cemetery. Our boat tied up right under it, so that we had a good view of the native monuments on the steep hill above us. Scores of little yellow, blue, red, green, and white kennel-like houses were scattered along the top of the hill, the homes of the ghosts of the departed, into which the Indians now and then put food for the spirits. Above each house was a cross, showing how Christianity is combined with the native superstitions. On the roofs of the graves were laid many mirrors, which flashed in the sun, as well as such belongings of the dead as guns, snow-shoes, bags of tobacco, and other treasures. It must have been a tedious business to get the bodies up to that lofty perch, yet to this day, I am told, canoes sometimes arrive with the remains of Indians who have asked to be buried there.

The natives of Nulato are dirty and their houses are not as well kept as those of the Upper Yukon tribes. The squaws object to having their pictures taken, and when I pointed my camera at some of them, they wrapped their shawls around their heads and threw themselves down on the ground.

The next town below Nulato is Kaltag, the starting point for a winter trail across to Unalalik, which shortens the way to Nome by five hundred miles. To the coast by this portage it is some eighty or ninety miles, while by the river it is six hundred. Kaltag is a trading post and a government telegraph station. It also has a wireless tower which was erected by private parties to maintain communication with the Iditarod gold fields.

While our steamer took on fuel oil, I set out on a short tramp into the country. Passing through the village of a dozen one-story cabins all fastened with padlocks because the Indian owners had gone off for a feast, I found myself in a virgin wilderness.

The ground was covered with moss and spotted with stunted spruce trees and bushes loaded with blueberries, cranberries, and squawberries. The moss was so deep that I seemed to be treading on a feather bed. Everywhere I went my feet sank in to the ankles. The moss felt cold, and pulling some up, I found the bed of perpetual ice just below. The matted roots were heavy with moisture though bare of soil.

On this walk I had my first experience with the Alaska mosquitoes. To my surprise, these pests were not fierce, and their bites not as severe as those of the New Jersey species. Though I had neither gloves nor head-net I suffered no great discomfort. This, I am told, is very unusual, as generally the mosquitoes are almost unbearable. They come in May and June, shortly after the breaking of the ice. At that time everyone who goes

The young Indians like to have their pictures taken, but the older squaws object and hide their faces. The old Eskimos believe the photographer carries away with him control of the soul of his subject.

The population of the great basin of the lower Yukon is numbered only by hundreds. Ruby, the principal town, is supported mainly by the gold mines on Ruby Creek, once the scene of a stampede.

Within two years after gold was discovered in the district near by, Iditarod had produced six million dollars' worth. The town is reached from the lower Yukon by going up the Innoko and Iditarod rivers.

through the country must wear a head-net and have his hands protected by gloves. It is best to wear boots, for the mosquitoes bore their way through the eyelet holes in one's shoes, and their bites raise great buttons of flesh on each side of the tongue. I have heard of men being killed by the mosquitoes, and they say the horses and other animals go almost crazy from the bites if they are left out in the woods.

Leaving Kaltag, the Yukon flows almost straight south for a distance of one hundred and fifty miles or more to the Holy Cross Mission, near which the Innoko River comes in. The Innoko gives access to the gold fields known as the Iditarod. The camp is reached by sailing up the Innoko to Dykeman at the head of navigation of the Iditarod River, a branch of the Innoko. The distance is about three hundred and fifty miles, and from there to the camp is seventy-five miles farther. In two years after its discovery the mines of the Iditarod district had yielded six million dollars' worth of gold. A single claim has produced forty thousand dollars' worth of gold a week throughout a season. Many of the claims have been bonded or bought by the Guggenheims, who are now operating large dredges there.

Between Kaltag and the Holy Cross Mission is Anvik, an Indian settlement with a Russian church, and still farther down the river is Andreafski, established by the Russians in 1853. Andreafski is now a little trading station on the banks of the Yukon with a great oil tank, at which the steamers stop to take fuel. The town is populated almost entirely by Eskimos, about the only whites being the storekeepers.

From Andreafski the Yukon widens until it is soon

three miles from one bank to the other. Then it branches
out into wide channels, each leading to the sea. Its
many mouths form a great fan-like delta one hundred
miles wide. In flood time the whole country is under
water. Islands grow up in a night and new sand bars are
sighted every voyage. In places the stream is so wide
that one can see little except a vast expanse of yellow
water rimmed by the sapphire sky. Close to the shore
grows grass as green as that of Holland, and the boat
seems to be moving through one vast pasture.

The Government has done little to improve the navigation of the Yukon. The only lights on this mighty
stream, with its winding course, its scores of tributaries,
and its thousands of shifting sand bars and islands, are
where the river flows into the ocean. Some of the captains put up their own marks to aid them in subsequent
voyages. As we passed through the delta the captain
of our steamer showed me a barrel in the middle of a
large sand bar. The sand bar was under water during
the last trip, when he had anchored the barrel there to
locate it. The captains all keep records of each trip,
noting the changes and handing their sketches over to
the captains following them up or down stream.

CHAPTER XXIII

THE CITY OF GOLDEN SANDS

I AM in the Hotel Golden Gate in Nome, the City of Golden Sands. To-day when I stood on Front Street at high tide and threw a stone into the ocean it ricochetted over a beach which was once a gold mine. News that gold had been discovered in the beds of creeks near by was already beginning to bring prospectors to this part of Seward Peninsula when, in 1899, gold was found right on the beach here. It was discovered by a United States soldier, who panned out enough every day or so for an extra meal. Then "Missouri Bill" made his big strike, getting out twelve thousand dollars' worth in one day. Soon men poured in by the thousands from all parts of the world to wash out this easy money from the sea sands.

The gold was in a kind of ruby sand which lay in beds from six inches to two feet deep for forty miles along the shore. As the miners came in each picked out a space, drove in a stake where he stood, and drew a mark on the sand around him as far out as he could reach with his shovel. Out of such small holdings within less than two months a million dollars' worth of gold dust had been washed from the beach in front of Nome. Just west of the town two men cleaned up thirty-eight hundred dollars in three days.

When the beach mining was at its height, the people

183

went crazy. Mining cradles were in great demand and the price of lumber rose to four hundred dollars a thousand feet. Coal brought from fifty dollars to one hundred dollars a ton, and cabins and shacks of one room sold for six hundred dollars each. Wages at once jumped to ten dollars a day, and during a part of the time to two dollars an hour. Then the sands began to play out. In 1900 those in front of Nome yielded three hundred and fifty thousand dollars, but the next year they had dropped to one seventh as much. It is the same with the other beach mines along the coast. Some of them yielded hundreds of thousands of dollars, but they were soon washed out.

Still, as I walked up the beach this afternoon I saw men taking gold out of the sand. In one place they had put up an engine and stretched a rude tent above it. Connected with the engine was a pipe about six inches in diameter which carried the water to the top of a sluice box twenty or thirty feet high. The men were throwing the sand into the box and the stream was washing it away, the gold being caught in riffles or iron gratings in the bottom of the box.

Farther north some men were rocking out the gold in hand cradles, and there was patchy mining going on all along the beach. I saw a woman laying out a claim and fencing it with poles. She seemed to resent my inspection. She was a positive woman and did not want visitors.

I am told there is still gold in these sands in front of Nome and that more comes in at every high tide. One can get colour almost anywhere by washing the sand. A low-grade deposit amounting to something like fifty cents a cubic yard is said to run for miles along the seashore, and machinery may yet be invented to get this gold out profitably.

I doubt not that there is a fortune under the planks of Front Street, and that if the buildings were cleared away from the tundra on which they stand it could be mined at a profit. Some of the houses have cellars which yielded enough pay dirt to cover the cost of the digging. The gold is scattered through the earth in patches or pockets, and there are probably many pockets yet undiscovered.

Back of Nome one can see the tailings from which the gold has been taken. There is a plain about four miles wide running from the shore to a low range of mountains, composed of three ancient beaches which have grown up throughout the ages. From these beaches millions of dollars' worth of gold has been mined.

I shall not forget my landing at Nome. It was early in the morning when our steamer cast anchor a mile or so out. We were taken from the ship by a steam launch to a landing above which rose a great tower connected by a cable with another tower of an equal height on the mainland. Passengers and baggage were taken from the ocean tower to the land in a platform cage which swung dizzily along on the cable high above the billows.

The city of Nome is a town of shreds and patches, the raggedest municipality I have yet struck in Alaska. There are houses enough for ten thousand people, though the population is to-day not one tenth of that. The skyline looks like the jaws of a boy just getting his second teeth. The buildings are scattered along streets paved with plank, gravel, or the sand of the seashore.

At the upper end is the Eskimo village. It is composed of tents, rude cabins, and shacks of boards, most of them put up by the placer miners and now occupied by squatters and Eskimos. The town proper is farther down the beach. The chief street is Front Street, a wide road paved with thick planks and lined with houses of one or two stories. Some of the buildings contain excellent stores, but there are many vacancies, and signs of "To Rent" are to be seen in every block.

There are but few big buildings in Nome. The largest is the Golden Gate Hotel, a dreary four-story barn with numerous bay-windows across its front and a view as desolate as that of Poverty Flat. The building is of light wood, which carries sound like a fiddle box. The moving of a bed on the ground floor sends a noise to the rooms in the attic. The place is golden only in the high charges for any petty service the guest may want. It costs me ten cents to press the electric button which brings the bellboy, and the bills for laundry are beyond computation.

To strangers with the proper introductions perhaps the most interesting place in Nome is the Log Cabin Club, famous all over Alaska for its hospitality. Its picturesque home is a cabin furnished in keeping with its rustic style. The table in the centre of its huge main clubroom is thirty feet long and five feet wide. It seems to be a single thick slab and is so polished that one can see his face in it. The front door is of logs and the great hinges are of hand-wrought iron.

When Nome was started there was no lumber to be had, and the first homes were tents. Later, frame houses were built over the tents, or as an annex to them. Many small shacks went up, and then came rambling buildings of two or three stories. Even to-day there are but few large houses and many a home has only three or four rooms. One reason for this is the cost of fuel and the difficulty of keeping the houses warm during the cold winter months.

The little buildings have to have high stovepipes, in order that their draught may not be cut off by the taller structures about them. The result is a little cottage will often have a galvanized stovepipe as high as itself rising above it. Looking down on the town, one sees a thicket of these smokestacks springing out of the roofs. They look like handles to the houses below, and make one think of so many Irish shillalahs, the chimneys being the handles and the houses the knobs on the ends of the clubs.

Many of the houses have gardens, for Nome is so far north that, though the summers are short, the sun works eighteen to twenty-four hours then and the people are able to grow lettuce, turnips, and other green stuff. Nearly every woman has some flowers in her front windows and some have flowers growing outside. Entering, you find these homes very well furnished. They have their pianos and other musical instruments. They are well equipped with books and magazines, in fact, with all the furnishings of the cultured homes of the States.

On the street are many women and men as well dressed as those of our cities, and there are others clad in the rough clothing necessary for hard labour in the Far North. There are miners wearing shoes laced to their knees, or white or black rubber boots to the waist. There are Eskimos in *mukluks* and skin garments. Their fat Mongolian features look out of fur hoods with bristles as long as a hat pin. Some are clad in parkas of fur or cotton, with their feet in boots of sealskin to the knees. There are little Eskimo women with babies tied to their backs. The faces of the little ones peep out over the shoulders of their mothers. The Eskimos look queerest when the rain comes, and this just now is most of the time. Then the natives put on waterproof coats made of the bladders of the walrus, a skin as thin as paper, which turns the rain and keeps one dry in the wettest of weather. This skin is in small pieces sewed together in bulbous patches.

Among the most striking business features of Nome are the curio shops, stores selling mining materials, and those dealing in furs of every description. Some of the latter have polar bear skins costing from forty dollars to seventy-five dollars apiece, glacier bear skins worth one fourth as much, and brown bear skins of great size. The stores have also white fox skins, reindeer hides, and skins of the ermine, which are as white as snow with a pinch of black on the end of the tail. The places selling mining supplies and hardware are especially large. I went through one hardware store that does a business of several hundred thousand dollars a year. Nome is a wholesale centre for the mining camps not only of the Seward Peninsula, but also for those of Arctic Alaska, and for much of north-eastern Siberia as well.

The provision stores carry stocks out of proportion to the size of the community, especially in the fall when full supplies have to be laid in for the long winter months. The last steamer comes late in October. From then on for six months or more the country is icebound, and such goods as are brought in must be on dog sleds. Freight charges for such supplies double their price.

Ships anchor far outside at Nome, and passengers are swung ashore on a platform suspended on a cable stretched from a tower built in the water to another tower on the beach.

The Log Cabin Club is the centre of the gay social life of Nome, when for seven or eight months it is shut in by the ice stretching away to the Siberian shores.

THE CITY OF GOLDEN SANDS

Just now, in the heart of midsummer, the weather is as soft and warm as in New York or Massachusetts. The air is so full of ozone that one seems to be breathing champagne. It is light the clock around and I can read my newspaper at midnight. Along in October the Nomeites will first sight blocks of ice floating down from the north. Perhaps the day after the water will take on a slushy look and in a little while Nome will be frozen in for seven months of winter. The thermometer drops to below zero and stays there, sometimes going to forty below, and back from the coast, still lower.

Many of the people leave Nome to spend the winter in the States, returning the following summer. Those who remain adopt a dress much like that of the Eskimos. They have fur coats, shoes, and boots, and protect their hands with fur mittens. Most of the citizens are confined to the town at this time, but there are trips with dog sleds across country, and except during blizzards there is communication between Nome and Council City.

I am told by the residents that the winter is the most interesting time of the year. Then the people have dances, socials, fairs, and amateur theatricals. It is quite the thing to go across country on skis from the town to the creeks and mining camps. Nome has a ski club, and tournaments are held, in which prizes are awarded, both for jumping and for speed. Sleighing with dogs is another amusement. A common winter sight is milady, wrapped in furs, sitting in a dog sled, with the driver running behind, holding on to the handle bars. Such sleds are used to go to dances held in the neighbouring camps, and the men run races with each other.

I like the Nomeites. There are but few drones among

them, and most of them are good boosters. They do not expect their city to have the population it once had but they say that owing to the large area of low-grade gold earth about it Nome is bound to be a mining centre for generations to come. They say also that it will always be the chief port of the Seward Peninsula, a territory which has vast mineral resources yet to be developed.

CHAPTER XXIV

CREEKS THAT MADE MILLIONAIRES

SEWARD PENINSULA, which forms the extreme western end of Alaska, is the Golden Horn of the North American continent. It is twice as big as Maryland and half the size of Ohio, and a great part of it is peppered with gold. The district has already produced more than eighty million dollars' worth of gold dust and nuggets and the country has hardly been scratched. Dr. Alfred H. Brooks, the head of the Alaska division of the Geological Survey, has estimated that there are more than two hundred million dollars' worth of gold mixed with its gravels, and the probability is that the total output of minerals will be fifty or more times the amount we paid for Alaska.

I have just returned from a trip with Jafet Lindeberg through the greatest gold mines of the Seward Peninsula. They belong to the Pioneer Mining Company, founded by Lindeberg, Bryntesen, and Lindbloom, the "three lucky Swedes." Since then more than six million dollars' worth of gold has been taken out of that creek, and tens of millions have come from the coastal plain through which it runs. The Pioneer Mining Company now owns about three thousand acres of gold-bearing earth and is capitalized at five million dollars.

When gold was discovered, Lindeberg and his partners washed out the first dust by hand, melting the frozen

191

earth with hot water. To-day the washing is done with the finest of mining machinery. Rivers of water have been carried over the mountains to supply the hydraulic giants, and the gold-bearing earth is forced up through pipes to a height of fifty feet into sluice boxes, in which the gold is washed out. Some of the company's land is phenomenally rich. Three hundred acres, or about one tenth of it, will run, so Mr. Lindeberg told me, from seventy-five thousand dollars to one hundred thousand dollars of gold to the acre, or in all from twenty to thirty million dollars. The remaining twenty-seven hundred acres carry more or less gold, and the company has enough work in sight to keep it busy for many years.

I have seen much of Jafet Lindeberg, who, with John Bryntesen and Erik Lindbloom, made the discovery that resulted in the great gold fields of Nome. None of the three men had had much experience in gold mining. Bryntesen had come from the iron mines of Michigan to search for coal. Lindbloom had emigrated from Sweden to San Francisco, where he had worked as a tailor, and came to Alaska on hearing of the gold discoveries at Kotzebue Sound. Lindeberg had come from Norway to aid the United States' expedition which took reindeer from Norway to the starving miners at Dawson. Having heard of Klondike gold, he took the reindeer contract so as to get to the mines. When he landed with the deer he heard that gold had been discovered on the Seward Peninsula and came on north to St. Michael. He was prospecting near there, along the Fish River, when he fell in with Bryntesen and Lindbloom, and the three decided to go westward and test the country about the Snake River, at the mouth of which Nome is situated. They had

The people "inside" do not let the snows and long twilights of winter keep them at home. The men try to beat each other getting their sweethearts by dog sleds to the dances in the mining creek towns.

In hydraulic mining mighty streams of water are directed against the hillsides of gold-bearing earth, thawing it and forcing it through pipes up fifty feet to the sluice boxes where the gold is washed out.

tested a half-dozen creeks flowing into the river, finding more or less gold, when they made their discovery on Anvil Creek. That was the twentieth of September, 1898. The weather was already cold, but by using hot water they were able to wash the gravel, and took out eighteen hundred dollars' worth of gold within a few days.

The Pioneer properties are in and about Anvil Creek and include the site of the original discovery. The chief agent in getting out the gold is water, which bursts forth from pipes in streams as big around as a telegraph pole and often several hundred feet long. The force of these streams is so great that they would cut a man in two if he tried to cross one. They are so swift you cannot pierce them with an ax. They are sent against the hills and lift up rocks and gravel and shoot them in clouds through the air. At one point of my trip one of these streams came between me and the sun, and the sand, gravel, and water composing it took on all the colours of the rainbow.

I stood for awhile and watched the men working. They were clad in slickers and white rubber boots. The pipe from which the stream came was so delicately poised on a pivot that it could be moved with the touch of a finger and made to carry the gold-bearing earth where the man directing it willed. The water boiled and foamed as it struck the glacial ice in which the golden gravel is bedded. It melted the ice, tore the earth away from it, and carried the mass of earth and gravel to the hydraulic lifts. In one place I saw such streams moving mountains of gravel, and everywhere they were forcing the gold, sand, and gravel up great pipes into the sluice-boxes.

With Mr. Lindeberg I watched the torrent rushing down the sluice-boxes. The force of the flood is so enormous

that if one should fall into it he would be crushed to
a jelly. If he were caught near the bottom of the pipe
leading up to a sluice he would be drawn into it by the
suction. Such an accident happened not long ago.
A miner fell and was sucked into the hole. Every bit
of blood was taken out of his body and his arms and legs
were torn off.

After we had examined the sluice-boxes, Mr. Lindeberg took us to the sides of a hill and demonstrated the
richness of the gold-bearing sand of that part of the mine.
He drove a shovel into the hill and carried a couple of
quarts of the sand and gravel to one of the little streams
that ran through the bed of the pit. He dipped the
shovel into the water and moved it slowly about, washing
away the dirt and the sand. At the end he showed us a
good-sized pinch of pure gold in grains ranging from the
size of coarsely ground coffee to that of fine table salt.
My daughter, who was with me, expressed a wish to wash
out some gold. She scooped up about a hatful of earth
and succeeded in getting out about seventy-five cents'
worth of gold.

In my talk with Mr. Lindeberg, I asked him to tell me
something about the changes in mining. Said he:

"We started by digging the earth with pick and shovel,
and we used the old-fashioned rocker to wash out the
gold. Later on, we made sluice-boxes and had horses and
scrapers. Then came the steam shovel, and now we are
doing most of our mining with water and the hydraulic
lifts.

"There has been a great change in the amount of gold
saved. Ground that could not be worked at a profit in
the old way now pays very well. With our hydraulic

sluices we are able to thaw the glacial formation down to where the gold-bearing gravel lies. We can strip this off with the water, and within a month or so the air will thaw the gravel to such an extent that we can force it into the lifts and get the gold out. After the glacial earth has been removed we find that the gold-bearing material runs to a depth of forty feet or more. It varies in richness, but there is so much of it that we expect to be mining for an indefinite period to come."

This far north the mining season is short, running only for ninety to a hundred days of summer.

I spent some time to-day in the melting room of the Merchants' and Miners' Bank here at Nome. The gold smelting was done in a little room adjoining the bank in a furnace that looked much like a kitchen stove. In the shelves around the walls were melting pots of one kind or another, and under them were bins of soda and other materials. When the lid of the stove was lifted I observed that it was lined with fire clay, and I was shown that it had a blowpipe connected with it. It was as hot as the "burning fiery furnace" into which the heathen Nebuchadnezzar cast the three Israelites.

The assayer was a young man from Sidney, Ohio, and a graduate of the Ohio State University. He is melting about two million dollars' worth of gold every year. watched him at work. First he put some soda and other chemicals into two half-gallon pots of graphite. Then he poured in about two quarts of gold dust and nuggets, handling the stuff as if it were so much cornmeal. Setting the pots on the blazing bed of the furnace, he covered the whole and sent in a draft which raised the temperature to around twenty-five hundred degrees Fahrenheit. It takes

195

only eighteen hundred degrees to melt gold, so the stuff was soon a liquid mass which boiled and bubbled. When he opened the furnace the stew was a golden red and the pots themselves were red hot. He lifted them off with pincers and poured the molten mass into steel moulds.

As the gold cooled, the impurities in it rose to the top as slag, which crumbled off, leaving a brick of pure metal worth thousands of dollars. The assayer dumped it into a wooden tub filled with cold water and a few moments later took it out and scrubbed it off with an ordinary nail brush. He then wiped it with a fifteen-cent towel, and showed it to me as bright and shining as a new wedding ring.

From a shovelful of gravel at Anvil Creek, which has yielded some $6,000,000, my daughter "panned out" about twenty-five cents' worth of gold. Jafet Lindeberg, one of the three "lucky Swedes," stands at the right.

Leading parts in the northland drama are played by the "huskies" and the "malamutes," the chief means of winter transportation and the heroes of the All-Alaska Sweepstakes, one of the world's most exciting sporting events.

CHAPTER XXV

THE DOG DERBY OF ALASKA

I HAVE just returned from a ride on the Pup-mobile over the Dog Car railroad that carries one from Nome across the gold-bearing plains to the mountains. The track is a narrow gauge built for steam engines by Charles D. Lane in 1900. The road did not pay and its only trains are little cars drawn by dogs, the nearest thing to a railroad now running on the Seward Peninsula.

The Pup-mobile consists of a platform on wheels with one or two rough seats fastened to it. The motive power is a team of from seven to fifteen dogs harnessed to the front of the car by a long rope, and directed by the voice of the driver, who calls out "Gee" to turn them to the right, "Haw" to turn them to the left, and "Mush" to make them go faster. At the front of the team is a leader with his traces fastened to the end of the rope, and behind him, two abreast, come the rest of the team. The last two are perhaps eight or ten feet from the car. Each dog has a harness much like that used for a horse. The collars are of soft leather, well padded, and the tough leather traces are fastened to the collars and upheld by straps across the dog's back. There are no bridles or halters, and the sole direction is by the voice of the motor-man. The dogs obey quickly, they are eager to run, and seem to enjoy pulling the car.

Our ride was out over the tundra which lies between the

foothills of the mountains and Bering Sea. The personal conductor was Mr. Fred M. Ayer of the Wild Goose Mining Company, who is noted as a mining engineer, and also as the owner of some of the best racing and freight dogs of this part of the world. The tundra consists of the decomposed vegetation under which is two or three feet of ice mixed with muck and blue clay. There are many soft spots filled with water, and many "niggerheads," or round masses of vegetation that turn as you step on them. In places on our trip the roadbed had sunken and water covered the track. At such places the dogs ran out on the banks to the water, and sometimes they made their way through the shallower pools. Now and then they broke into a gallop and we fairly flew over the rails. I am told they go twice as fast pulling a sled over the snow. The names of the dogs were: Rover, Blizzard, Leo, Bubbles, Ginger, Arrow, and Ring. All were picked animals and all have taken part in the annual races to Solomon and Candle.

The dog races of Nome are the great sporting events of the Far Northwest. They are to Alaska what the Derby is to England. They are talked of from one year's end to the other and as the time approaches, the dogs which are to compete are the subjects of never-ending discussion. Thousands of dollars are bet on the races and nearly every man and woman has a wager of some kind or other.

The greatest race is the All-Alaska Sweepstakes, run every April from Nome to Candle City, on the Arctic Ocean, and return. I am told that as much as two hundred thousand dollars have been bet on that race, and that the prizes have ranged all the way from fifteen hundred to ten thousand dollars. At one time, when the prize was ten thousand dollars in gold, the money was presented in a massive silver loving cup. The owner of the winning team poured the coin into the lap of the driver, keeping the cup only as a souvenir of the event.

The distance in this race is four hundred and eight miles and the usual winning time is between three and four days. In 1910 it was made by Colonel Ramsey's team, driven by John Johnson, in seventy-four hours, fourteen minutes and forty-two seconds, which was the record until Leonard Seppala, the Norwegian driver of Mr. Lindeberg's Siberian team, beat it by forty minutes seven years later.

In addition to the All-Alaska Sweepstakes there are races every March from Nome to the Solomon River and back. This is known as the Solomon Derby and is over a distance of sixty-four miles. One year's winning team did this in six hours, running at an average speed of more than ten miles an hour.

Among other features of the Solomon River Derby is the Burden Race, in which the dogs run seventy-five miles, carrying one passenger and fifty pounds of baggage. The passenger is usually a woman, the wife, daughter, or sweetheart of the owner or driver. This trip has been made in less than eight hours. The Burden Race to Council City always ends in a ball.

I asked Mr. Ayer, winner of one of the Solomon Derbies, how the dogs were prepared for the race. He replied: "They are trained, groomed, and carefully fed for months beforehand. A part of the diet is fish, fresh mutton, and eggs, and during the race they get one meal of hamburger steak per day. Camps for food and water are established along the road. For three days prior to the race they are not taken out of the kennels, but for three weeks before that time they are exercised in long-distance runs.

"According to the code of the Nome Kennel Club, to avoid any suspicion of cruelty, the drivers must bring back every dog, dead or alive. The whip usually tied to the racing sled is to be used in case of a fight between the dogs but never to urge them on or to beat them. Blankets are carried along for the dogs as well as green veils for their eyes should the sunlit snow be too glaring for them, and flannel moccasins for their feet in case the ice cuts them up. At the relay camps at night every dog gets an alcohol rub."

Continuing in response to my questions, Mr. Ayer said:

"I do not think that the native Alaska dogs are the fastest or best for racing purposes. My team is mostly made up of fox hounds, and, as a rule, they can beat the malamutes in pulling, endurance, and speed. I never carry a whip and do not yell at the dogs. They will respond to a word, and it is easy to keep them at a speed of from eleven to fourteen miles an hour. They enjoy the race and seem to realize what is expected of them. They will be as fresh at the end of fifty miles as at the beginning."

Most of the racing of Alaska is under the direction of the Nome Kennel Club, founded by Albert Fink to improve the dogs used to transport miners and supplies. This club was organized before racing was thought of, but the sport is doing much to improve the strain. Of late years many Russian stag-hounds, Great Danes, and Missouri bird-hounds have been brought in. Crossing them with the native stock tends to produce better animals. There are here a large number of Siberian dogs which are smaller than the malamutes and look like wolf dogs in miniature. They are noted for their endurance. The races are famed for their fairness and absence of trickery. The only case in which an attempt has been made to beat the favourite team by fraud was in the Candle Race of 1914, when a blanket stuck with porcupine quills was laid on the track and lightly covered with snow, so that any dogs that ran over it would have been lamed. The plotters, who had directed their own teams to go out of the course to avoid this trap, would surely have won had not the blanket been found just before the race.

During the long winter every postal card and every letter, newspaper, and magazine that comes to Nome has to be brought over fifteen hundred miles of ice and snow by dog teams. The mail is taken from Fairbanks to Ruby, Iditarod, and Fort Gibbon by dogs, and, in fact, the whole of the interior of this great territory is dependent upon dogs for its winter transportation. In the summer the dogs are sometimes used by the prospectors as pack animals, and at the time of a gold stampede their value rapidly rises, especially if a stampede occurs during the winter. In the summer time you can get a good dog for twenty-five dollars. In the winter you may have to pay one hundred dollars for the same animal.

There are men in every large town who do little else than drive dog teams. The winter mail and freight are taken across the country on narrow sleds about sixteen feet long. Such sleds will hold eight hundred pounds, and it will take from nine to nineteen dogs to haul them. The mail contractors are paid by the month. some of them making as much as ten dollars a day.

One of the dog-freighters tells me that the Mackenzie

River husky is about the best all-around trail dog to be found in the North. The husky, like the malamute, is a cross between a dog and a wolf, and is an animal long known in Alaska. It was used by the Indians before the Hudson's Bay Company came to the Northwest three centuries ago. The husky is very hardy and noted for its good disposition.

I asked how the dogs are handled on the trail.

"Each driver has his own methods," was the reply. "It is very important that the animals be treated well. If the trip is to be long and hard, the dogs should be favoured for two or three days at the start. This is to get them seasoned so that they will last throughout the journey. A good driver will save his team in every possible way. He will ride only when going down hill, and most of the time he will run in front, keeping his sled in the trail by the gee-pole. In cold weather one would rather run or walk than ride. I have driven fifty-four miles in a day with the thermometer 53 degrees below zero. I ran almost the whole day and at the end it seemed to me as though my lungs were scalded. I have sledded when the thermometer was 72 degrees below zero."

"How many hours can you drive in a day?"

"We try to make eight or ten hours, but it is often best to drive only six. The stops have to be made according to the trail and the roadhouses. We always shelter the dogs at night if possible, and most of the roadhouses have kennels for them. If there is no shelter the native dog will bury himself in the snow or climb upon something above it. He bites the icicles out of his toes when he stops for the night. The feet of a dog are as important a factor in travelling as the feet of a horse. A close-built

THE DOG DERBY OF ALASKA

foot with round balls and thick skin is essential to a trail dog. There must also be a very little hair between the toes, otherwise the snow catches there and balls up and forms icicles that lame him."

"What do you feed the dogs on such trips?"

"We usually carry dried salmon along to feed on the trail, and, at the end of the trip, give them cooked meals of rice, tallow, and fish. They get but one meal a day, unless the running is hard, when they have a lunch of dried salmon at noon. In the latter case it is necessary to let them rest two hours after lunch, otherwise they get sick."

The stories of Alaskan dogs are legion, and their exploits surpass those of the famous St. Bernards of the Alps. There are huskies and malamutes which have travelled tens of thousands of miles in harness, and tales of how they have saved the lives of their owners when almost frozen to death or lost in the snow. Baldy of Nome is the hero of one of these stories. Baldy was the leader of Scotty Allan's team in the All-Alaska Sweepstakes. During the race he felt that the sled was running light, and, looking back, could see no signs of his master. He thereupon turned the team and went back over the trail several miles until he found Scotty lying pale and unconscious on the snow. He had been stunned by running into one of the iron posts marking the trail. Baldy stopped and licked the pallid face of the senseless man. He then set up a howl and scratched away at his driver's breast until Scotty came to, and, crawling back on the sled, motioned him to go on with the race. This Baldy did and came out ahead.

The story of this dog has been told in a little book, entitled "Baldy of Nome," written by Mrs. Esther Birdsall

Darling, who has, better than any other writer, commemorated the virtues of the Alaskan dog. Mrs. Darling has owned several teams that have won the All-Alaska Sweepstakes. Every dog lover will appreciate this one of her poems:

Sometimes when life has gone wrong with you
    And the world seems a dreary place,
Has your dog ever silently crept to your feet
    His yearning eyes turned to your face?
Has he made you feel that he understands,
    And all that he asks of you
Is to share your lot, be it good or ill,
    With a chance to be loyal and true?
Are you branded a failure? He does not know—
    A sinner? He does not care—
You're master to him—that's all that counts—
    A word, and his day is fair.
Your birth and your station are nothing to him;
    A palace and hut are the same;
And his love is yours in honour and peace,
    And it's yours through disaster and shame.
Though others forget you and pass you by,
    He is ever your faithful friend—
Ready to give you the best that is his,
    Unselfishly, unto the end.

From October to May, the United States mail carrier making the last lap on the overland trail from Fairbanks, over seven hundred miles away, is the man most welcome in Nome.

The steam laundry at Treadwell makes deliveries by dog team the year round. Dogs are often used as pack animals in summer as well as in winter by prospectors and people living in the hills.

Interest in the sweepstakes has improved the breeding of the racing dogs. Well-bred pups like these are in great demand. A number of Alaskan dogs saw service in the Alps during the World War.

The Pupmobile is the nearest thing to a railroad on Seward Peninsula. The dogs gallop along with their little car on rails laid for an unsuccessful steam road into the gold country about Nome.

CHAPTER XXVI

THE day is coming when reindeer meat will be sold in our American markets just like beef and mutton. This reindeer meat will come from Alaska. It will be shipped in cold-storage steamers and trains to all towns of the United States and will form the basis of a large packing industry.

There are now about two hundred and fifty thousand reindeer in the territory, and if the herds continue their present rate of increase it is only a matter of a few years before they will pass the million mark. It is estimated that Alaska can support ten million reindeer, and eventually the American housewife should be able to buy juicy steaks and roasts from Alaska as cheaply as those from our Western prairies. In fact, the industry has already reached the point where the Alaskan reindeer meat packers are urging Congress to protect them by a high tariff from competition in Norway and Sweden, which enjoy low costs of production and cheap freight rates to the United States.

The reindeer meat packing industry of Alaska is at its beginning. The first shipments were made about eight years ago, when twenty-five reindeer carcasses were shipped to Seattle. The meat was sold at from twenty to twenty-five cents per pound, and sales have increased each year since. Just now they are beginning to slaughter the deer for this season's shipment. I saw the work going on in a slaughter house back of Nome. The butcher shop is a large galvanized-iron building with corrals adjoining and passageways through which the deer are dragged into the slaughter house. I climbed to the roof and looked at the animals. There were fifty in each corral. They were as fat as butter and in splendid condition. These reindeer had enormous antlers, but they were not at all fierce. I had expected to see larger and heavier animals. Though of the average reindeer size they were not taller than three-month-old Jersey calves. The dressed carcass usually weighs about one hundred and fifty pounds, but government experts predict that careful breeding will shortly double this weight.

The deer I saw slaughtered belonged to a stock company organized at Nome to develop the industry. The company is a close corporation, with an authorized capital of seven hundred and fifty thousand dollars owned by men of large means. One, for instance, is Jafet Lindeberg, who, as I have said, was employed by the United States Government to bring a herd of reindeer from Norway to Alaska about 1898, during the time of the great famine in Dawson. The idea then was to land the reindeer on the Alaska coast and drive them over the mountains to the Klondike to feed the starving American miners. The deer were landed, but the undertaking was not a success, as far as giving the miners a large supply of food was concerned.

"Do you think a market for the meat can be created in the United States?" I inquired of Mr. Lindeberg.

"Yes," he answered. "There is already such a market in Europe. Norway and Sweden, as well as Finland and

Russia, have been shipping large quantities of reindeer meat for years to the chief European centres and even to the United States. Once when I was at Panama I saw reindeer meat from Norway among the government supplies bought for the Canal Zone employees. The northern part of Russia consumes more reindeer meat than either beef or mutton.

"With lower freight rates, I expect deer meat to compete with the present domestic and foreign meat supplies of the United States. It is delicious, and there will be a demand for it among the meat-eaters who like to have a change of diet now and then."

The reindeer meat packers say that the day will come when the packing houses here will have as many by-products as those of Chicago. At present they are able to sell the skins and horns only, in addition to the meat, but in the future the blood will be used for tankage, the hoofs for the making of glue, and certain of the bones for other purposes. The horns are sold by the pound to men in Nome, who ship them away to be made into knife-handles. The hides are in demand for buckskin gloves and for shoe uppers. Some of the skins are tanned and sold as furs. Dyed reindeer fur is more beautiful than the ponyskin coats worn in the States. The fur is finer and the skins are lighter.

More than thirty years ago sixteen reindeer were brought across Bering Strait from Siberia to establish the first reindeer colony at Unalaska in the Aleutian Islands. That experiment was not successful and it was some years later before a real start was made. The Government began to import them in 1892 and continued for ten years, being stopped by Russia's prohibition of further exportation of the animals. In 1902 nine herds had been established and the Government owned some two thousand deer worth about fifty-six thousand dollars. In addition, the natives had twenty-eight hundred valued at seventy-one thousand dollars. To-day there are one hundred and fifty thousand reindeer in native hands.

The cost to the United States Government of introducing reindeer into Alaska was three hundred and thirty-five thousand dollars. All told, only twelve hundred and eighty head were imported. Besides the more than two hundred thousand there now, approximately a hundred thousand have been killed for food or for shipment to the States. As it is estimated that the total increase from the original reindeer herds has been worth six million dollars, the original investment of the Government has increased about two thousand per cent. in value in thirty years.

The industry of reindeer raising has been developed through a system of apprenticeship. If a native youth wants to become a herd owner, he makes a contract with the school authorities to take a year's training, at the end of which he is given four female and two male deer. At the end of the second year he may keep five females and three males, with annual increases until the fourth year, when he is given a herder's certificate and left with six females and four males. He may then use the surplus males for food or sale. When his herd is between fifty and a hundred and fifty strong the herder is required to take on an apprentice and put him through the period of training, and as his herd increases he must add more apprentices.

According to the present laws, the Eskimos and Indians cannot sell their female deer, and private parties can

The reindeer furnishes food, clothing, transportation, and an income to the Eskimos, for whom the animals were introduced into Alaska. Young Eskimos are apprenticed to expert herdsmen until prepared to start herds of their own. This is one of the prize winners at a reindeer fair.

There are already a quarter of a million reindeer in Alaska, which some day may support ten million. In summer, driven by mosquitoes and a craving for salt, the herds make straight for the sea coast.

Alaska reindeer meat is regularly shipped to the States from Nome where slaughter packing houses have been established and where it is expected the industry will some day furnish a considerable portion of our food supply.

acquire reindeer only from the Laplanders who brought them over and the missions which have some deer of their own independent of those belonging to the Eskimos.

As to the number of deer Alaska can support that has been put by the experts at a possible ten million. The whole country is well adapted to reindeer raising and a lot of it is fit for nothing else. All told, it is estimated that there are in the territory two hundred thousand square miles, or an area nearly five times as large as the state of New York, upon which the animals can pasture. They graze upon a peculiar kind of yellowish moss which covers the greater part of northern Alaska. It is hard and tough and rather like coral. It seldom grows over three inches high, but spreads out over the ground. The reindeer will dig down under the snow with their hoofs to get at it.

Among the men who have helped to build up the reindeer industry in Alaska is Mr. W. T. Lopp, head of the government schools of the territory. Mr. Lopp proposed to bring deer across Bering Strait from Siberia at about the same time that Dr. Sheldon Jackson brought his first deer to the Aleutian Islands. A little later a number of deer were brought from Siberia and put in charge of Mr. Lopp at a station near Bering Strait, and from then until now he has had much to do with the reindeer owned by the natives. All of the reindeer herds so owned are under the charge of the Bureau of Education, and to-day Mr. Lopp may be said to be the patriarchal head of the industry. The Eskimos, for whom Mr. Lopp has done so much, call him "Tom Gorrah," or "Tom, the good man."

At one time, Mr. Lopp with four Eskimos drove a herd of deer seven hundred and fifty miles across country to relieve a party of whalers who were starving on the coast of the Arctic Ocean. This trip lasted two months, with the average temperature twenty or more degrees below zero. Part of the journey was over the floating ice of Kotzebue Sound, and when they got to the end of the ice the reindeer had to swim a short distance to the mainland.

At first Siberians were imported to teach the natives to handle the deer, but they did not succeed, and it was not until Mr. Lopp trained the young Eskimos that they were able to make much progress. To-day they are expert in breeding and caring for them. They have large herds, some men owning as many as sixteen hundred reindeer. One such might be called the Eskimo reindeer king. He is one of the men who accompanied Mr. Lopp in his rescue of the whalers. His deer are worth forty thousand dollars.

Said Mr. Lopp to me: "Deer herding can be learned as easily as sheep herding, and the Eskimo boys readily take to the business. Six or eight herders can take care of a thousand head of deer. The animals have to be driven about to where the moss patches are and watched lest they stray too far away. The herders live in tents or temporary huts. In the winter the deer are liable to stray several miles from camp, and the boys go out in the morning to round them up. Some of the animals have bells on them. They are easily frightened and will scatter like a flock of sheep if approached by dogs. They chew the cud like a cow, and if left to themselves will feed for a time and then lie down."

The herders do not drive the reindeer but follow them. In summer the deer make straight for the seashore, not only because they crave the salt, which they do not find in the interior, but because they are driven by the mosquitoes. The sea breezes blow away the mosquitoes.

Mr. Lopp tells me that attempts to use the reindeer to transport freight and mail have not been successful. Many of the stories that have been published as to the speed of the reindeer are, he says, untrue. The ordinary deer cannot go more than forty miles a day, and it cannot make more than twenty-five miles a day on long journeys. The reindeer is not hardy, and five or six days is as long as one should be driven at a time.

"The trouble is," said Mr. Lopp, "the deer has to get its own food on the way. The nutritive qualities of the moss are not as great as those of hay. You would not expect to drive a horse a long distance on hay, and you cannot drive a reindeer a long distance on moss, especially if it has to travel all day and hunt for its moss at night. Only in the coldest parts of Alaska are reindeer used as teams, and there by the Eskimos only. The usual sled load is about three hundred pounds, although as much as sixteen hundred pounds has been carried by a single deer.

"An interesting development in the reindeer industry of Alaska," continued Mr. Lopp, "is the holding of two annual reindeer fairs. One of these is held at Akiak on the Upper Kuskokwim River, and the other at Mary's Igloo on the Seward Peninsula. These fairs are like the great stock shows of the United States, but their only stock is reindeer. The Eskimos bring their deer in from many miles around. They compete for prizes in lassoing, butchering, driving, feeding, and herding. They have races of many kinds, and there are also prizes for the best kind of harness, sleds, and fur clothing. The prizes are contributed by the merchants of Nome, Seattle, and elsewhere. The fairs, which last for several days, are the great events of the Eskimo year."

The last Mary's Igloo fair began January 11th and lasted several days. Part of the time the thermometer was thirty-five degrees below zero, yet the people slept on the snow in tents, without fire, and all were comfortable in their sleeping bags of reindeer skin. The first event was the butchering of deer by three different methods and a discussion as to the best. In this contest two Eskimos drove their knives to the heart at one blow. Another severed the jugular vein at the first stroke.

The lassoing contest ran through three days, and was won by the man who lassoed the most deer in ninety minutes. There were eight hundred deer in the herd used for this purpose, and the winner lassoed eleven in the time allowed.

The wild deer driving contest had fourteen entries. Each of the contestants had to enter a herd, and rope, throw, harness, hitch up, and drive a hornless, unbroken bull one half mile to the river and return. He had then to unhitch, unharness, and remove the halter, all unassisted.

Altogether these fairs are proving a great success, and they promise to increase in interest and profit as the years go on.

Here is the way Uncle Sam himself sums up the reindeer industry of Alaska and what it has done for the Eskimo:

"The object of the importation was originally to furnish a source of supply for food and clothing to the Alaskan Eskimos in the vicinity of Bering Strait, nomadic hunters and fishermen eking out a precarious existence upon the rapidly disappearing game animals and fish. Within less than a generation the reindeer industry has advanced through one entire stage of civilization the Eskimos in-

St. John's in the Wilderness at Allakakat is right on the Arctic Circle, is the farthest north Episcopal mission and was erected by Archdeacon Stuck, noted for his work among the natives.

Maybe one reason Eskimo children are always so jolly is the fact that their mothers never punish them. These people believe the soul of some ancestor, dwelling in every child, will haunt the harsh parent.

habiting the vast grazing lands from Point Barrow to the Aleutian Islands; it has raised them from the primitive to the pastoral stage; from nomadic hunters to civilized men, having in their herds of reindeer assured support for themselves and opportunity to accumulate wealth."

CHAPTER XXVII

AMONG THE ESKIMOS

I SAW my first Eskimos along the Lower Yukon. I met them again on the Island of St. Michael, and I find them here on the Seward Peninsula, where there are said to be thirty-five hundred.

Many people think that most of our Eskimos live along the coast of the Arctic Ocean. This is not true. Four fifths of them are to be found south of the Arctic Circle and the majority of them live on the coastal plains sloping down to Bering Sea. There are many Eskimos in the deltas of the Kuskokwim and Yukon rivers and their settlements are to be found also on the Alaskan Peninsula.

So much has been published about the Eskimos, one might think them an important part of the human race. As a matter of fact, they number, all told, not more than thirty thousand, and of these only ten or fifteen thousand live in Alaska. There are a few thousand in Greenland, some of whom are civilized; a few in Labrador, also civilized, and a greater number scattered through the northern part of the Canadian Dominion from Hudson Bay to the mouth of the Mackenzie River. There are also a few in Siberia, but nowhere are they of any importance except as a racial curiosity and in a small way as trappers of furs for the world's markets.

The Eskimos have a style of dress all their own, but many of them, especially in the towns, wear much the

214

same kind of clothing as the whites. Many of the women wear blouse-like parkas of calico trimmed with fur and hoods of cloth fringed with wolverine which stands out from their faces. This is the most popular fur for parkas, because in winter the breath does not freeze into icicles upon it as on other furs. The parka comes down over trousers tucked into long boots, or *mukluks*, of hide.

No matter what their dress, it is easy to tell the Eskimos. Their faces are Mongolian in type. I have seen many just like them in my travels through Siberia and along the Great Wall in north China. The Eskimos' eyes slant like those of the people of the Desert of Gobi and their faces are of the same bronze or copper colour. They are lighter than the North American Indians but they have the same high cheekbones. Their flat faces are square rather than long with little fat noses. The young men and women have rosy cheeks, and their lips are bright red. Most of the elderly women have tattooed stripes extending vertically from the lower lip down the chin to indicate that they are married, and now and then you see a man with a cuff button of bone thrust through the flesh near the edge of his mouth. The Nome Eskimos have black eyes and jet-black hair, which the women wear in long braids down their backs. These people have a friendly, honest look. They are full of fun and it takes but little to bring out a smile. They are naturally intelligent and good traders.

I wish I could show you the Eskimo babies. They are the brightest, sweetest, and I might add the dirtiest, little pieces of human clay that I have yet met with in my travels over the world. They are full of fun and romp about, mimicking their fathers and mothers and everybody else. Most of them are dressed in furs, and some look like large fuzzy balls. As their parents have a susperstition that if the children be photographed their souls will be under the control of the photographer, even though he be far away, they run from the camera. It required considerable coaxing for me to get my Eskimo children's photographs, and I was able to succeed only by pointing the camera in another direction and then turning quickly and making the snapshot before they understood they were being taken.

Another Eskimo superstition is the belief that in every child is the soul of one of its ancestors. Therefore, they will never punish their children for fear of insulting some respected great grandfather or mother. A story is told in Nome of an Eskimo whose son was rather severely thrashed by a teacher at one of the government schools. The father promptly shot the schoolmaster. Then a tribal council was called to see what was to be done, for the Eskimos knew the man would be punished by the United States. By the decision of the council, the murderer was made to dig his own grave and then he chose his nephew to shoot him as he stood beside it.

Many of the natives now speak English, and their children go to the government schools. Twenty-one schools are maintained on the Seward Peninsula, and about eight hundred Eskimo children attend them. Some of them have good minds and many reach a high proficiency in reading and writing. One of the little girls recently went from here to Plattsburg, New York, where she entered the fifth grade. In a class below her in the same Eskimo school here in Alaska were two boys, one a full-blooded Eskimo and the other the son of a white man.

AMONG THE ESKIMOS

The white boy, who had been to school in the States, thought he could easily beat the native. At the end of the first week the Eskimo was at the head of the class, a place he held throughout the year. That boy studied arithmetic, including percentage, interest, commission, freight, and profit and loss. He could calculate the cost of whalebone from the time it came from the whale until it was turned into goods and brought back to Alaska.

These people are always smiling or laughing. They sing, and seem to be fond of music and dancing. I went last night to one of their dances held in an old schoolhouse not far from the Eskimo section of Nome. The schoolhouse had but one room about thirty feet square. It was walled with windows, and the light of the midnight sun made the interior as bright as day. On a bench under the windows sat the musicians, eight Eskimos dressed in native costume, and the room was filled with dancers. The music came from drums like tambourines, each consisting of a hoop as big around as a dishpan over which skin was tightly stretched. Each man pounded his drum with a little white rod the length of a walking stick. Some of the drums were larger than others, and the eight musicians produced all the notes of the octave. They sang as they played and kept perfect time.

The first dance was by five sturdy young men clad in long skin boots and trousers and shirts. All wore gloves of skin or fur, and all were bareheaded. The dancing was largely a series of postures. The men stamped the floor, they sprang into the air, they swung their arms this way and that, keeping time to the music. They sang the while in loud, raucous tones, their voices changing in expression according to the story of the song. Now they

217

seemed angry, as though singing of war, and again laughing when the tale was comic. Much of the dancing was like that of Russia, and one or two of the dancers were natives of Siberia. Later women and girls entered the dance, and at one time a young woman, with a baby on her back, stood in the centre and led the fun.

I cannot describe the enthusiasm of the Eskimo onlookers. Around the walls, standing up or sitting on their heels, were scores of these copper-skinned people, their slanting eyes ashine, and their hands clapping as they lost themselves in the music. The crowd was more appreciative than any I have ever seen at a concert or dance in the States.

After the dancing was over we went outside the schoolhouse for an exhibition of blanket-tossing. Twenty or thirty of the natives surrounded a tanned walrus hide about ten feet square, holding it low with their hands. Then an Eskimo boy jumped into the middle of the hide. He stood upon his feet, and at a word they jerked the hide taut, sending him up into the air. As he fell they came closer together and then again threw themselves back, tossing him higher and higher, and continuing to do so as long as he could keep his feet. Later an Eskimo girl took the boy's place, and then one or two of the strangers stepped on the hide and were tossed to the sky amid the hilarity of their Eskimo friends. We took up a collection, distributing the proceeds among the performers.

The day has long gone by when the Eskimos will give a polar bear skin or a bale of fox skins for a fishhook. They now know the value of their furs and bring them to the best markets. The other day the king of the Diomede Islands, in Bering Strait midway between North America and Asia, brought the annual fur catch of his people here to Nome for sale. The furs consisted of the skins of fox, polar bear, and other animals, worth several thousands of dollars. I watched the sale which was held in the hotel billiard room. The skins were spread out over the tables, and the old chief, clad all in furs, sat half doubled up in a chair smoking an Eskimo pipe, accepting or rejecting the bids. His face was seamed with wrinkles, as though with tattooing, and he reminded me of the Maori chiefs I have seen in New Zealand. His skin was dark brown, but his bristly hair was as white as the fur of his polar fox skins. They told me he was honest and much respected. They said he was wealthy from an Eskimo standpoint, being worth perhaps as much as ten thousand dollars and owning a schooner that cost him three thousand dollars.

The Eskimos about Nome make their living by fishing and hunting and selling ivory carvings. I am surprised at the exquisite workmanship on the curios they bring to the hotels to sell to the tourists. They use the tusks of the walrus, carving upon them images of men, bears, seals, and wolves. They make cribbage boards of these tusks, and paper knives, and handles for canes and umbrellas. A very large walrus tusk was recently carved and sent to the President of the United States.

Among the carvings sold are some of mammoth ivory from the tusks of prehistoric animals which roamed Siberia and Alaska thousands of years ago. I have seen many such tusks since I came to this part of the world. They have been unearthed along the Klondike River, and are to be seen in Dawson and Fairbanks, either preserved indoors or standing against buildings out in the open. At a mining camp outside a miner's cabin on the north fork of the Klondike I found one as thick through as my leg.

All of the Eskimo carving to-day is done with steel tools, but there is work in existence that dates back to the Stone Age. The older Eskimos say that their ancestors used tools of flint, and it is known that they have been carving ivory for many generations. Some of the very poorest of them, and those that live in the most out-of-the-way places, are noted for their fine work. They seem to do it for pastime, and make many toys and dolls for their children. They have a way of softening the bone, horn, or ivory before they work it. To make the carvings more distinct they etch lines on the surface with a black paint made of a mixture of gunpowder and blood. This, when put on the freshly cut bone, makes a permanent stain.

The Eskimos are rapidly changing. They live differently from those described in most books of Arctic travel. On the Seward Peninsula they have houses of wood and skin and the snow house is comparatively unknown, except in the heart of winter. Some of their winter houses are cellars four or five feet deep and twenty or twenty-five feet square. Poles of driftwood are laid about the cellar to heighten the walls and timbers are placed across the top. Then dirt and sod are piled around the hole until they have what looks like a great mound of earth. In the centre of the top is an opening about as large as the page of a newspaper, across which is stretched a sheet of seal or walrus bladder to give light to the house below. The house is entered by a tunnel connected with a shaft or well six or seven feet deep in which is a ladder. Around the walls of the living room is a platform, which is the sleeping place of the family. Such houses are so warm

Many Eskimos still wear their distinctive native dress. The man on the left is wearing a waterproof coat of walrus bladders, and both have on mukluks, or high boots of walrus hide.

The kayak is a light framework of driftwood covered with seal or walrus hide. The Eskimo makes the opening water tight with laced-up skins and can turn over and over in the sea without shipping any water.

The Eskimo dance is a series of postures in time to the singers' raucous cries and the beating of walrus-skin drums like tambourines. The dances are often followed by exhibitions of blanket tossing.

that the Eskimos often go almost naked while indoors. The dwellings are dark, badly ventilated, and often infested with vermin.

Some of the Eskimos near the white settlements are changing the style of their architecture. They are building homes above ground, buying window sash and glass panes and doors like ours. Many of them are now using cook stoves in place of the old seal-oil lamps, and the white traders tell me that the Eskimo women are learning to cook. They bake an excellent bread with the aid of yeast made from hops, which they buy at the store. These traders laugh at the story, so often published, of a tallow candle being the stick candy of the Eskimo boy. They say the natives are fond of fat, but that their chief use of it is in connection with other foods.

I asked one of these traders to tell me what goods he sold to the Eskimos. He replied:

"Everything under the sun. The staples are sugar and flour, especially sugar. They like sweets, and one Eskimo will eat more sugar than a whole family of whites. We sell them all sorts of canned goods, such as peaches, apricots, jams, and preserves. Of late they have been buying clothes, including underwear and socks. They even buy thermos bottles to take along with them on their sealing trips. They want steel fishhooks and the best of guns. The Eskimo knows a good rifle. He usually buys a repeater and will pay a good price for it."

CHAPTER XXVIII

SCHOOL REPUBLICS OF THE ARCTIC!

ESKIMO villages with town councils elected by the people!

Eskimo schools governed as republics organized by the pupils!

Coöperative stores run by the natives to get the most for their work and their money!

Christian communities modelled upon the Golden Rule as much as any in the United States!

These are some of the features of civilization developed by Uncle Sam among the natives of Alaska. The work was started by the missionaries shortly after we took possession of the territory. A decade later the Government came to the aid of the missionaries; and later still it took up the job as an independent undertaking. The advance has been steady, and now Uncle Sam is really the great father of his copper-skinned children of the Far North. He has already spent more than a million dollars upon their schools and is now laying out something like two hundred thousand dollars a year in educating and civilizing them. He is watching over their health. He is promoting their industries. He is teaching them self-government and making them American citizens. He is, in short, upbuilding them in every possible way.

This work is being done by the Bureau of Education at Washington through its Alaskan Division with headquarters at Seattle. It has superintendents travelling over the country and studying methods for the betterment of the natives. The chief of the Alaskan Division is William T. Lopp, who came to the Bering Strait as a missionary teacher to the Eskimos when Benjamin Harrison was President. He has covered the entire Arctic coast with reindeer and has visited most of the interior on dog sleds. He covers thousands of miles every year on his inspection trips.

According to Mr. Lopp, Alaska is about the largest school division on the face of the globe. The territory is divided into five districts, each of which has its own superintendent. One of the districts is twice as big as Illinois, while each of the four others is, on the average, larger than Missouri.

Every one of the sixty-seven government schools for the Eskimos and Indians of Alaska has its own building. These houses are usually one story, and are made of frame or logs. They are heated by wood and are lighted during the dark days of the Arctic winter with kerosene oil or gasolene. In most of the schools five-hour sessions are held for five days of each week. The terms vary in length according to the seasons and the occupations of the locality. Lessons are cut short when the big hunts are on; and the killing of a whale on the ice may give the children a vacation for a week.

There are one or more white teachers in every school and every teacher is a social worker. The schoolhouse is the community centre, the chief meeting place of the people. The little Eskimos are taught to honour Old Glory, which floats over all school buildings. The children are shown the bad effects of drink and are not allowed to use tobacco in school. This is a great reform. Tobacco has always been common among the Eskimos, who learned its use from visiting whalers. It was formerly a rarity to find a child over ten years of age who did not smoke, chew, or use snuff. Along Kotzebue Sound the Eskimos mix their smoking tobacco with shredded willow pith to make it go further, and they char the fungus of the spruce tree and mix the powder with finely cut black Kentucky tobacco for snuff.

The use of alcoholic liquor, long one of the curses of these natives, is now on the decline. The poorest of whisky and alcohol is smuggled in by the whalers and traded for furs. The Eskimos of the Far North long ago learned how to distil alcohol from molasses, sugar, and flour, mixed with water and boiled in an old oil can. Into the can was inserted a gun barrel fitted with dough or clay to render the joints airtight. This gun barrel was then passed through a block of ice, which condensed the steam from the mixture so that it came out drop by drop as a crude spirit.

Sanitation is being taught by the teachers and doctors Medical directors under the Bureau of Education visit the schools and instruct the teachers how to care for the natives. There are now nine doctors and fourteen nurses continually working among these people, waging war on tuberculosis and other prevalent diseases, but the number is not sufficient, and larger appropriations from Congress are needed to provide an adequate medical service.

The teachers do all they can to instruct the people how to take care of themselves. There are bathtubs in most of the schools, and many of the children now get baths once a week. Even the grown-ups occasionally come in for

The Eskimos are always begging for schools, "to make us smart like white man." The children go happily to learn the three R's even in the coldest weather. Their moccasins are lined with grass to keep their feet from frostbite.

Kivalina, nearly a hundred miles north of the Arctic Circle, has a native town council. Five Eskimos look after such matters as the community supplies of wood and dried fish. Self-government is fostered by the schools.

At Selawik, on the Arctic Circle, the Government has a flourishing manual training class. The school republic laws forbid the wearing of the fur parka inside and fines are imposed for dirty faces or uncombed hair.

a wash. The teacher at Kivalina, one of the Eskimo villages north of Bering Strait, says that the bathtub is one of the chief features of his school. During a single term four hundred and ninety-two baths were recorded at the Kivalina school.

In these baths soap is now used, and the disgusting makeshifts of the past have been abolished. In some of the villages the old-fashioned sweat baths still prevail. These are held once a week during the winter. The bathhouse is made of logs and sod. A fire is built on the earth in the centre, and the smoke comes out through a square hole in the roof. When everything is red-hot the coals are covered and a skin is placed over the roof hole so that no heat escapes from the building. Perspiration is induced by beating the body with bundles of willows. The Eskimo bathers sit on a platform at one end of the house, and the heat serves in place of towels for drying them. Sometimes they rush out from this bath and pour over themselves water from holes in the ice.

I have been greatly interested in the Eskimo school republics established all along the coast of the Arctic Ocean, as well as in the Seward Peninsula and in the Yukon and Kuskokwim basins. There is one at Wainwright, between Icy Cape and Point Barrow, which has enacted its own school laws and governs itself under the teacher's guidance. All pupils who can read in the first reader are eligible for membership. The officers consist of a president, mayor, and judge, each with a term of one month. There is a council, which meets every Friday afternoon, when the president takes the chair and laws are enacted. No bill can become a law unless it is passed by the council and signed by the mayor.

Among the laws are:

"No citizen shall speak Eskimo in the schoolroom.

"No citizen shall whisper or look behind in school time.

"No citizen shall be noisy or rude. He shall not wear his skin parka into the schoolroom, and he shall be fined if he comes to school with a dirty face or uncombed hair."

The laws define the duties of the citizen-pupils and the work each is to do in keeping the school clean. They provide for records of attendance, of the game killed by the village hunters, of the weather, and also of the amount of paper, pencils, and books used.

The mayor of this school has three police officers. One is a truant officer, one a health officer, and another the monitor of the kindergarten. One of the police officers is always present in the schoolroom, even during the recess and after hours, when the schoolhouse is used as a sort of club.

At Kivalina the school republic has a president, vice-president, judge, two peace officers, two health officers, and two commissioners of work. The health officers watch over the cleanliness of all the children in the village. They make everyone clean himself of vermin, and when a new child comes to school he is taken to the bathroom where his hair is combed and his body rigidly inspected. He is made to wash his hands and face, and if his clothing is dirty he is sent home to have it washed or changed. The commissioners of work are responsible for the manual labour of the school, such as taking care of the fires, sweeping the schoolroom, and bringing in ice and snow for the bath tank.

Kivalina, like nearly all the Eskimo villages of the Far North, has a town council. The council is composed of five men. Three are old Eskimos, and the other two are younger men who can read, write, and speak English. This council takes charge of all matters relating to the village, including supplies of food and fuel. One year the stock of firewood was not sufficient; the next summer, under the direction of the council, driftwood was brought down on rafts from a beach twenty miles away, and a municipal woodpile large enough for the following winter was built. The council is now considering the supply of dried fish for next season and will establish municipal fish traps along the rivers.

The Eskimo town at Noatak, on the Noatak River, some distance above Kotzebue Sound in Arctic Alaska, has a government consisting of five trustees who settle all disputes among the people. It has also annually elected peace officers. These men have kept liquor from coming into their village. The teacher there says that not one drop of liquor was brought into Noatak during the whole of last winter.

One of the most interesting schools of Alaska is that at Point Barrow, the farthest north school in the world. The settlement there consists of six or eight white men in addition to the teacher, and about two hundred natives. The whites are engaged in whaling. The Eskimos fish and trap and catch whales and seals. They have also reindeer which add to their income, and on the whole they are well-to-do.

The schoolhouse at Point Barrow cost six thousand dollars, and includes the home of the teacher. It has a blacksmith shop with portable forge and the boys are taught how to use the white man's tools. They learn carpentry and make all sorts of things from dog chains to coverings for canoes. The shop itself was built by volunteer labour.

The school at Selawik has a sewing department and a sewing machine. The machine is used by the women of the village, and girls come from miles around to learn how to make garments. It is used by the young men, too, in making sails for their boats.

In one school on the Arctic Ocean there are three classes in cooking each week. The girls make bread, rolls, biscuits, and doughnuts, both at school and at home. Sourdough biscuits and hot cakes are now to be had in every igloo, and they have great feasts on Thanksgiving and Christmas, sometimes cooked for the whole village by the girl pupils.

The advance in sewing among the Eskimos is remarkable. Not many years ago a great part of the sewing was done with bone needles and the only materials were skins. The skins were so hard that they had to be chewed in the mouth before the needle would go through, and there are many Eskimo women with teeth ground down to the gums by their work as seamstresses. Every school now has its sewing class, and in some of them an hour a day is devoted to making garments of one kind or another. The smaller girls hem towels or dishcloths and make gingham aprons for the girls of the cooking class. In one school every girl above the primary grade has made a dress for herself. The older girls also make dresses for the smaller children. In some of the schools they are embroidering on cotton the birds, flowers, and animals of Alaska. Instruction in darning and mending is given to both boys and girls.

The Eskimo children are learning how to handle money

The doctor at Kanakanak hospital calls at forty-three villages. Sometimes he goes by launch, sometimes by reindeer sleigh, sometimes by dog-sled. He brings back with him all the more serious cases.

Jolly young Eskimos and their pups find a welcome at the Moravian mission station at Bethel on the Kuskokwim. Formerly reached only by the native kayaks, it is now a port of call for river steamers.

Furs used to be very cheap in Alaska but now the Indian trappers have learned their value and often send their best skins to the States by parcel post to get better prices.

and are passing from the stage of barter to credit and cash. Arithmetic lessons include problems on the buying and selling of goods, the selling of furs, and the importation of articles from the outside. At Point Barrow the advanced classes use the price lists in the mail-order catalogues, and estimate what things cost in furs. They compute the expense of sending fox skins to Seattle by mail, and figure out the value of bear skins, whalebone, and ivory.

Money values are thoroughly explained and the relations of time and distance are taught. In the past these things had little significance among the Eskimos. Distance was reckoned by the number of sleeps during a journey. The Wainwright School, for instance, is three sleeps south of Point Barrow and one sleep north of Icy Cape.

CHAPTER XXIX

FUR SEALS AND FOX FARMS

AS I write, the steamship *Victoria* is carrying me across Bering Sea. We have just left the Pribilof Islands, where there are now more than half a million fur seals. Of this number over a hundred and fifty thousand are breeding females, each of which can be relied upon to yield one baby a year. Of the babies one half will be males, whose skins will some time be sold in the fur markets of the world, adding to the enormous profits we have already cleared from the islands.

But what are the Pribilofs and just where do they lie on the map of the world? They are really rocky volcanic peaks in the midst of Bering Sea, so small that they would not make a fly speck on a chart of the Pacific Ocean the size of a billiard table. They have an area, all told, of less than sixty square miles, and are about the most forbidding looking places on earth. The islands are composed of alternate stretches of sand and broken rock, in some cases backed by cliffs rising four hundred feet high. They are in one of the gloomiest parts of the ocean. In the winter they are surrounded by ice floes and icebergs, while in summer they are wrapped in fog. The sun seldom shines upon them, and it is only by means of the compass and chart that ships are able to make their way there. The nearest land is the Aleutian Chain over two hundred miles to the south.

FUR SEALS AND FOX FARMS

From time immemorial the Pribilofs have been one of the chief breeding places of the fur seal, and since their discovery they have supplied most of the sealskins of the world.

There are to-day only three seal rookeries, or breeding places, of any importance. One of these belongs to Uruguay, one to the Russians, and one to the United States. The first is the Lobos Islands, off the mouth of the Rio de la Plata. The Russian rookery is in the western part of Bering Sea. The United States rookery on the Pribilofs is the largest and most profitable of all. From it more than two million skins were taken during the latter part of the last century, and even now, under the strict government regulation of seal killing, it sends to the great fur sales at St. Louis some fifteen thousand skins every year.

The Pribilof Islands were named for the Russian sea captain who discovered them just ten years after our Declaration of Independence was signed. The Russians had heard from the Aleutian Islanders a tradition that the fur seals came from the north and they scouted about over Bering Sea for eighteen years before they found just where the breeding place was. Pribilof spent three years searching for them, and he cruised for weeks near the islands without being able to find them. One story relates how he heard the seals barking and then ran in to the Island of St. George, which was covered with the animals. A few weeks later he discovered St. Paul, and a half million skins were taken that year.

The chief market for the furs was China, and the Russians grew rich from their sales. At one time they took so many skins that the killing was stopped for some years, the females being spared. This was the case at the time we bought Alaska, when the herd contained, it is estimated, from two to five million animals. After the United States took possession the islands were leased by the Government to the Alaska Commercial Company, which paid a rental of fifty-five thousand dollars per annum and a royalty of two dollars and sixty-two cents on each skin taken. That company killed almost two million seals during the twenty years it held the Pribilofs. After that they were leased to the Northern Commercial Company at sixty thousand dollars a year and a tax of about ten dollars a skin. The latter company took several hundred thousand skins. At the expiration of its lease in 1910 the Government took over the islands. The sealing industry is now managed by the Bureau of Fisheries under the Department of Commerce.

The fur seal comes to the islands only during the summer. For the rest of the year his life is spent in the sea. He arrives at the Pribilofs in the late spring, and as winter comes on, makes his way southward through the Aleutians, and down as far as California. Some of the large males winter in the Gulf of Alaska, while the younger ones will go as far south as the latitude of San Francisco. The females go very far south. In coming back, the adult males get to the breeding grounds about the first of May. The females and the older bachelors stay away until June, the two-year-olds come along in July, and the yearlings in the latter part of August and in early September.

A full-grown bull often measures six or seven feet in length and six feet between the tips of his outstretched fore flippers. He weighs from one hundred to five hundred pounds. The cow seals are between four and five feet long and often weigh up to one hundred pounds. The pups when first born are about a foot long and weigh only three or four pounds. They are born on the land, and the mothers have to teach them to swim. They begin to learn at two months of age, and soon become so skillful that at the end of the season they go away with their mothers and remain for six months in the ocean without landing at all.

The fur-seal industry is just a stock-raising business, and the animals can be controlled in the breeding season even more easily than horses or cows. The males do not begin to breed until they are five years old, when they develop a wig, or mane, which distinguishes them from the younger animals. The cows begin to bear at three years and continue for a decade or more. The males under five years old and those unable to secure and control harems are called bachelors. The superfluous males are the ones killed for furs.

The seals are polygamous, and each bull of full size claims the right to as many cows as he can appropriate. In some cases the fiercest of the bulls have had as many as seventy-five cows, but experts have found that each harem bull should have only about thirty-five cows to keep a herd at its best.

In their summer migration to the Pribilofs each of the old bulls picks out a spot on the rocks, near the water, about fifty feet in circumference, which he intends to use as a home for himself and his harem. About a month later the cows begin to come, and he sees that he gets his share, fighting any other bull who attempts to come into his territory.

A short time after the cows arrive each gives birth to a

pup, and from that time on she goes out to sea now and then to get food. She often swims as far as three hundred miles away to find good feeding grounds. The bulls, which are fat upon their arrival, eat nothing for several months, or until near the end of the breeding season. After that they occasionally go out for a meal but come back to the islands.

There is very little sea food about the Pribilofs, and at present the nearest feeding grounds are about one hundred miles away. The best are on the submerged plateaus, or banks, situated a little north of the Aleutian Islands. The seals eat chiefly squid, but are fond also of herring, smelts, salmon, and other kinds of fish, upon which they gorge themselves whenever they can.

They can sleep in the water, resting on their backs, with their hind flippers held aloft, and their noses just above the surface. While on the land they sleep the greater part of the time, and one can frequently see the master of the harem and his cows, and even the pups, all fast asleep.

During the summer the pups suckle their mothers, living upon milk until the approach of cold weather, when they have learned to swim and can catch their own fish and squid. As winter comes on the cows and pups start away first and the bulls and bachelors follow some time later.

I am told that the best furs are those taken from the animals of three and four years, and the Government aims to kill only the surplus bachelors of those ages. The cows are all kept for breeding. The killing, which is done after a regular system, begins about the last of June and ends before the first of September. Each seal selected to be killed is stunned by a blow on the head with a heavy club and while he is still unconscious he is stabbed to the heart and bled.

The dead seals are laid out in rows to be skinned by the natives. They leave on the skin a layer of fat from a fourth to a half inch thick, and work so skilfully that the skin comes off as a sort of bag with two round holes at the front where the fore flippers went through. The most expert can skin a seal in two minutes.

The next process is salting and curing the skins, which are then packed up in pairs and shipped to the markets. Formerly all of them were sent to London, the world's market for raw furs. There they were graded according to size and quality, and sold at auction in lots of one hundred. In 1910 the average price obtained by the Government for about thirteen thousand skins taken on these islands was thirty-three dollars. Since the World War the Government's fur auctions have been held at St. Louis. In a recent year, fourteen thousand, eight hundred and fifty-two seal skins were sold at an average of one hundred and fifteen dollars a skin.

By the treaties made in 1911 the killing of the animals at sea has been largely stopped. We have our revenue cutters on guard about the islands, and we watch for Japanese, English, or American sealing pirates. In the past, a fleet of such boats watched for the seals as they swam to and from their feeding grounds and as they made their way northward and southward during the year. The pirates killed the cows as well as the bulls to such an extent that they took about nine hundred thousand skins in the thirty years prior to 1911. They destroyed more skins than they secured, the estimates being that, for every skin taken, four or five seals were killed and lost. Moreover, many of the females so destroyed were with pup or had pups on land which were left to starve. If the mother seal dies, there is no hope for her young, for the seal will not suckle any but her own offspring. The total losses from pelagic sealing ran high into the millions.

Besides the seal fisheries on the Pribilofs, the herds of blue foxes maintained there by the Bureau of Fisheries are sources of considerable revenue to the United States. Nearly a thousand skins have been sold in a year, bringing in eighty thousand dollars. In the Pribilofs the fox herds are allowed to run at large, but in the Aleutians and the islands of Southeastern Alaska, where many foxes are raised, they are usually kept in pens on regular fox farms.

Fox farming appears to be one of the big coming industries of Southern and Southeastern Alaska, mainly on the coast or islands. Climatic conditions seem to favour especially the blue foxes, which are decidedly more prolific than the black or the silver foxes, though the skins of the latter bring the best prices.

I have visited some of Alaska's fox farms. At a distance, such a farm looks like a great chicken yard with walls of woven wire and little coops inside. The wire is much like chicken wire, but is made of tough steel, and reaches as high as that about a tennis court. At the bottom it is sunk about four feet and is then bent over so that it runs under the ground for two feet to prevent the foxes from burrowing out from under it. At the top the wire has an overhang of two feet. This is to keep the foxes from climbing out of the pen. Each fox pen has its own kennel made of boards. It is entered by a board chute up which the fox runs when it goes in, but some-

The bull seal reaches the Pribilofs about May 1, picks out a place on the rocks for his family home, and then fights for his share of the cows when they arrive in June.

Raising foxes for their fur is a growing industry in Alaska, where many of the fox farms have paid big dividends. These silver-gray puppies were valued at one thousand dollars each.

times a wooden pipe a foot square serves as an entrance. The foxes run in and out of these pipes and usually carry their food inside to eat it.

Usually but one pair of foxes is kept in a single pen. The animals are so timid that they have to be handled carefully, especially in the mating season, when they are sensitive to strange sights, noises, and smells. Most of the fox farmers will not permit visitors to enter their property for fear they will frighten the foxes. When excited the animals grow crazy and sometimes eat their young. On the other hand, they get acquainted with their keepers and some become so tame that strangers can handle them. During my visit to a fox farm on the Tanana River my daughter, who was with me, picked up two little silver-gray fellows the size of kittens and hugged them to her while I made a snapshot. Those foxes were worth a thousand dollars apiece.

The baby foxes, often kept in "nursery" pens to themselves, have long bushy tails, little sharp noses, and eyes sparkling like jet. In the same pens are sometimes baby martens with heads not bigger than a baby's fist and eyes the size of a black-headed pin. The marten has a gorgeous yellow throat. The rest of its fur is a rich brown. It is really a sable, and is sometimes known as the Alaska sable, the best of which are equal to the sables of Russia.

On this same farm I saw one litter of foxes being mothered by a cat. She had three baby foxes which when grown will be worth from five hundred dollars to one thousand dollars apiece, and possibly more. The mother of these foxes was a very nervous animal and the farmer feared she might kill her young, so they were taken away and given to the cat in place of her kittens, which seemed to be a satisfactory arrangement for both cat and baby foxes.

It seems that it is necessary to have cats around a fox farm for such complications. There is a story that one man in eastern Canada lost a litter of silver foxes because he would not pay a high price for a cat. The mother of the foxes had died, and in looking around to find a cat in the proper condition, the farmer discovered but one. The owner of the cat, appreciating his need, said he would not sell his cat for less than five hundred dollars. The fox farmer indignantly refused. The result was that he lost five little foxes that might have been worth twenty-five hundred dollars, and all for a five-hundred-dollar cat. One fox raised by a cat at Fairbanks had a pelt valued at eight hundred dollars.

There is a great demand among the fox farmers for wild foxes for breeding. One has paid as high as one thousand dollars apiece for black foxes and one hundred dollars and upward for red ones. There is a closed season for killing foxes, but some of the farmers have been paying the Indians for the live young they catch, and shipping them to the east as ranch-bred. Not long ago the government fur warden found forty-two live young in the hands of Indians and turned them all loose. This number included sixteen blacks worth at least one thousand dollars apiece. When they let the foxes go, from sixteen thousand to twenty thousand dollars fled off into the woods. The Indians could not help themselves for fear of the law.

When an Indian finds a fox nest he watches it until the closed season is over and then tries to catch the foxes with traps so protected by wrappings that they will hold the animals without injuring them.

CHAPTER XXX

THE ALEUTIAN ISLANDS

AMONG the least known parts of Uncle Sam's dominions are the Aleutian Islands, the shores of which I am now coasting. I have crossed Bering Sea and travelled along the Alaska Peninsula, a great tongue of land extending from the southwestern end of the territory as far as from New York to Cleveland. I have skirted the coast under the shadow of the Katmai volcano, which a few years ago spread a coat of ashes broadcast over the land near by, and have seen something of the Island of Kodiak, the largest in Alaska, where the Government is now experimenting in dairy and stock farming. The whole of this region is practically unknown.

Bering Sea is twice as big as Hudson Bay. It has a greater area than the Gulf of Mexico. It is as long from north to south as from Chicago to New Orleans, and its width is greater than the distance between the mouth of the Hudson and the Missouri River at Omaha. The sea is colder than the Pacific Ocean, from which it is shut off by the Aleutian Islands, and the climatic conditions are such that it is usually shrouded in fog. It is noted for its storms, and during the winter a great part of it is covered with ice.

When we left Nome the water was smooth and we had no wind to speak of all the way to the Aleutians. The

239

sky was bright, with fleecy clouds floating here and there through it, while now and then a fog bank or so was to be seen in the distance. There was not enough breeze to raise white caps. There the colour of the water was green. A day or so later it changed to a deep blue, caused by the greater depth, or possibly by the clouds. The northern half of Bering Sea is so shallow that if you could drop the Washington Monument down into it the aluminum tip would reach above the surface of the waves. Farther south, along the Aleutians, it reaches a depth of almost two miles. Near the islands are the great banks, somewhat like those of Newfoundland, upon which feed tens of millions of cod and halibut. They are among the best fishing banks of the world and are a big asset in our aquatic wealth.

As we came south, I talked with the captain about his voyages. During the open season from June to October he makes five or six round trips from Seattle to Nome. The ships often break their way in through floating ice and go out chased by Jack Frost. The ice comes to Nome almost in a night. It freezes first along the beach, and the whole sea becomes mushy. The water is covered with white caps of slush. Then a cold spell will come, and the sea will freeze far out from the shore. The ice may not be thick at first and it breaks with the tide and floats away. If the wind blows toward the land, it is driven on to the beach and banks up. When the winter is established the ice may extend from Nome as far as Nunivak Island, and floats in from the Arctic Ocean through Bering Strait.

When the ice breaks in the spring it goes almost as fast as it comes in the fall. A channel may form between the shore and the solid frozen body, and there may be a river

The most valuable Indian baskets are woven by the Aleut women, and are made of grasses and tender spruce roots, coloured with native dyes. Sometimes it takes a whole winter to make one basket. The art is dying out as the young girls are losing their interest in basketry.

After the return from a lucky whaling trip, especially if belugas have been killed, the natives dress in full regalia and have a "whale dance."

of water with banks of ice on each side. Sometimes the earliest passengers are landed upon the ice and the ships are frozen in.

I shall not forget my first sight of the Aleutian Islands. We had passed no land for two days when we came to the Island of Unimak, at the end of the Alaska Peninsula, which forms the beginning of the great chain of islets reaching from Alaska almost to Asia. The islands lie in a crescent, like stepping stones over the sea. They form the arc of an enormous circle reaching from the western to the eastern hemisphere. Unimak lies on our side of the world, but Attu, the last of our islands, is in the Orient fifteen hundred miles distant and not very far from Kamchatka. At our coaling station on the Island of Kaska, which is in the eastern hemisphere, the evening twilight has not disappeared when the sun is rising in Maine. John Bull often boasts that the sun never sets on British possessions. The same is true of Uncle Sam's dominions, when we take in Attu Island and the Philippine Archipelago.

The Aleutians are the heads of volcanoes which have been almost drowned in the sea. The Island of Unimak has two active volcanoes. Shishaldin, the highest of these mountains, has an altitude of more than nine thousand feet. We could see it plainly as we sailed through Unimak Pass. The foothills were green, but far up the sides the grass was lost in the snow of the mountains and the peak was hidden in clouds. During our passage the sun seemed to set between the ship and the island. There was a great black cloud floating in the sky between us and Unimak. Out of the bottom of the cloud came four broad shafts of light, making a translucent veil between the ship and the island, and losing themselves in the sea. Through the rainbow-hued shafts we could plainly see the smoky outlines of the island beyond. The rays of the sun seemed to mark the end of this side of the world and Unimak to belong to the other side. Above the black cloud from which came the rainbow veil the sky was a brilliant blue, and higher still were golden clouds painted by the hidden sun. It was a combination of sky and land and sea that I have never seen in any other part of the world.

Unimak, the largest of the Aleutian Islands, guards the chief pass into Bering Sea. Near it is Unalaska, upon which is Dutch Harbour, one of the safe ports of the territory. The harbour is on a bay backed by hills sloping gently up from the water until they are lost in high mountains behind. Captain Cook landed there just two years after we declared our independence of England. The Aleutians had been discovered by Vitus Bering in 1741, but Cook was the first one to tell the English much about them. He found the natives gentle and inoffensive and said that they might serve as a pattern to the most civilized nation on earth. He described them as short, plump, and well formed. The women wore garments of sealskin, and some of the men had clothes made of birdskins, with the feathers next to their flesh. The men had holes in their lips in which they wore buttons of bone. Their houses were holes in the earth covered with a framework of driftwood and held up by whalebone. They entered through a dark tunnel, going down a ladder. The principal room was from ten to twenty feet in diameter. They used lamps for heating, and their household utensils consisted of bowls, spoons, and buckets, the latter made of straw closely woven.

THE ALEUTIAN ISLANDS

When the Russians took possession there were about thirty thousand of these Aleuts on the islands. They were hunters and fishers and were skilled in catching the sea otter, then about the most valuable fur known. The Russians exploited the Aleuts to such an extent that they were almost exterminated. They have continued to decrease since we bought Alaska, and it is doubtful whether there are a thousand of them living to-day. At Dutch Harbour and on some of the other islands the people are now living in buildings erected by the whites, but on many of the islets they have homes half underground, living much as they did when Captain Cook came. They are very poor, and now that the Government has made a bird and game reservation of the Aleutians, their condition is worse than ever. According to the present law, one has to have a permit from the Government before he can hunt game in these islands. Dr. Lester Jones, who, as a representative of the Department of Commerce, travelled among them a few years ago, said that some of the islanders live eight hundred miles from a post office and that getting a hunting permit might mean thirty-four hundred miles of canoe travel back and forth to the mail. It would probably take several months to get such a permit and there could be no surety as to just when the reply would arrive.

I am surprised at the climate of the Aleutians. Their summers are cooler than Sitka, while their winter weather is milder than that of either Tennessee or Kentucky. At Unalaska the average January temperature is thirty degrees above zero. All of the islands are damp and foggy. The rainfall is about ten inches a month, and Unalaska is said to have two hundred and fifty rainy days in the year.

ALASKA—OUR NORTHERN WONDERLAND

On the island of Akutan is one of the two whaling stations now operated in Alaska. The other is at Port Armstrong on the southern end of Baranof Island, about a thousand miles north of Seattle.

Conditions have greatly changed in the whaling industry since some of our Yankee forefathers made fortunes in the business. In place of their little sailing ships, large steamers, painted sea-green, are used. The harpoon is now fired from a three-inch gun and attached to a cable operated by a steam winch, which pulls in the whale after it has been speared. The whaling vessels have air compressors for inflating the bodies of the whales after they have been killed, so that they can be more easily towed through the water. The best whalers to-day are Norwegians who are found in all the seas where whales are hunted. The largest catches are in the world's southernmost waters, the number taken in oceans of Europe and North America being hardly one fourth of the whole.

Whale beef is said to be both palatable and nutritious and has occasionally been sold in American markets. A single whale will furnish as much meat as one hundred of the largest Shorthorn cattle. The flesh is ordinarily used only for fertilizer, along with the bones, and sells for very little money, while the oil brings only a fraction of the former price, and the once enormous sales of whalebone have shrunk to almost nothing. It has been suggested that the fish canneries might put up whale meat during the several months each year that they now stand idle.

Whale fishing in Alaskan waters is very dangerous, for if the vessels stay north too long they run the risk of being caught in the ice. Once three hundred whalers from a fleet of eight vessels were forced to winter at Point Barrow

As the Eskimo whaler waits for the ice pack to go out so he may harpoon his prey in the open sea, he often spears a seal as it comes up to a hole in the ice to breathe.

The beluga whale is almost pure white and is often twelve feet long. So-called "porpoise leather" is made from its hide, and often as much as one hundred gallons of oil are obtained from a single carcass.

The people of Kodiak are far ahead of natives in other parts of Alaska. The island quickly recovered from the thick blanket of volcanic ash showered on it by Mt. Katmai across Shelikof Strait.

In Unalaska may still be seen the barabaras, used long ago by the Aleuts. Over a shallow circular excavation was erected a framework of driftwood or whalebone which was covered with sod.

and would have starved to death.if the United States Government had not sent a relief expedition with a herd of reindeer for food.

It is questionable whether the Aleutians will ever support any considerable population. So far they have no whites except a few fox farmers who are trying to raise blue foxes. There has been some talk of using the islands for dairying, but there is a difference of opinion as to whether it would pay. The climate is so damp that grain will not mature, though grasses of all kinds grow in abundance, and on the lowlands there is more or less grass throughout the year. The soil is a vegetable mold mixed with volcanic ash. The country is very rugged, and there are no places where farms of any size could be made.

There is no doubt that cattle can be raised on the Island of Kodiak, but Kodiak is not one of the Aleutians. It lies far to the eastward, being only about two hundred miles west of Seward. It is south of the Alaskan Peninsula, and separated from it by Shelikof Strait. Kodiak is the largest of the Alaskan islands. Its area is almost as great as the state of Connecticut and it raises some of the finest grass that waves under the American flag. The island is for the most part treeless and the hills are covered with green. The Russians raised cattle there and Americans had farms under cultivation as far back as 1880. The government stock farm is at the eastern end, about fifteen miles from the harbour and town of Kodiak. The town has several hundred people, nearly all of whom have gardens in which they raise cabbages, potatoes, and turnips. Some of them keep cattle and put up some hay to be used during the snowstorms.

The experiment station has barns and silos and all the

equipment of a modern cattle farm. The fields are fenced with barbed wire and the stables are of modern construction. There is a dairy building equipped with separators and other butter-making machinery, and experiments in breeding cattle suited to the climate are carried on. So far the best animals have been found to be Galloways, as they have long coats of hair which afford protection from the rainy weather. They are good rustlers and feed out, of doors a great part of the winter.

Though hardy cattle, the Galloways are poor milkers, and it is now proposed to cross them with the Tibetan or Mongolian yak. The director of the Russian experiment station at Irkutsk, Siberia, states that the yak crossbreeds readily with domestic cattle. The hybrids are more or less sterile, but some of them are breeders, and if a strain could be established it would be of great advantage to Alaska. The Siberian yak are good for milk and beef and also as draft animals and burden bearers. The Canadian Government has given the Fairbanks station a male and a female yak, bred in the Dominion national park at Banff, so that crossing them with the Galloways can now be tried.

The hills of Kodiak Island are still covered with the ashes of the Katmai volcano which fell there in 1912. The volcano is only ninety miles northwest of Kodiak, and the ashes were carried over the island by a wind which blew for two days during the eruption. For forty-eight hours ashes fell like snow until they had covered the whole island to a depth of eighteen inches. There were numerous slides of ashes down the hills and mountainsides, and where they drifted they swept away fences and almost buried some of the experiment station buildings.

Some of the sheep and calves were suffocated, and the livestock outside the barns were without feed during two whole days. When the eruption stopped, the vegetation was covered with this volcanic dust and almost all the pasture was destroyed. When the rains came the ashes flowed into the creeks and formed dangerous quicksands. The sheep would lie down at night in what seemed perfectly dry places and by morning find themselves so mired that they could not get out. To make matters worse, the bear of Kodiak, unable to get pasturage on the hills or fish from the streams, came down from the mountains to prey upon the stock.

All the springs were choked up and it was necessary to dig a well to water the cattle. At last hay was shipped in for feed, and later some of the stock was taken away to be kept over winter.

Though it was feared the eruption had ruined the island for agricultural purposes, grain was planted the next year, and it was found that the ashes have acted upon the soil like a thick coat of fertilizer. The grass has come up through it and is growing better than ever. The crops are thriving, and the present condition of the island is better than it was before.

The great shower of ashes from Mount Katmai led to the discovery a few years later of the "Valley of Ten Thousand Smokes," which was added to the wonders of the world by the tremendous eruption.

While making a study of Mount Katmai for the National Geographic Society, Professor Robert F. Griggs, of Ohio State University, found adjacent to the volcano a valley from which arose tens of thousands of clouds and pillars of steam and other hot gases. Subsequent expeditions sent to Alaska by the Society and headed by Professor Griggs made complete explorations not only of the valley of the smokes but of the surrounding area.

Professor Griggs found that the eruption of Katmai, with a force many times greater than that of any other volcanic upheaval, blew off the entire top of the mountain. It formed a crater three miles wide, at the bottom of which is now a vitriol-green lake of unknown depth. The explosion also opened a great fissure in the earth, underlying the Valley of the Ten Thousand Smokes and extending many miles beyond. Explorations showed that the valley with its numerous branches has a total length of thirty-two miles and an area of seventy-two square miles. Instead of ten thousand smokes, there are believed to be millions of vents, craters, and fissures, through which clouds of vapour are bursting forth from the bowels of the earth. The region is a veritable modern inferno. One member of Professor Griggs's party likened it to "the devil's private corner of hell." In some places the hot gases rush out with a roar, in others they make a grumbling sound, while in still others they only whisper. Temperatures high enough to melt zinc have been recorded. All the ground is hot, and the explorers regularly cooked their meals over the smaller vents. Much of the surface is burned red, while the evil-smelling gases have left brilliantly coloured incrustations at the edges of craters and fumaroles. The region contains a lake of warm water in which float miniature icebergs, and the valley is filled, according to the few who have ever seen it, with such startling phenomena as to give a weird, uncanny impression of being in another world.

As a result of the reports of the Katmai expeditions,

President Wilson set aside the Mount Katmai region as a national reservation like Yellowstone Park and the Grand Canyon. Thousands will in future years visit this spectacle of the tremendous volcanic forces of the earth in operation. Mount Katmai is only twenty-five miles from the coast which lies near one of the main steamer routes to Alaska. If a motor road were built, the tourist might leave his steamer after breakfast, ride through the volcanic region, and be back in time for dinner on board ship.

The scientists who have studied the Valley of the Ten Thousand Smokes believe that it will remain in its present state for many years, and that it represents on a vastly greater scale what was the condition in the geyser area of Yellowstone Park countless ages ago.

CHAPTER XXXI

THE CITY OF SEWARD

SEWARD is the southern terminus of Alaska's new railroad and, so the Sewardites say, the country's chief ocean port of the future. Its citizens are already comparing it with Stockholm, which has almost four hundred thousand inhabitants, and they claim that it will be the gateway to resources equal to those of the four Scandinavian countries. They point out that Norway, Finland, Sweden, and Denmark, which are in the same latitude and have much the same climate, have a population of over fourteen millions and say that Alaska will some day have twenty millions or more.

Seward is situated on the great Gulf of Alaska at about the middle of the southern coast of the territory. It is on Resurrection Bay, a magnificent inlet at the lower end of the Kenai Peninsula, so surrounded by mountains and guarded by islands that within its harbour ships are as safe as alongside the docks of Hamburg or Liverpool.

The city is as far from Ketchikan, where the Seattle steamers make their first stop, as the distance from New York to Cleveland. It is only five or six days from Seattle, although without stops the voyage could be easily made in less than three days. By the new railway line it is within five hundred miles of Fairbanks from which a great part of interior Alaska can be reached by the river steamers.

But come with me as I climb the wall of the great mountain that rises straight up on one side of Resurrection Bay and get a bird's-eye view of the town. Leaving the wharves and passing through the business and residential sections, we shall make our way through the moss, and after pulling ourselves from one tree root to another, shall finally stand high over the harbour.

The mountain wall rises sheer above Seward to a height of several thousand feet, losing itself in the great range that bounds this side of the harbour and fading away into the snow-capped peaks behind. The first hundred feet is covered with green trees, some of which are two feet in diameter. They cling to the rocks and grow straight up, forming palisades, as it were. Among them are bushes, making a jungle that reminds me of the lower slopes of the Himalayas. There are giant ferns under alder trees and salmonberry bushes, the whole growing out of a deep bed of moss into which our feet sink as though into feathers.

At the left, looking out through the dark spruce, we can see the white glacial waters of Lowell Creek roaring as they rush foaming over the rocks down into Resurrection Bay. They cut their way through the upper part of the town and pass under the railway embankment which circles the harbour.

Turning about, we can see Resurrection River, which comes in at the end of the bay, and across the inlet another mountain wall rises before us. Its peaks are of black volcanic rock, and in its hollows nestle glaciers of pale green ice that the sun turns into emeralds. High up on the mountainsides are patches of snow gleaming like silver against the black cliffs, and below, rising a thousand or more feet from the water, is the great blanket of forest green that covers southern Alaska.

This forest-clad wall extends to the end of the harbour where it drops into the sea. Beyond it are the mountainous islands that guard the bay and make it almost landlocked. At first sight the land seems continuous, but there is a narrow passage between Fox Island and the Kenai Peninsula so that the shipping of the world can sail in and out.

The bay itself is about sixteen miles long and is protected on all sides from the gales. Its waters are from six hundred to twelve hundred feet deep, so deep that the only anchorage outside the wharves is at Sunny Cove off Fox Island, where, for an area of about three hundred and twenty acres, the water is shallow enough for ships' anchors to reach bottom.

I have visited most of the great harbours of the world, including the Golden Horn, at Constantinople, the landlocked channel of Sydney, Australia, and the wonderful Bay of Rio de Janeiro. The harbour of Seward is as beautiful as any of these, and has wonders that the others know not. Its surroundings of green, mixed with glaciers and snow, are like those of no other harbour on the face of the earth. The whole is a mighty amphitheatre of green lowland and blue waters, of snow-capped mountains and glacier-clad hills, roofed by the clear sky.

It is in the arena of this amphitheatre that Seward has so recently come into existence. On the north side of the bay and running back to the mouth of Resurrection River is a plain giving enough space for a large city, but as yet having houses only on a spit of land that juts out into the sea. There the ships lie at the wharves built upon

One Easter Sunday, more than a century ago, the Russians discovered a magnificent deepwater harbour on Kenai Peninsula and named it Resurrection Bay. Here, when several years passed with no supply ship from home, they built the first vessels launched by white men on the western shore of North America.

The laying of the Alaska Northern Railway developed Seward from a scattered settlement to a go-ahead Alaska town. The railway paid the half-breed wife of a renegade "squaw-man" four thousand dollars for the site.

Glacier-scoured and snow-capped mountains tower above Resurrection Bay, while close to the shore are dense spruce forests and wild red-top grass. The forests are carpeted with deep moss as soft as a feather bed.

piles. The business section of the city is back of the wharves, where for perhaps one third of a mile the ground rises, giving excellent drainage. Here the streets climb the hills and then go over a slope that rolls gently on until it reaches the mountain wall in the rear.

The better houses are pretty bungalows and artistic cottages. Nearly all have smooth green lawns with flowers and plants. The houses, though small, are comfortable and well furnished. They have electric lights and all the modern conveniences. Board sidewalks have been built, and a bridge of planks crosses the ravine through which flows Lowell Creek.

The new homes of Seward are beyond these bungalows. There the west bank of Resurrection River has been laid out in town lots and real-estate signs are scattered among the tents and shacks. There are many tents with walls and floors of boards. The average board shack, which may form the home of a family of from two to a dozen, is not more than ten by twelve feet in area.

The business section of Seward already fills two or three streets close to the wharves. The main street has been macadamized and concrete sidewalks have been laid. The business buildings are of one and two stories. Some of them are of frame, others are of galvanized iron. Midway in one block I saw a shed consisting only of an iron roof upheld by poles. It had chairs under it and was labelled the "Royal Bootblack Parlour."

Seward has a number of restaurants and several hotels. I am living in a hotel facing the harbour, with a half-dozen small glaciers in sight over the way. I have two connecting rooms, lighted by electricity and heated by stoves, the charge for which is two dollars and a half per day. On the same floor is a porcelain bathtub which I can use for fifty cents extra and have hot water therewith if the order is given beforehand. As is common in Alaska, the hotel has no eating accommodations, but I get excellent meals at the restaurants on the main street two blocks away, where I can dine fairly well for seventy-five cents.

The port of Seward is ice-free the year round. Deep-draft vessels can come in on any day of the year. The winter climate of this coastal region is not much colder than that of Seattle or Portland, and it is warmer than either Norfolk or Baltimore. The temperature ranges from fifty to eighty-five degrees above zero in summer and from thirty to fifty degrees above zero in winter. Once the thermometer fell to seven below zero but that is the coldest on record. The rainfall is about the same as that of Ohio and Virginia, the total precipitation being forty-two inches per year.

It seems strange to think of going bare-footed in Alaska, but the children of Seward do that all summer long. They go bathing in the waters of Resurrection Bay, and swimming parties to Lake Kenai, some distance back in the country, are among the features of their picnic excursions.

When the Government took over the Alaska Northern company's railroad there was a big jump in land values. Business property trebled and quadrupled in price, and the same was true of the suburbs. The prices of land are high, but it will be long before the city will come up to the expectations of its owners. The present additions to the townsite are at the head of Resurrection Bay, where tents have been erected, frame buildings put up, and families located. For ten miles up the valley of Resurrection River men have taken up homesteads, and farms the size of garden patches are being cultivated here and there. Some of the homesteads were applied for ten years ago, but owing to government red-tape as to titles the applicants have not been able to complete their ownership.

Resurrection Bay was named by the Russians, who discovered the harbour on an Easter Sunday. There was a white settlement here when the first public buildings of Washington began to go up on the banks of the Potomac. The first residents were Russians, who had a colony on Kodiak Island about two hundred miles distant. They came here to build ships, choosing the place on account of the harbour and the timber near by. The first ships built on the western shores of North America were constructed here, and one of them was launched when George Washington was still serving his first term as president. Later, when the seat of the Russian administration was transferred from Kodiak to Sitka, the shipyards were given up.

After the Russians left, Resurrection Bay was frequented by the Indians, who came here to hunt and fish; and then, perhaps a hundred years later, a white man named Frank Lowell, a sailor from Maine, settled where Seward now stands. He had a wife of mixed Indian and Russian blood, and was one of the class popularly known as "squaw men." After he had lived here for ten or twelve years, along about 1890, Lowell deserted his wife and his five children and emigrated to Kodiak. Mrs. Lowell remained and was on the ground and claimed ownership at the time that the Alaska Northern Railway Company selected Resurrection Bay as the southern terminus of its line. She received four thousand dollars in cash and thirty-seven town lots from the company for her claims.

CHAPTER XXXII

ACROSS KENAI ON HORSEBACK

IMAGINE a wild virgin region larger than Massachusetts with almost three fourths as much good land as the Bay State, with warmer winters and cooler summers and with rainfall sufficient to raise hardy crops. It is a country of surpassing beauty—a region of rivers and lakes and beautiful valleys, with mountains equal to the Alps in their grandeur and with glaciers surpassing any known to the continent of Europe. Let the country be one of big game, moose, bear, and deer, wild fowl of all kinds, and fish without number. With this picture in your mind you will have a glimpse of the Kenai Peninsula of Alaska, one of the richest districts tapped by the new railroad.

I can tell you something of Kenai, as I have just crossed the peninsula. Leaving Seward, I went as far as Mile Twenty-nine on the Alaska Northern line, which Uncle Sam took over, and then went on horseback over the mountains through Moose Pass to the little mining camp of Sunrise, not far from the eastern end of the Turnagain Arm. I saw scarcely a dozen people while on the way. The country has hardly been prospected, and there are parts of the interior that have never been trodden by the foot of white man.

The railroad trip from Seward to Kenai Lake is one of the wonder rides of the world. You go up the valley which ends in Resurrection Bay amid the most magnificent of mountains. It is as though Switzerland came down to the ocean, and you could ride under its glaciers and snows through valleys and hillsides of vivid green. There are rushing streams and winding lakes. There are great canyons and forest-clad cliffs. There are open parks made by Nature carpeted with ferns and wild flowers and grass growing waist-high. Lungs and nostrils are filled with the sweet air from the spruces on the mountainsides.

Six miles from Seward is Bear Lake, set in the midst of a natural park surrounded by snow-capped mountains on the sides of which hang glaciers of sapphire and forests of emerald. The region is called Woodrow Park after President Wilson. There is a roadhouse on the edge of it near a clear, rushing trout stream. The place is a picnic and summer resort and the bungalows scattered about under the trees remind one of a Chautauqua or a camp-meeting ground.

Going on to the north, we passed tiny homesteads cut out of the woods. At Mile Twelve I saw an abandoned log cabin which had been occupied last summer by some city chaps who had come there to hunt. They had expected to stay a week or ten days but had remained more than two months. Nevertheless, their actual cash outlay for food during that time was less than ten dollars. They spent five dollars for flour, potatoes, and coffee, and the rest of their food was the fish, game, and berries they found in the woods.

Beginning at Mile Nineteen, Kenai Lake winds about through the mountains for twenty-seven miles. It is only a mile or so wide, and no one knows how deep.

Soundings have been made to thirteen hundred and fifty feet below the surface but the bottom was not reached. The mountains are snow-capped, and high up on the sides of the green, below the snow line, you can see the trails made by the mountain sheep. The surroundings are mirrored in the crystal-clear waters of the lake.

At Mile Twenty-nine, where I left the railroad and took horses to go across country to Sunrise, is the roadhouse of Oscar Christensen, a wily Swede who has a half-dozen horses which he rents out for all that the traffic will bear. He charged me sixteen dollars a day for two horses and a guide, and told me that I could pick up the guide on the way.

Before leaving I dined at the roadhouse on moose meat or Alaska beef cooked over the coals by a six-foot pioneer. His kitchen stove was a range made at Hamilton, Ohio, and in the living room adjoining were chairs and tables and a rosewood Victrola with several dozen records on top. There were flowers in the windows. Around the wall were spring beds. The stove of the living room was a section of hydraulic pipe as big around as a flour barrel with legs of gas pipe. It was long enough to take in a whole stick of cord wood.

After leaving the roadhouse, I spent the better part of two days riding through the forest to Sunrise. The horses were fairly good, but the saddles were excruciating. I am accustomed to riding and cover about fifteen hundred miles every winter in the parks about Washington. But this ride across Kenai was another story. Our horses were broad-backed Percherons, and the saddles were a high-pommelled variety so made that they threw one far to the front. It was like sitting on a sawbuck with ill-fitting stirrups. It brought an entire new set of muscles into play and gave me the sensations and pains of the man who takes a long ride for the first time. I found it impossible to go out of a walk, and when we came to a mining camp, after fifteen hours in the saddle, I was so stiff that I had to be lifted from the horse. The next day I walked part of the way and had to be lifted off and on whenever I rode.

During my journey we thought we were lost. The guide failed to turn up as expected, and when he did so, it was already dark. He took us along the sides of cliffs, over a trail where the forest fires had made it exceedingly dangerous, and where we had to jump the logs in the darkness with no telling what might be on the opposite side. I slept the clock round after reaching Sunrise.

I despair of making you see the beauties of this trip. I rode through one little valley after another with the grandest of mountains everywhere in sight. I wound along streams where great red salmon the colour of raw beefsteak flashed through the water. I skirted beautiful lakes wherein were mirrored towering mountains with their wonderful vegetation and curious outlines. The colour effects made me think of paintings in which the pigment is laid on in great patches to get striking effects of light and shade. I passed through acres and acres burned over by forest fires where the grass had grown shoulder high and the flaming fire-weed stood six feet tall. In places the woods were carpeted with stunted tree ferns.

Sometimes the forests of spruce were green, sometimes frosted silver, sometimes pure white. The silver and white trees were dead or dying from forest fires, and their lace-like branches, turned to ivory, looked like the most exquisite carvings.

And then the live things we saw on the journey. I have already spoken of the salmon. We could see the trout in the streams, and I am told that all are full of grayling and other fine fish. I met one man on the way who had stopped for an hour at the head of Trail Lake and caught twenty-seven trout, pulling them out as fast as he could throw in the line. I could easily have caught salmon and trout with my hands in the smaller streams.

Now and then during the journey I started up coveys of grouse, some as big as chickens. They ran along in front of my horse for hundreds of feet like turkeys, and did not seem to be much afraid. At a cabin where I stopped for dinner, a miner cooked some ptarmigan he had just killed.

Later on I saw the tracks of brown bear here and there on the trail, and once or twice scared up porcupines which scuttled away through the grass. My guide told me to be careful not to ride over a porcupine, for my horse would surely be lamed by its quills.

Here at Sunrise I have had plenty of fresh game to eat. We have had roast and broiled moose and caribou steak with wild cranberries on the side. Wild fowl is plentiful and there are excellent fish from Six Mile River and Turnagain Arm. Now and then bear meat is brought in, and at times one can get mountain sheep. The bear meat is not popular. It tastes like tough beef. The mountain sheep is the most delicious of all the game found in Alaska. Most of the food here comes from the wilds and can be had for the taking, which makes the cost of living cheap.

As for the future of this Alaskan frontier region, it would

The Kenai Peninsula is a wild virgin region with rivers and lakes and beautiful valleys, with glaciers surpassing any in Europe, with flashing streams full of trout and salmon, with forests abounding in moose, deer, and wild fowl.

Kenai is a sportsman's paradise. There is a record of a hunting party
which in a two months' stay spent only ten dollars for food. They lived
mostly on fish, game, and berries which may be had in abundance for
the taking.

seem to lie mostly in its farms. The Agricultural Department experts who went over this region a few years ago have estimated that there are on the Kenai Peninsula and in the Matanuska and Susitna valleys something like four million acres of fairly good land. Some of it is covered with swamp and muskeg which will need draining, but at least one third of it will require clearing only to be made ready for crops. There is enough land of this kind to make more than eight thousand farms of a quarter of a section each, or four thousand farms of three hundred and twenty acres, which is the amount of land now allowed for a homestead in Alaska.

There is good forage almost everywhere in this part of Alaska, and, according to the farming experts, much of this region will be used for stock raising.

The pioneer farmer on Kenai Peninsula cannot succeed without a struggle, however. The greater part of the land is covered with moss, which, in places, is a foot or so deep. The soil is wet, and so sour that it needs lime. It seldom produces good crops at the start but needs to be broken up and exposed to the air to sweeten it. There are vast quantities of muskeg, a sort of marsh consisting of peat so saturated with water that it is boggy during the summer. It is no good whatever except when well drained.

Most of the peninsula is well wooded. The best trees are in the lowlands and on the lower slopes of the mountains, the timber stopping at about two thousand feet. The woods are in groves of spruce, hemlock, and poplar, with patches of bushes and open meadows between. The trees are usually small. A few of the spruces are more than two feet in diameter, but many are no bigger around than telegraph poles. The poplars grow in dense

261

forests. They are tall, straight, and beautiful. There are cottonwoods in the lowlands that reach a thickness of two or three feet. So far, much of the timber is protected by the government reservations, and in Seward they pay high for lumber, which has been brought from Puget Sound, notwithstanding the fact that there is fairly good timber ten or twelve miles away. Indeed, most people in Alaska think the country is over-conserved and that Uncle Sam's fears for posterity hang like Sindbad's "Old Man of the Sea" around the neck of the territory.

CHAPTER XXXIII

OUR NORTHERN GAME PRESERVE

IN ALASKA the United States has one of the finest hunting grounds for big game in all the world. As the country is opened up by railway lines and motor roads, more and more American hunters will take advantage of the territory's splendid opportunities for sports, which are now but little known. They will swarm over the Kenai Peninsula after the giant moose and the great brown bear, they will chase the caribou over the Tanana valley, and will climb the Alaska Range to kill mountain sheep and goats. They will even make excursions to Mount McKinley, and some may go farther north to hunt the mighty walrus and the polar bear.

The Government has prepared for the coming of the hunters by enacting stringent laws defining the open seasons for certain animals, and has set aside great game preserves, one of which surrounds Mount McKinley. Every non-resident of Alaska is required to pay from fifty to one hundred dollars for a license to hunt in the territory with an additional payment of one hundred and fifty dollars to kill moose south of latitude sixty-two.

Moreover, the hunter is limited in the number of animals he may kill, and even the residents cannot ship out their meat, or send their heads as trophies, without a special license from the Government of Alaska. It will cost the sportsman forty dollars to export one moose, but he can send four deer, two caribou, two sheep, two goats, and two brown bear for ten dollars. The law forbids hunting of game animals with dogs, or the use of shotguns larger than ten gauge.

The open season varies in different parts of the country. North of latitude sixty-two brown bear may be killed at any time, and moose, caribou, sheep, and sea lions from August 1st to December 10th. Walrus may be killed from May 10th to July 1st, and grouse, ptarmigan, and other birds from September 1st to March 1st.

It is unlawful for any person, in any one year, to kill more than two moose, one walrus or sea lion, three caribou, three mountain sheep, three brown bear, or eight deer; and he must not have in his possession on any one day more than twenty-five grouse or ptarmigan.

On the Kenai Peninsula it is necessary to have a licensed guide who will charge from five to ten dollars a day. The guides, who may be either white men or Indians, are appointed by the Governor, and their names are published.

During my trip across the Kenai Peninsula I saw several sportsmen from the big cities of the States. Most of them were after the moose, which is abundant in that region, and they were enthusiastic over their prospects.

It is now prohibited to shoot moose in Southeastern Alaska, and it was not so long ago that the restriction on killing caribou in the Kenai Peninsula was abolished. It is estimated that there are still vast numbers of caribou on the barren lands of the Far North. They live there in the summer and go southward in great herds for the winter. Several years ago a drove of thirty thousand came within a mile of Dawson and fed there on the hills. Men went out in automobiles to see them and great numbers were killed. The animals did not seem to be afraid of man, and even the automobiles did not create a stampede.

About forty-five miles from Fairbanks is a hill known as Porcupine Dome, where, the hunters say, the caribou of that region come together to start south in companies. They move in droves of thousands. After spending the winter in the south, they begin to straggle back again in herds of one hundred or so along in February and March. Caribou are still seen as far south as the Lynn Canal, over a thousand miles from their summer home.

The chief food of the caribou is reindeer moss, and their favourite feeding grounds are the treeless parts of the territory, including the tundras along the coast of the Arctic Ocean, and down to the Pacific side of the Alaska Peninsula. They scatter widely in summer and collect in bands in the fall. Each herd has its leader, and it is said that if the leader is killed, the rest of the herd becomes panic stricken and stampedes back and forth until another caribou takes command.

One large drove of caribou collects almost every year along the watershed between the Yukon and Tanana rivers. The hunters from Forty Mile, Eagle, and Circle and the other mining towns of that region rely upon it for a part of their meat supply.

I have seen a number of moose since I came to Alaska. I have watched them swimming in the Yukon flats as we passed through on the steamboat, and have picked out several with my field glasses along the banks of the streams. They range over the timbered parts of the territory and are especially plentiful on the Kenai and Alaska peninsulas. Unlike the caribou, they feed in the mixed woods of spruce, poplar, and birch along the river bottoms and on the sides of the hills. During the winter they browse on the willows and young alders, digging the bushes out of the snow.

The Kenai giant moose is the largest of the deer family. Antlers are offered for sale which measure six feet from tip to tip, and now and then one finds a pair that is more than six feet in width.

The moose are at their best at the close of the summer, when they have grown fat on the rich vegetation. They are most easily caught when the mosquitoes are so bad as to drive them into the rivers and lakes. In the winter they are hunted by men upon snowshoes. The moose are so heavy that they sink into the snow to their bellies when they get out of the sheltered places, and will make for a lake or a river where they can travel over the ice from which the snow has been blown. It is not uncommon to find a baby moose, or calf, as a pet in the mining towns. The calves are born during May and June, and follow the cows until the next spring.

The most delicious meat of Alaska is that of the mountain sheep. It brings higher prices than any other game in the market, but it is difficult to get and the supply is never abundant. A hunter at Fairbanks told me that he once saw six hundred sheep in one drove. He thought himself lucky to have killed two before they got out of sight. These wild sheep are different from those of the Rocky Mountains. Their coats are more like hair than wool. The Dall sheep, named for William H. Dall, the Alaskan explorer, is pure white with horns of jet black.

Mountain sheep are most numerous in the Kenai Peninsula and in the Alaska Range. There are some about Mount McKinley, where good hunting grounds may be reached by railroad. There are also large numbers in the Endicott Mountains, north of the Yukon, where for the most part they graze far above the timber line.

Some attempts are now being made to domesticate the mountain sheep. The lambs are caught and raised in captivity. A farmer near Copper Centre, about one hundred miles from Valdez, is trying to cross the sheep with some he has imported from Montana and other Northern States. He has been successful with some of his rams and has bred from about a half-dozen mountain ewes. The cross results in a large, tame animal whose fleece is a combination of hair and wool. The wool is thick and close to the hide, while the hair extends out beyond it. The meat is said to be superior to that of any except the wild mountain sheep itself.

Bears are to be found almost everywhere in Alaska. No less than thirteen different varieties are recognized by the scientists. There are four general types: the brown, the grizzly, the black, and the polar bear. With the exception of the polar bear, the brown bears are the biggest known. The largest of all are found on Kodiak Island, in the Alaska Peninsula, and about Yakutat, not far from Cordova. I have seen brown bear skins which were more than ten feet long and six feet wide with fur upon them three inches thick. I priced one in a store at Juneau and it was sixty-five dollars. At Nome all furs were cheap. I bought skins there of two baby grizzlies for ten dollars each, and sent them home by parcel post. They weighed just under twenty pounds, and it cost two dollars and forty cents to have them landed in Washington. Polar bear skins of enormous size are sold at Nome for sixty and seventy dollars, only a fraction of the price they would bring in the States.

As for the common black bear, there are so many of them about the mining camps that they often break into the cabins when the owners are away. Every camp and village along the Yukon has one or more tame bear cubs which will eat out of your hand and go through tricks upon order.

The polar bears of Alaska are found in Bering Sea and along the Arctic Ocean. The hunter who wishes to kill such game should go to Nome in the spring and travel over the icefields northward into the Arctic. The bears move north and south with the ice drift. They come as far south as the Seal Islands and have been found as far north as latitude 79. Their food is chiefly seals and fish. The great bears lie near holes in the ice where the seals come up to breathe and grab them when their noses show on the surface.

These bears are perfectly at home in the water, and have been seen swimming in the Arctic sixty miles from land or ice. I am told by the hunters that they usually run on the approach of a man, but that they will attack one when they are hungry. There is a story told here about an Eskimo at Point Barrow who got in the track of a bear which was running from a hunting party. The Eskimo, who was shooting ducks, sent a charge of shot into the bear, who turned back, knocked the Eskimo down with one of his paws, bit off the top of the man's head, and resumed his flight.

There is only one animal in the polar region that can successfully fight the polar bear. That is the great walrus, which often weighs more than a ton. The bears

It is estimated that there are still several million caribou on the barren lands of the Far North, where they feed on reindeer moss.   In winter great herds go south, often as far as a thousand miles from their summer homes.

The lynx lives in deep forests and bush country, where it preys on birds, rabbits, and other small animals.   It is trapped for its soft, thick, pale fur.

will attack the baby walrus, but they are afraid of the sharp ivory tusks of the grown-ups, which are sometimes two feet long. A full-grown walrus has been seen on the body of a dead whale, keeping away a polar bear hungrily swimming around it.

A striking feature of Alaskan game is the provision that Nature has made for their protection. Some of the birds and animals change their colour in winter so that they cannot be seen against the snow. The ptarmigan, for instance, which is one of the finest grouse of Alaska, has a summer plumage of mottled brown while its winter coat is snow-white. The same is true of the rabbits, which are gray in the summer but snow-white in the winter. The rabbits of Southern Alaska are twice as large as those of our Eastern States, although not so large as the Arctic hare. They are sometimes called snowshoe rabbits, because their feet are so large and soft that the animals can go over the snow without sinking.

Rabbits are so numerous that they form the food of many wild animals. They are eaten by wolves, dogs, and bears, and even by the mink and the lynx. The eagles and ravens prey upon the rabbits, and Indians hunt them in companies, driving them to a centre and then shooting them. They are also snared or shot to feed the foxes on the fox farms. I met one fur farmer who had killed twenty-seven hundred rabbits in one year as food for his foxes.

Notwithstanding this, the animals multiply so rapidly that they would overrun the country were it not for a plague that periodically kills them by thousands. I have been told that this plague comes every seven years, and that it is usually followed by an increase in the moose and other wild game. When the rabbits are plentiful there are but few moose, and when rabbits are scarce the moose are abundant. This may be from the fact that the rabbits injure the pasturage over which the moose feed in the same way that sheep will destroy it for other live stock. In the winter the rabbits live on the bark of the willows, eating it down as the snow melts. In this way they destroy great thickets by girdling the trees.

CHAPTER XXXIV

THE BIGGEST THING IN ALASKA

THE biggest thing in Alaska is the government railroad. By that I do not mean so much its five hundred miles of tracks, its cars and equipment, or the number of tons and passengers it will haul, but what it stands for in the future of the territory. It means the building of feeder wagon and motor roads and the construction of other railroads. It means cheaper coal, lower freight rates, lower living and mining costs. It means more lands and resources flung open to the settler and the prospector. It means a new era of development and prosperity for Alaskans.

The act providing for government railroads in Alaska, passed March 12, 1914, authorized the building and operation of railroads here to an extent not to exceed one thousand miles and at a cost of not more than thirty-five million dollars. On this authorization President Wilson bought the Alaska Northern Railway and decided to extend it to Fairbanks, a distance of four hundred and seventy-two miles, at a cost of something like twenty-seven million dollars. The construction of the road was entrusted to the Alaska Engineering Commission. Surveys began in June, 1914, and dirt began to fly the following May. Steel was joined all the way from Seward to Fairbanks in the early spring of 1922. To-day Pullman cars and diners flash through wilderness formerly trav-

271

ersed only by dog sleds. Mail now gets to Fairbanks from Seattle in nine days instead of from one to three months. Freight reaches its destination in three weeks' less time than formerly.

The original appropriation of thirty-five million dollars would doubtless have been sufficient except for the war conditions that brought higher wages and material costs. Later appropriations brought up the total for getting the line into full operation to fifty-six million dollars, or just about eight times what we paid for the territory. Eleven millions of the money provided by Congress were used in building wharves, laying out townsites, paving streets, constructing waterworks and sewerage systems, and developing coal mines along the right of way.

According to Colonel Frederick Mears, chairman of the Engineering Commission, the Alaska railroad has cost about eighty thousand dollars a mile, inclusive of rolling stock and terminals, or sixty-seven thousand, six hundred per mile exclusive of same. By way of comparison, in 1918 the property investment per mile on railways in the United States was something over eighty-three thousand dollars.

The three men originally appointed on the Alaska Engineering Commission were W. C. Edes, Frederick Mears, and Thomas Riggs, Jr., all of them extremely well fitted for their work. Just previous to his appointment, Mr. Edes, a Western railroad builder with thirty years' experience, had been in charge of construction of the Northwestern Pacific Railroad out of San Francisco. Colonel Mears had been in railroad work for ten years in the West and in Panama. Mr. Riggs, later Governor of Alaska, had been in the United States Geological

Survey and immediately before his appointment was in charge of the Alaska international boundary survey, so that he was entirely familiar with the territory.

While the road was built not as a revenue getter, but to open up the country, in the opinion of men who have studied the situation, in four or five years it will be on a self-supporting basis. It is estimated by the Commission that ultimately the revenue will be in the neighbourhood of one million dollars per annum, which does not include any estimate for coal movements from the Matanuska fields to tidewater for the United States Navy.

While the southern terminus of the line is at Seward, the beginning of the old Alaska Northern Railway, bought by Uncle Sam, new construction began at Anchorage on Ship Creek, which became headquarters for the Engineering Commission. Anchorage, which rose amid the stumps of the trees that had such a little while ago to be cut out for its growth, is now a thriving railroad town with pretty homes, stores, government shops, an electric lighting system, sewerage and waterworks, and one of the finest public schools in all Alaska. The school library contains more than a thousand reference books. Though it is a mere infant, its population numbers over a thousand, and it is, next to Juneau, the largest town in the territory. It already has a lively social life, with its parties and dances, motion-picture theatres, and recreation park. There are many fraternal organizations as well as a Farmers' Association, a Fair Association, and an energetic Woman's Club.

I was so fortunate as to see Anchorage in the stump, tent, and shack stage, though it was growing marvellously fast. I give you my notes just as I penned them when I

273

was on the spot, seeing how Uncle Sam's engineers and executives were putting through their big job:

I have come from Sunrise, the little mining settlement on Kenai Peninsula, to Anchorage, the headquarters of the Alaskan Engineering Commission. Anchorage sprang into being when the President, like Aladdin, rubbed the rusty old lamp of Congress and wished for that appropriation of thirty-five million dollars for railroads in Alaska. The town is the nearest port to the Matanuska coal fields, and when navigation in Cook Inlet is open, which is from five to seven months of the year, it will have, perhaps, the bulk of the coal trade. It is for this reason that the people here expect a big city at Anchorage. They look forward to it as a smelting and manufacturing centre as well as a commercial port, and are already talking of it as the financial heart of Alaska.

I found the people of Seward jealous of Anchorage. They claim that their port will be the only real city at the southern end of the railroad, because Resurrection Bay is free of ice throughout the year. All steamers going to Anchorage have to travel several hundred miles farther. They must come up Cook Inlet, the great bay on the west of the peninsula extending about two hundred miles into the land. The inlet in places is upward of fifty miles wide, but it narrows at the northern end, and is only a few miles across in Knik Arm, where Anchorage is situated. The lower part of the inlet, owing to the warm Japanese current, is open throughout the year. The upper part freezes along in October or November, and for a great part of the winter ships cannot come in. The place is one of high tides. The sea rises from forty-five to sixty-five feet in the arms of the inlet, and rushes in twice a day in a wall forming a bore of somewhat the same nature as those in the Bay of Fundy or in the Hugli River, up which one goes to Calcutta.

I had some experience with the tide in coming from Sunrise to Anchorage. We had to leave Sunrise when the water was high, which was not until midnight. Our boat was a launch about eighteen feet long, with a twelve-horsepower gasolene engine. There were bench seats around the side and only a canvas for cover. The owner of the boat was a German storekeeper of Sunrise, and the engineer was his son, a boy of eighteen. The man refused to go unless he got at least $30, but we managed to drum up seven passengers, Mr. George Parks, of the government land office, five prospectors, and myself.

It took us about eight hours to go the hundred miles, and the German was over six days getting back home. We went out of Turnagain Arm to Fire Island, and after lying there for an hour to avoid the rough water, came on through Knik Arm to Ship Creek, and had to wait several hours more before the tide rose so that we could land. We might have taken a dory and tramped to the beach, but the mud at Anchorage is of a blue glacial clay as sticky as glue. The steamers usually anchor some distance from shore and all freight is landed in lighters. The government wharf is high up on piles, and there are platforms a little below the floors of the warehouses upon which the lighters are anchored. They come in when the tide is high, and as it falls are upheld by the platforms so they can be unloaded at leisure.

I like the way our engineers are handling their job. There is no red tape here at Anchorage; "fuss and feathers" are absent. The engineer commissioners are as plain as pipe stems, tramping along with the men and going about the work on foot or on horseback. The two-story house put up for the Commission here would not rent for over fifteen dollars a month in the States. Most of the clerks do their work in tents or log cabins. The forestry department is a two-room shack with folding cots. The commissary building is of logs, and the stables near by, where from fifty to one hundred horses are lodged, are of canvas. The hotel, or messroom, for the men and government employees is a log cabin where three meals are served for a dollar a day. I have yet to meet an official who puts on any airs. Most of them go about with their pants in their boots, and the clothes worn by the three commissioners would hardly bring the value of the wool in them at a second-hand store.

The railroad men receive higher wages than those paid for similar work in the States. The labourers employed are of all nationalities, while not a few are Alaskans. The engineers tell me they find it difficult to get Americans to do the rough work. They all want to be foremen, bosses, or timekeepers. They are willing to work hard as prospectors and miners, but they do not like to handle the pick and shovel at so much per day. The Alaskans are doing much of the clearing and have taken many contracts for ties.

To-day I went over the part of the roadbed near Anchorage. The new railway looks as if it might form an exhibit in a national exposition. It goes through the woods, but the land on each side of the track has been cleared and ditches drain away every bit of the water. I have never seen a better-looking roadbed anywhere. It

The first section of the Government Railway from Seward north toward Anchorage was bought ready built from the Alaska Northern Railway. Fifty miles from Seward it loops-the-loop for four miles through the mountains.

In the mountains where the heaviest snows occur much of the track has been roofed over with enormous sheds. Most of the line is in a region of only moderate snowfall, and all-year operation of the road is assured.

compares favourably in appearance with that of the Pennsylvania or the New York Central.

The engineers have the advantage here of building along hills formed of gravel, and all that has been necessary to get material for the fills has been to drive cuts into the hills at the side of the track. These cuts are then roofed over and the cars are run into the bank and loaded by gravity. I understand that this is the character of much of the route between here and Fairbanks and that a large part of the track will be easy to keep in repair.

A great deal of apprehension has been felt by many who do not understand Alaskan conditions over the difficulty of keeping the road open in winter. The Commission expects to have comparatively little trouble from the cold or the snowfall. The heaviest snows are near the coast, and snow sheds will be established there and in the region about Turnagain Arm. There is much less snow in the interior. The maximum fall at the summit of the main mountain range is only about seven feet, and this can easily be controlled by rotary snow ploughs attached to the engines. At Anchorage the snow seldom reaches a depth of more than two feet and the deepest snowfall is not over three feet.

During my stay at Anchorage I have learned about the country through which the railroad will go from Mr. Thomas Riggs, Jr., who has personally gone again and again over every foot of the ground. He tells me that most of the region has not yet been fully prospected. The land is covered with moss and other vegetation which so hides the rocks that it is hard to tell what there is. It is known, however, that the road will give easy access to many rich gold deposits, and it is certain that mining camps will spring up here and there all along the way from Seward to Fairbanks. There is quartz gold near the line of the Alaska Northern, and there are quartz and placer mines in other parts of the Kenai Peninsula.

Forty miles north of Anchorage is Willow Creek, which has a number of mines, with a ten-stamp mill. A little farther north is the Talkeetna River, where there is good farming land. That part of the country is made up of plains and valleys spotted with groves and covered with grass. A short distance to the west of it are the Yentna and Skwentna mining districts, where prospectors are taking out placer gold.

One of the most promising mining districts along the new railroad is near Broad Pass, where the line crosses the mountains at an altitude of twenty-four hundred feet above the sea. The pass is about five miles in width, and there are mountains on each side of it eight or nine thousand feet high. Off to the west can be seen Mount McKinley, sixty-five miles away, and on the east are the Cathedral Mountains and Mount Hayes, which is almost as high as Fujiyama or Pike's Peak.

To the west of Broad Pass discoveries of low-grade quartz gold are reported. Farther over in the foothills of Mount McKinley is the Kantishna mining district, which has gold, antimony, and other metals. There are sixty-odd miners and trappers there now, and some of them are doing quite well.

Farther along the line are the Nenana coal fields, and then comes the Tolovana gold region, not far from the route between Nenana and Fairbanks. But most important of all the mining regions so far discovered is that around Fairbanks itself. The Tanana Valley Railroad, a narrow-gauge road extending for forty miles north from Fairbanks into the placer-mining district, has been purchased and is a part of the government railway system. This gives this rich mining district a direct rail connection with the outside.

The Alaskan mining regions will profit exceedingly by the cheap fuel that will come over the railroad. Those of the Kenai Peninsula, the Matanuska valley, and all south of Broad Pass now have cheap coal from the Chickaloon coal fields, whereas those on the northern side of the pass and in the Tanana valley may be supplied by the great coal deposits of the Nenana region. The Chickaloon coal, which is from the Matanuska fields, is said to be equal to the Pocahontas. A branch of the railroad runs out from the main line at Matanuska Junction to Chickaloon. The Government has mined and tested many hundred tons of it on the vessels of the navy and it is found to be excellent. It can be used for cooking and it will be the first Alaskan coal of commerce.

The Nenana fields are of vast extent. The railroad passes through them, and it is down grade all the way from there to Fairbanks. The coal deposits extend from the railroad eastward for a distance of perhaps one hundred miles. Outcroppings can be seen on the cliffs and in places the veins are forty feet thick. The coal is a high-grade lignite suitable for all local commercial purposes. It is not good enough to bear exportation, but it will be of enormous value to the miners in the interior.

In order to appreciate what this coal means to the mining regions, it must be remembered that most of the gold deposits are in frozen ground. The frost and ice go down to bed rock. The earth has been frozen for ages, and it has to be thawed out by fire or steam. A single gold mine would often consume from ten to twelve cords of wood a' day, and before the railroad could bring cheap coal nothing but wood could be used. The fact that wood costing over thirty dollars a cord is giving way as mine fuel to lignite coal costing six dollars a ton, delivered, will result in enormous areas of low-grade gold-bearing regions being worked. It means the opening of many new quartz properties, and a great increase in the valleys and benches where the gravel can be washed over by dredging and hydraulic sluicing.

In addition to the cheap coal supplies to be furnished by the government railroad, Southeastern Alaska is much interested in the twenty-two-mile Alaska Anthracite Railroad from a point on Controller Bay to the Bering River field where there is coal equal to the Matanuska variety. It is the field which the Guggenheims were popularly supposed to be gobbling when the great excitement about conservation in Alaska began, and it is, to a certain extent, accessible to Cordova and the Copper River Railroad.

There are now about five hundred farms in the Matanuska and Susitna valleys not far from Anchorage, and there are many new homesteads in the Tanana valley. All of these farms are being operated with a view to supplying the local market and they are raising considerable produce but by no means enough to supply the demands. The railroad commission is trying to bring about a system of coöperation between the merchants and the homesteaders which will lead to less importation from the outside and a greater sale for local products. Many of the farms are springing up around the new towns being laid out at every possible traffic centre.

CHAPTER XXXV

MOUNT McKINLEY, THE "MOST HIGH"

MCKINLEY, the highest mountain on the North American continent, was known to the Indians as Denali, the "Most High." It was used as a landmark in their journeys and stories of it form a part of their folk lore. Most of the world's great peaks rise from a high plateau. Mount McKinley, with its snow-crowned head four miles aloft in the clouds, towers up from a low tundra shelf. No other mountain known rises so high over its own base. It is this which gives it such an effect of supreme height and grandeur.

I have seen Mount McKinley from the hills of the Tanana valley near Fairbanks. It is visible in many parts of Alaska and as more and more tourists visit it and Mount McKinley National Park it will become as well known as Fujiyama, Mont Blanc, or Pike's Peak. It will rank as one of the scenic wonders of the world and the grandest mountain on earth. If you will take an aeroplane and shoot straight up for four miles you will be on a level with its summit; and when you stand on its slope at the end of the road, where the automobile will land you after leaving the cars, you will have a mountain view which cannot be equalled in the Alps, the Andes, or the Himalayas.

I have travelled through all of these regions. I have

seen most of the greatest mountains of the world. Take Aconcagua, the giant of the Andes. It actually is a half mile higher above the sea than Mount McKinley, but the best views of it are to be had only when you are a mile and a half or two miles above the sea, and then you see it over other peaks which dwarf its altitude. One of the best places to see Mount Everest is on the southern slope of the Himalayas. I saw it from Tiger Hill, not far from Darjiling, where I was about a mile and a half above the sea. I started out in the darkness and waited there for sunrise. The air was clear and the sun's rays made the mighty peak look like frosted silver, but one could not realize that he was gazing at the highest known point of the globe. Mount Everest is almost six miles above the sea, but my view was cut off by Kinchinjinga, which is only one thousand feet lower, and that mountain was dwarfed by the other giants between.

Each of these wonder mountains has its own features of scenic grandeur, but none can show the stupendous height effect of Mount McKinley. The north side of the mountain rises almost precipitously and, standing on the northern foothills, one has an unobstructed view of seventeen or eighteen thousand feet of mountain walls.

I can give you a close view of Mount McKinley only from hearsay and from the magnificent pictures of Belmore Browne, the noted mountain climber of the Camp Fire Club of America.

Mr. Browne is an artist, an explorer, and the author of the "Conquest of Mount McKinley." He has attempted the ascent of Mount McKinley both from the south and the north, and at one time he succeeded in reaching within a few hundred feet of the top. He has been over the great part of the region which has been inclosed in the park, and has given the committees of Congress a graphic representation of the wonders of the mountain and of the great droves of wild game to be found on the slopes. I have secured some of my best impressions of the park from him.

I have also talked with Charles Sheldon of the Boone and Crockett Club of New York about his experiences on the slope of Mount McKinley. He is another of the great authorities on this out-of-the-way game region. He built a cabin on the mountainside some years ago and spent a winter or so there studying the game of the country and collecting specimens for the U. S. Biological Survey.

In addition to these two men, I have met in Alaska members of every party connected with the attempts to climb the mountain—with the exception, that is, of those in the party of Dr. Cook, of North Polar fame.

The great mountain was known to the Russians and was mentioned by George Vancouver, the navigator after whom Vancouver Island was named. He came into Cook Inlet and reached the site of the present town of Anchorage in 1794. His records describe his view of "stupendous snow mountains apparently detached from each other." He must have seen Mount McKinley, Mount Foraker, and others.

It was not until eleven years after we took over Alaska that two prospectors named Mayo and Harper made a trip three hundred miles up the Tanana River and on their return mentioned an enormous ice mountain they had seen in the south.

In 1889 another prospector named Densmore gave an

enthusiastic account of the mountain, but it was not until
1896 that W. A. Dickey, a Princeton graduate, travelled
through the Susitna valley and made an extended description of it. Mr. Dickey named it after President McKinley,
recording that name in a letter published in the New
York *Sun* in 1897. Dickey estimated its height as
twenty thousand feet. A little later George Eldridge
and Robert Muldrow of our Geological Survey took its
height by triangulation at twenty thousand three hundred
feet, the generally accepted figure, although I have seen
estimates which make it two or three hundred feet higher.

Another remarkable survey was made of a part of the
region by Dr. Alfred Brooks and D. L. Reyburn in 1902.
They were the first men to set their feet upon the slopes of
Mount McKinley. I have talked with Doctor Brooks
about his experiences. He made a reconnaissance survey of
the western and northwestern face and was the first to lay
out a plan for attempting an ascent. Doctor Brooks estimates the height of Mount McKinley at 20,300 feet, of
Mount Foraker at 17,000 feet, Mount St. Elias at 18,024
feet, and Mount Logan at 19,539 feet.

And now as to the ascent of this giant peak. The
first man to attempt it was James Wickersham, a former
delegate to Congress from the territory. Judge Wickersham has told me how he caught sight of it from far up
the Yukon when he first came to Alaska, and determined
to do what he could to reach its summit. It was in May,
1903, after holding his first term of court at Fairbanks,
that he set out with four men and two mules. He went
down to Tanana in a steamer and ascended to the head
of navigation on the Kantishna. He left the river and
struck across the country to the base of the mountain,

McKinley, the loftiest peak on the North American continent, was known to the Indians as Denali, the "Most High." With its snow-crowned head four miles aloft in the clouds, it towers above a low tundra shelf. No other mountain rises so far above its own base.

The first real ascent of Mt. McKinley was not made until 1910, when some miners climbed the north peak. Three years later the party headed by Archbishop Stuck reached the top of the south peak.

but he tried to ascend by the Peters Glacier, and was stopped by the enormous ice-covered cliffs of the north peak. He came back saying that only a balloon could ever take one to the top. He spent a week in attempting the climb, and it was only when his provisions gave out that he returned to Fairbanks.

The next attempt was made by Doctor Cook, who claimed that he stood on the peak, and gave an illustrated lecture at Washington, telling how he got there. This, like his North Polar expedition, was afterward shown up as a fraud.

The first real ascent of Mount McKinley was made in February, 1910, by a party of mining prospectors backed by three saloon keepers of Fairbanks. The prospectors were Thomas Lloyd, Charles McGonogill, William Taylor, and Peter Anderson. One of the saloon keepers was "Big Bill McPhee," whom I met in Fairbanks. He and the two others each put up five hundred dollars for the journey, which sum sufficed for the needs of the party. I had a talk in the Tanana Club at Fairbanks with Tom Lloyd, who headed the party, and also with Taylor and Anderson, with whom I travelled on the Tanana River from Nenana to Chena.

The men got to the foothills about the first of March, 1910. Lloyd, who had been hunting mountain sheep in the region, led the party up the slope by easy passes and made his way over the great Muldrow Glacier. It took them about twenty-five days to get to the head of the glacier with their dogs and supplies, and it was on the tenth of April that Taylor, Anderson, and McGonogill made the final part of the ascent, crawling over the ice by means of irons strapped to their moccasins and with hooked poles in their hands. They did not tie themselves together with ropes, and there was no cutting of steps. It was every man for himself, and they gradually climbed the ice of the north peak of the mountain, carrying a fourteen-foot flagstaff with them. They planted this on the peak where it stands to this day.

The top of the mountain is somewhat like a horseshoe. It is an extinct volcano and the south point is perhaps three hundred feet higher than the north point. Tom Lloyd, Pete Anderson, Billy Taylor, and Charlie McGonogill could easily have gone over and climbed the south peak, but they wanted their flag where they mistakenly believed it would be seen by telescope at Fairbanks, one hundred and fifty miles away.

The honour of the highest ascent goes to the party headed by Archdeacon Stuck, who with Harry Karstens, the Alaska scout and guide, reached the top of the south peak in 1913. Belmore Browne had come within about one hundred feet of it the year before that, but an earthquake, which had shaken down the great ice masses, and the blizzard which came up at that altitude prevented his getting to the summit.

As to the feat of Harry Karstens and Archdeacon Stuck, I got the story of it from Harry Karstens as we sat and chatted together in Big Bill McPhee's store at Fairbanks. Harry Karstens is a young trapper and hunter famous for his nerve on the trail. He is a noted guide and takes out rich hunters when they come to the Yukon. He brought the first mail into Fairbanks and took the first letters into the Kantishna. He made the trip up the mountain in partnership with the archdeacon, the latter furnishing one thousand dollars for the expenses against Karstens' experience, the understanding being that the two were to divide the proceeds from Archdeacon Stuck's book and lecture describing the ascent. The men were fifty-two days on the way, of which fifty days were spent going up and only two coming down. You can get a graphic description of the journey by reading Archdeacon Stuck's book entitled "The Ascent of Mount Denali."

Mount McKinley dominates the greatest of the Government's reserves, Mount McKinley National Park. This park has an area of over twenty-five hundred square miles, or more than twice that of Rhode Island. There are rich grass valleys; there are beautiful woods of spruce, cottonwood, and birch; there are waterfalls and rushing streams. Mighty glaciers sweep down the mountain sides. Muldrow Glacier is thirty-five miles long. The largest glacier of the Swiss Alps is only sixteen miles in length. Here and there great lava-flows from the old volcanoes make patches of vivid brown and green and purple and red.

Wild animals throng the whole area and, now that they are protected by the Government, will make the park the largest and best-populated game preserve of this continent. The only place I know that at all compares with it is the strip two miles wide running from Mombasa, on the east coast of Africa, to Lake Victoria, six hundred miles inland. That strip, a mile wide on each side of the railroad, fairly swarms with zebra and antelope of various kinds.

It will be the same in the Mount McKinley Park. That region has thousands of caribou, or American reindeer. Belmore Browne saw one hundred and twenty-five in one herd, and they sometimes move back and forth over the park in droves of thousands. Charles Sheldon tells me that he counted five hundred mountain sheep in one day. The park is also the haunt of the bear and the beaver. It has moose in the low timber and bushes along the streams and there are foxes, rabbits, and lynx, and the many varieties of birds found in Alaska. It will be the most interesting place for the study of natural history. Protected by law, most of the animals will become so tame that they will not run at the approach of tourists, and will be preserved for all time among the wonders of our fauna.

Heretofore this region has been practically inaccessible to the ordinary traveller, but the railroad will make the region almost as easy to reach as any of our national parks. At one place the trains pass within fifteen miles of the park. Moreover, the foothills of the northern slope of the mountains are such that roadways can be easily made up one little valley after another so that tourists may go by wagons or automobiles right to the foot of the mountain.

The bridge at Hurricane Gulch, 284 miles up the line from Seward, is over 900 feet long and 300 feet above the stream below, and an important link in the transportation chain which will reduce living and mining costs in Alaska.

Down to Cordova, the "copper gateway of Alaska," come the trainloads of ore.   Sometimes a single vessel leaving this port will have an ore cargo worth nearly $1,000,000.

CHAPTER XXXVI

CORDOVA, two hundred miles across Prince William Sound from Seward, is the copper centre of Alaska. The ore coming down to the port is from only two or three mines, but they represent one of the most extensive and richest of the copper areas of the world. More than four hundred copper locations have already been made, and the ore belt is known to be over seventy miles long and twenty miles wide. These deposits are so rich that Alaska may become as noted for its copper as it has been for gold.

The first trainload of ore that came down to Cordova contained metal to the value of more than a half million dollars, and that now on the wharves is worth from twelve to fifteen thousand dollars a carload. The ore is brought down from the Kennecott mines in sacks, each containing from one hundred and fifty to two hundred pounds of ore carrying twenty-eight dollars' worth of copper.

The ore of the Kennecott mines is so rich in copper that it can be dug from the earth, turned into metal, and put on the market at a cost of a few cents a pound. The average ores they are now taking out are over twenty per cent. copper, and a large part of them carry as much as seventy-two per cent. In comparison, the copper ores of Arizona yield about five per cent., those of Montana about three, and those of Michigan less than one per cent. Do you wonder that the Kennecott mines pay?

The native metal was used by the Copper River Indians before white men entered the territory. Old spear- and arrow-heads of it have been found in the sluice boxes of the miners, and ceremonial knives of copper are even now employed by the natives in cutting the salmon taken at the beginning of the catch.

Long before the Russians sold Alaska to us, they had discovered that copper existed there. They had nuggets and small household utensils of beaten copper. They found no large deposits, however, and it was not until a generation after we had taken possession that prospectors, on their way from Prince William Sound to the Klondike, learned about the Copper River region. In the same year the United States Geological Survey reported a similar copper belt on the northern slope of the Wrangell Mountains, about two hundred miles south of Fairbanks.

The most important discovery was that of the Kennecott mines, which were developed by the Morgan-Guggenheim syndicate. These deposits were discovered in 1900 by two miners prospecting near here, and a little later the property was investigated by Mr. Stephen A. Birch, a young mining engineer, who brought it to the attention of the capitalists and organized the projects which have made it one of the greatest copper mines of the world.

It was through a talk with Mr. Birch that I learned the story of the discovery. Said he:

"It began with the mining excitement that followed the rush to the Klondike. Among the prospectors then

290

moving about here and there over Alaska were eleven working under a partnership agreement. These men went in pairs, first drawing lots to see which section of the country they should take. The district of the upper Chitina River was drawn by Clarence Warner and Jack Smith, who had tramped so extensively over the mountains of Arizona that he was known as the 'Arizona Centipede.'

"Toward the end of the summer of 1900 Warner and Smith had gone carefully over the section allotted to them but had found nothing and were about to leave in despair. Their grub was fast diminishing, and when they came to the Kennecott River they decided to end their work by prospecting the land between Kennecott Glacier and Nikolas Creek and, if nothing was found, to give up for the year. They had gone only three miles when Warner sprained his ankle on one of the rocks, and the two sat down by a stream to rest. While eating their lunch, Smith called Warner's attention to a large green patch in the rocks on the side of the mountain. He said it looked strange and that they ought to go up and see just what it was. Warner replied that Smith might go if he would, but he didn't intend to climb that far to look at a sheep pasture. He thought the green patch was grass and that it was one of the feeding grounds of the mountain sheep found on the hills of this part of Alaska.

"Discouraged by Warner's objection, Smith was about to give up when he saw in the bed of the stream a piece of float or chip of mineral-bearing rock. He picked it up and he and Warner studied it together. They broke it in two. As the fracture had a silvery look they thought it was silver. They found more of the float in the creek, the pieces increasing in number as they walked up the stream and gradually leading them to the spot they had thought a sheep pasture. Then they saw that the outcropping was copper from what proved to be the richest copper mine ever discovered.

"Now the first thing a prospector does after making a strike is to select a name for his find," continued Mr. Birch. "The question was what they should call the new mine. Old Jack Smith, who was ahead of Warner and first saw the possibilities, turned to his partner and said: 'By God, Warner, she's a bonanza.' To which Warner replied: 'Well, Jack that's a good name for her. We'll call her 'The Bonanza Mine.'

"And a bonanza it has proved to be. After only four and one half years' operation it yielded over eight million dollars in dividends, and then began earning at the rate of more than six millions per annum. So far no one knows the actual extent of the deposit, and it is safe to say that it will be paying dividends for generations to come."

When the prospectors returned to the rest of their party at Valdez, Mr. Birch was there on behalf of himself and certain capitalists of New York City, looking for promising mining investments. The prospectors told him about their discovery and showed him the specimens of ore, and he agreed to make an examination the following spring if they would give him an option upon it.

The next season Birch returned to Alaska and found the deposit all and more than had been claimed. He then secured a new option, agreeing to pay one hundred thousand dollars to each of the eleven members of the party. To make this option perfectly valid, he had to

The wise explorer anchors his tent and belongings securely to supple trees so that they may not be blown away, while his dogs tuck their noses into their long bushy tails and keep warm.

A prospector's sprained ankle led to the discovery of the copper deposits which, as the Bonanza mines, paid dividends of six million dollars in a single year. The ores here are the richest known.

secure the signatures of the eleven prospectors and all who were interested with them. Some of the men had been grub-staked by others, so that the money had to be divided among thirty-two claimants, each of whom had to agree to the deal. The establishment of the titles involved several lawsuits, one of which was carried to the Supreme Court of the United States, and it was five years before the Alaska Syndicate was able to begin actual development work.

Although this syndicate had to put approximately twenty-five million dollars into the property, including the expense of building the Copper River Railway, there is no doubt that they have got back the worth of their money. They have already received more than the purchase price in dividends, and the market value of the property is several times what it cost.

Further on in our conversation Mr. Birch spoke of the copper deposits on the Island of Latouche, in Prince William Sound. That island has rich copper lodes, but the ore is of an entirely different character from that of the Bonanza and the Jumbo near by. The Latouche mines are low-grade producers. Their ore is a chalcopyrite which averages about three per cent copper. It is quarried from the hillsides overlooking the water, and is treated by the flotation process.

The story of the discovery of the Latouche copper mine, which was told me by an old prospector at Seward, is quite as interesting as that of the Bonanza. The Latouche mine was the result of a mess of bad clams. A number of miners were sailing along the shores of Latouche Island when they stopped at a clam bed and dug up enough for a meal. They cooked the clams, but before eating them found that they were deadly poisonous on account of the copperas in them. One of the men suggested that the copperas must come from copper deposits near by, and that they had better stop and prospect the rocks. The outcome was the discovery of these great deposits of low-grade copper ore almost on the edge of the sea. The miners decided to develop the property for themselves, but the ore contained such a small percentage of metal that they could not make it pay. They kept on mining, however, with the idea that the deposits were so large that they ought to sell the property at a big price.

Finally, one of them named Beatson announced that he was disgusted and was going outside for the winter. He took some of the ore with him and went to New York, where he induced a rich relative to advance him thirty thousand dollars to purchase the property, with the understanding that Beatson was to retain his own share.

Beatson then came back to Latouche, but before he did so, he changed his money into thirty yellow bank-notes of one thousand dollars each, which he sewed inside the lining of his mackinaw. When he came to the mine it was with a sad face. He said that capital was tight and the public not prone to invest. He kept on preaching hard times and at last cast such a gloom over the camp that the others of the party decided to sell if they could get any kind of a price for the mine. They were in this mood when Beatson asked them to name a price, and they finally agreed on a few thousand dollars. Before showing his money Beatson asked: "Are you sure you would take that price if I could find the money?" When the other miners replied in the affirmative, he asked them to put their offer in writing. Thinking he was bluffing, they did so. He thereupon ripped open his coat and handed out the sum in one-thousand-dollar banknotes. The yellow bills looked so good that the men took them and the mine became his.

Beatson then began to develop the property and finally sold it to the Alaska Syndicate, which is now operating it at a profit. I have not learned the price but am told that it was high enough to drop Mr. Beatson into "Easy Street" for the rest of his life.

Copper mining requires capital, so that it has not attracted the small prospector as gold has done. Though it is said that a billion dollars' worth of copper is in sight in Alaska, and though one nugget weighing three tons has been found, so far mining costs have been so high that only ore with a large copper content will make the work pay. The ore has to be shipped to the States to be smelted, which means much re-handling besides the long and expensive haul. There is plenty of coal suitable for the smelters close to the copper regions. The Bering River fields lie a little east of Cordova near Controller Bay, which is now reached by the Alaska Anthracite Railroad. As soon as these fields are developed and cheap coal is available smelters will undoubtedly be built and operated close to the copper mines.

CHAPTER XXXVII

ON THE COPPER RIVER RAILWAY

SO FAR as I know, the Copper River and Northwestern Railway is the only line in the world that takes its passengers right to the foot of magnificent glaciers and allows them to examine these greatest wonders of Nature while the train waits. Within an hour of the arrival of our steamer at Cordova an excursion train started out from the wharf, and the tourists on board were carried a distance of about fifty miles up the Copper River Valley to the Miles and Childs glaciers, two mighty streams of ice that stand almost facing each other on opposite sides of the track.

Leaving Cordova, the road winds around the hills high over the water, hanging to rocky cliffs covered with dense vegetation. A little later it enters the mouth of the Copper River valley and skirts Eyak Lake, which fills a star-shaped depression scooped out by some ancient glacier. The lake is almost entirely shut in by high wooded mountains rising abruptly from the water's edge. After following the winding shores of this lake for four miles, the line crosses the Eyak River, which carries the glacial waters of the lake out to the sea. It is by this river that the boats from Cordova go into and out from the lake, and during the summer months the stream is gay with canoes, rowboats, and power craft of every description. The lake teems with fish and it has excellent trout. During the winter it is sometimes frozen over and is used for skating and sleighing. There is some fishing done then through holes in the ice.

Leaving the lake we passed through a forest of spruce, and wound our way over the Copper River Delta, crossing stream after stream from the great glaciers of the interior. The flats extend for sixteen miles east and west, a wide expanse of green level land, half swamps, with water here and there showing out of the green. Flocks of ducks and geese rose from these ponds as our train passed. We could often see walls of green ice from our train. The glaciers reached the clouds that dark, rainy day. The ice seemed to be looking at us over the trees.

We saw the graves of some miners who had tried in vain to get through to the Klondike by this route in the gold rush of 1898. A little farther on we crossed Long Island, and at Mile Thirty-four came to the bridge over Hot Cake Channel, so called because a party of engineers were shut up there during the railway construction and for weeks had nothing to eat but hot cakes.

All the way to the foot of the mountains the engineers had to wade through the mud to lay out the route, and it was hard to find a solid roadbed. At Mile Twenty-nine we were only thirty-two miles from the Bering River coal field, and twenty miles farther on came to the narrow passage between the Miles and Childs glaciers. Here the road crosses the Miles Glacier bridge which cost more than a million and a half to build, and then goes on its way up the mountains.

There are a number of smaller glaciers visible from the

train, but those we came to see are the Miles and the
Childs, the two mightiest ones in all the valley. Childs
Glacier is within a quarter of a mile or so of the track, and
Miles Glacier is in plain sight as you sit in the cars facing
the bridge. Of these two the Miles is by far the larger.
It begins in the snowfields of the mountains and
it is probably fifty miles long. Where it enters the
Copper River valley it spreads out in a great bulb,
which at the end is six and one half miles across. It
is about twelve and one half miles around the whole
front.

Our train stopped on a switch near the bridge, in plain
sight of both glaciers, and we had an hour or so to look
about. We left our cars and made our way to the termi-
nal moraine of the glacier, which is made up of rocks of all
sizes.

The vegetation had now disappeared and we stood on
the bank of a river with glacial waters that looked like
skim milk. We were right under a mighty ice wall that
ascended straight up from the water to a greater height
than that of the dome of our Capitol at Washington.
This wall is washed by the river. It extends along the
banks of the stream for a length of four miles and runs
back for more than ten miles up the valley. It is composed of broken and uneven cliffs of pale green ice from
which huge masses are continually falling.

We could see and hear the ice blocks breaking off as we
stood under the wall on the opposite bank of the milky
river. First came a cracking, which sounded like
a battery of heavy artillery. Then a mass of pure white,
weighing thousands of tons, broke loose from the glacier,
seemed to hang in mid air for an instant, then plunged

down into the stream with a thunderous roar, sending up a high cloud of spray. A moment later the mist had cleared away, and the ice block could be seen rising and falling, sending waves almost to our feet.

The breaking of the ice is caused by melting and also by pressure from the great ice river as it flows slowly down from the heights. The movement of the glacier varies in speed from time to time. During the years 1906, 1907, and 1908 it came forward only two or three feet a day, but in 1909 its motion increased to five or six feet, and in August, 1910, it was advancing at the rate of thirty or forty feet daily. After that it began to slow up, and in June, 1911, it was moving less than two feet per day. Scientists made careful observations and photographs of the Childs Glacier at the time of its greatest activity. They would come out in the morning to find tons of ice resting where their cameras had stood the day previous and to see a great tree perhaps a hundred years old prone on the ground with its butt beneath the glacier. The night before the same tree had been upright and the ice some distance away. In this movement the ice acted like so many ploughs, ripping up the earth to bed rock, and piling up the turf and bushes ten or fifteen feet higher than the level of the plain.

In view of what the engineers did in constructing this line, it would seem no idle boast to say they could even fight off the advance of a glacier. The route lay through one of the ruggedest mountain regions of the continent, with glaciers, glacial streams, rapids, and canyons to be conquered. In the delta flats there was hardly any ground fit for construction camps and the only fuel was green alders and willows. Sometimes it took six months to get material up the river from Cordova to the glacial region. Sometimes as the surveying parties got farther inland they worked with the thermometer at fifty below zero.

In summer much construction material had to be towed up the river by men pushing their way through the cottonwood thickets, while others waded in the stream to keep the boats off the rocks. In winter it had to be sledded over ice sometimes piled up in barriers, sometimes filled with dangerous pot holes.

The most remarkable engineering feat on the route, though, was the building of the eleven-hundred-and-fifty-foot bridge across the river between the Miles and the Childs glaciers. For a time the fate of the million-and-a-half-dollar investment hung by a hair. Thousands of piles driven deep into the bottom of the river and frozen into seven feet of ice formed the temporary foundation of the third and last span. The bridge builders were working with breathless haste to beat the spring thaw. Before they had a chance to make fast the last span, the ice began to move, carrying the span with it. While one gang chopped the ice with axes, and melted it with steam pipes, another, with block and tackle, not only stopped the moving span, but inch by inch dragged it back into place where at last it was bolted and riveted. Now around each pier is a row of eighty-pound rails one foot apart to act as an ice breaker.

Like the White Pass line, the Copper River Railway was built for business reasons and it went straight ahead in the face of these enormous difficulties. Construction began in 1906 and the one hundred and ninety-six miles of track was completed five years later. The total cost

The Copper River Railway is the only line in the world that carries its passengers right to the foot of magnificent glaciers. The river runs between Miles and Childs glaciers, each of which has a front of ice three miles wide.

One of the most beautiful trips in the world is through the Keystone Canyon from Valdez to Chitina, and thence down the Copper River Railway to Cordova.

was twenty million dollars, or about one hundred thousand dollars a mile, but the road has paid, for the route taps the Wrangell Range, the richest known mineral section of Alaska. This range has gold, copper, and silver, and the finest copper mines of the world.

CHAPTER XXXVIII

WOMEN ON AMERICA'S LAST FRONTIER

You toast the men of Alaska,
 God bless them every one,
They gave their best, they stood the test,
 Of the Land of the Midnight Sun.

But what of that brave woman
 Who mushed close by their side
She took the trail (they thought her frail),
 All hardships she decried.

The sweetheart, wife, or mother,
 She came for love alone,
She stifled fear, fought back each tear,
 And built anew the home.

A toast to the Alaska woman
 From Ketchikan to Nome,
She's worth more gold than earth can hold,
 A toast to woman—home.

I QUOTE these lines from the club book of the Kegoayah Kozga, or Northern Lights, the name of the up-and-coming women's club of Nome. This club reflects the dawn of woman's work in northern Alaska. The Kegoayah Kozga has its own house, a delightful little cottage on one of the main streets of Nome, and even has a surplus in its treasury. It has its civic events, its clean-up day, its annual entertainment for husbands of the members, and its yearly farewell party for those going "outside" for the winter. Its study classes run throughout the year. The women who belong to it are typical of the cultured women in other parts of the territory. They are well dressed, well bred, and well educated. Not a few are college graduates, and all are more hospitable than is common throughout the States. Many of them have lived in Alaska for years and their stories of conditions, present and past, are especially interesting.

It was not until 1898, when gold was discovered in the Klondike, that many women came to Alaska. Those who were here before that were chiefly the wives of government officials or of officers of the army and navy, some of whom lived at the posts and others at the chief towns along the coast. There were also the wives of missionaries at Sitka and other places in Southeastern Alaska, and occasionally the wife of a sea captain or trapper.

The first woman to establish a home on Cook Inlet was Mother White, the wife of a whaler who made voyages to Bering Sea and the Arctic Ocean. She built a log cabin store and roadhouse on the shore about two hundred miles from the site of the new town of Anchorage. There Miss Martha White was born, the first white child to see the light of day in that part of the world. When the work began on the government railway she was chosen to drive the first spike.

It is more than twenty years since Mrs. White established her store and roadhouse. She dealt with the Indians and trappers, and later on started a fish cannery and saltery. In one year she put up two thousand barrels of salted salmon. She made considerable money, which she invested in mining. She went in the gold stampede to

Sunrise, on Turnagain Arm, where she made so much that she might have retired in comfort. Then bad luck came. She put her winnings into unsuccessful properties and lost them. She went back to the roadhouse business and established little hotels at Hope City and Sunrise. These were a success and she gradually accumulated some property. In the meantime, her daughter was growing up and Mother White decided to leave Alaska and go to the States to educate her. She moved to Chicago and opened a little store there, which supported her until Martha's education was finished.

And then came that longing to go back to Alaska that permeates the souls of all who have made their homes here. It so obsessed Mrs. White that she left her daughter in Chicago and went alone to the North. With tears in her eyes, she told me how she went back to the mining camps of Hope and Sunrise. Many of the old prospectors whom she had known were still there, and she felt that here were her friends and her home. She returned to Chicago to get her daughter, and when the work on the Alaskan Railroad began she was one of the first on the ground at the new town of Anchorage. She came in with a stock of lumber and canvas, and before a rail was laid or any excavation begun she had put up tents down on the flats for eating and lodging. Her sleeping tent was equipped with bunks one over the other, like those of a sleeping car, and each bed brought her a dollar a night. When the new site for Anchorage was chosen, she built a frame hotel on the main street.

Another woman who has made good in Alaska is Mrs. Harriet Pullen of Pullen House, at which I stopped in Skagway. By her kindness to the old miners and stranded

Martha White, the first white child born on Cook Inlet, was chosen to drive the initial spike in the Government Railway.

The Alaska homesteader and his wife have no easy job. Both should be young, strong, and prepared to do everything for themselves, as help is usually scarce at wages always higher than in the States.

"I had delicious hot waffles, butter, and syrup at the Two Girls' Waffle House. The proprietors came from Seattle to Anchorage just at its beginning and set up a shack on the flats."

prospectors she has earned the title of "Mother of the North." Mrs. Pullen came to Skagway at the time of the gold rush to the Klondike. The daughter of a well-to-do settler on Puget Sound, she was a widow with three little sons at the time gold was discovered. She decided to go to the gold mines. She was almost penniless when she landed in Alaska, and when a miner came to the steamer to hire a cook for his camp she asked for the job and got it. She did well there, and later on became the cook for a boarding house, where her sourdough flapjacks, soda biscuits, and apple pies, were soon famous. Seeing that big money was being made in freighting goods over the mountains, she sent her first savings back to Seattle and brought in six horses from her father's farm. She also imported a wagon, and started freighting over the trail. She drove the horses herself, making her customers load their own goods. She got such high rates that she was soon clearing twenty-five dollars a day.

At the end of the first season she was one thousand dollars ahead, and this gave her enough to build a cottage and start a hotel. From that time on she has been able not only to live well and make money, but to give her children as good an education as our country affords. The boys went to school in Skagway, where they worked at odd hours and during vacation to help their mother. Later they were sent to the United States to college. The youngest boy was drowned at Juneau. One of the other two was the first appointee from Alaska to West Point, and another graduated at the University of Washington. Both sons did valiant service in the World War. General Pershing said he wished he had a regiment of Pullens.

Another woman came north from Juneau, where she had been working in a laundry. She was blonde, forty-five years of age, but so stout and rugged that she pulled her own sled, weighing two hundred and fifty pounds, from Lake Lindeman through to Lake Le Barge, and made her way on down to Circle City. She started a laundry and bake shop, selling her bread for from fifty cents to a dollar a loaf. Later on she came to the Klondike and staked out a claim on Eldorado Creek, from which she realized three hundred thousand dollars.

The women of the gold rush days did all sorts of things and underwent every hardship to get to the gold mines. Many were stranded at Skagway or Dyea, the ports at the foot of the mountains over which the trails led to the gold camps.

One woman over seventy-five years old came north with the rush. She had no money to get over the trail, so she started in selling newspapers at from twenty-five to fifty cents each, the current prices of those days. She was so old that she aroused sympathy, and a rich miner would often give her five dollars for a paper and tell her to keep the change. All this time she was sleeping in a piano box in a little cabin. Friends, fearing she would freeze during the winter, got her people in Montana to write her to come home. When she left Skagway she had two thousand dollars earned in her newspaper selling.

The old type of roughly dressed frontier woman is rapidly passing. The mining of the rich camps is going into the hands of large capital, and there are but few women who have big mining investments. Margaret Mitchell, who called herself the Quartz Queen of the Klondike, believed that the hundred and eighty-odd million dollars' worth of gold that has been washed out in grains and dust from the creeks and basin of the Klondike must have been ground off from rich veins near by. In her search for the mother lodes, for years she took up and bought quartz claims. Some of her properties are said to carry good values.

Margaret Mitchell was always one of the first to rush to every new mining field, and in this way got the nickname, "Stampede Mag." She also watched out for claims that lapsed through the carelessness of owners in failing to do the assessment work annually required. Every now and then she picked up a valuable claim, and sometimes one belonging to the big capitalists. I understand that when she jumped one such claim the millionaires had to pay her six thousand dollars before she would release the new title thus acquired. I met "Stampede" Mitchell and found her a bronze-faced, energetic woman of middle age, with a firm faith in the existence of quartz gold in the upper Yukon.

At Anchorage I often breakfasted at the "Two Girls' Waffle House." The "Two Girls" were bright-eyed, rosy-cheeked, plump young women who came from Seattle to Anchorage when it was first started and opened an eating place on the flats. When the town was moved to the hills they put their house on a wagon and moved with the times. Whenever I went to meals at their place the counter was filled, for their waffles served hot from the griddle with plenty of good butter, syrup, and coffee were enough to make a hungry man's mouth water.

I found many other women in business at Anchorage. Some were typists, others clerks in stores, and others proprietors of shops of their own. There was a woman barber on Fourth Street and one of the best dry-goods and notions stores in town was kept by a pretty red-haired girl under thirty. Another young lady who had come up from Illinois and was staying at my hotel told me she had always pined for the free life of the North and was going to open a millinery shop. She had a thousand dollars' worth of stock coming up from the States.

The larger towns of the Alaska of to-day have perhaps one half as many women as men. The tents and the shacks of the past have given place to comfortable homes with gardens and flowers, and the social conditions are not far different from those of the towns of the States. Every town of any size has a women's club like that at Nome. The Juneau Women's Club recently gave a reception to the Women's Club of Douglas Island. It was held in the city hall, and among the papers read was one on English literature, another on the cathedral towns of Europe, and a third on early English with readings from Chaucer.

The Fairbanks Club has been especially interested in civic matters. Its members write editorials for the local newspapers on how to improve sanitary and educational conditions; and they have done a great deal to help the town. The same is true of every women's club in the country from Ketchikan to Nome.

The clubs keep close watch on the schools, and all of them are more or less literary in character. The women of Alaska come from all parts of the world, and many of them have travelled extensively. They have broad ideas of public affairs and their discussions take a wide range.

But it seems to me I could write forever about Alaska. I have travelled widely over the world, visiting all the continents and most of the countries, but I have yet to find a place more delightful or more interesting than our mighty land of the North.

It is said of the River Nile that he who drinks of its waters always comes back to Egypt. I feel much the same about Alaska. Most of the prospectors, tourists, and travellers whom I have met in these journeys are making their second or third visit to these wonderful wilds. Just where the charm lies it is hard to say. It may be in the air, which fills one's lungs with such invigoration that one seems to be breathing champagne; it may be in the scenery, which is equal to any in New Zealand or Switzerland; or in the wildness which gives one the sensation of being an original explorer, like Christopher Columbus, or Hernando de Soto. The magic of Alaska is perhaps best expressed by Robert Service's "Spell of the Yukon."

> There's a land where the mountains are nameless,
>   And the rivers all run God knows where;
> There are lives that are erring and aimless
>   And deaths that just hang by a hair;
> There are hardships that nobody reckons;
>   There are valleys unpeopled and still;
> There's a land—oh, it beckons and beckons.
>   And I want to go back—and I will.

THE END

BIBLIOGRAPHY

THE standard historical works on Alaska are the volume on Alaska in Hubert Howe Bancroft's "History of the Pacific States" and William Healy Dall's "Alaska and Its Resources." A standard guide book is the "Rand McNally Guide to Alaska and the Yukon," first published in 1922. Following is a selected list of recent works:

BROWNE, BELMORE. "Conquest of Mount McKinley." New York, 1913.

BURR, A. R. "Alaska, Our Beautiful Northland of Opportunity." Boston, 1919.

CAMERON, CHARLOTTE. "A Cheechako in Alaska and Yukon." New York, 1920.

DE WINDT, H. "Through the Gold Fields of Alaska." New York, 1898.

DOLE, N. H. "Our Northern Domain." Boston, 1910.

DUNNING, W. A. "Paying for Alaska." New York, 1912.

GORDON, G. B. "In the Alaskan Wilderness." Philadelphia, 1918.

HEILPRIN, ANGELO. "Alaska and the Klondike." New York, 1899.

HIGGINSON, ELLA. "Alaska, the Great Country." New York, 1909.

JONES, E. L. "A Study of the Thlingets of Alaska." New York, 1914.

KENT, ROCKWELL. "Wilderness: A Journal of Quiet Adventure in Alaska." London, 1920.

MUIR, JOHN. "Travels in Alaska." New York, 1915.

POWELL, ADDISON. "Trailing and Camping in Alaska." New York, 1909.

SCULL, E. M. "Hunting in the Arctic and Alaska." Philadelphia, 1909.

SHELDON, CHARLES. "The Wilderness of the Upper Yukon." New York, 1911.

BIBLIOGRAPHY

STEPHENSON, W. B., JR. "Land of Tomorrow." New York, 1919.
STUCK, HUDSON. "Ten Thousand Miles with a Dog Sled." New York, 1914.
"The Ascent of Denali." New York, 1914.
"Voyages on the Yukon and Its Tributaries." New York, 1917.
"A Winter Circuit of Our Arctic Coast." New York, 1920.
UNDERWOOD, J. J. "Alaska an 'Empire in the Making.'" New York, 1920.
YOUNG, S. H. "Alaska Days with John Muir." New York, 1915.
"Adventure in Alaska." New York, 1919.

The nine departments of the National Government and the twenty-three separate offices or bureaus having duties and controls in Alaska are a prolific source of information on the territory. An exhaustive list of their publications may be had on application to the Superintendent of Documents, Government Printing Office, Washington, D. C. The following government documents deserve especial mention:

INTERIOR DEPARTMENT: Annual Report of the Governor of Alaska. General Information Regarding Alaska.
GEOLOGICAL SURVEY: Future of Alaska Mining and the Alaskan Mining Industry in 1919, by Alfred H. Brooks and H. V. Martin. Bull. 714.
Alaskan Mining Industry in 1920, by Alfred H. Brooks. Bull. 722.
BUREAU OF FISHERIES: Alaska Fishery and Fur-Seal Industries in 1920, by Ward T. Bower. Document No. 909.
Pacific Salmon Fisheries, by John N. Cobb. Document No. 902.
DEPARTMENT OF AGRICULTURE: Annual Report of the Alaska Agricultural Experiment Stations.
BUREAU OF AMERICAN ETHNOLOGY: Eskimo about Bering Sea. 18th Ethnology Report. 1897. Part I.
Thlinget Myths and Texts, by John R. Swanton. Ethnology Bull. 39.
Social Conditions, Beliefs, and Linguistic Relationship of the Thlinget Indians. 26th Ethnology Report.

INDEX

INDEX

Agriculture, future of, in Alaska, 60.
Akutan Island, whaling station on, 244.
Alaska, how named, 40.
Alaska Anthracite Railroad, new coal developments of the, 280.
Alaska Commercial Company, activities of, 143; fur seal monopoly of, 232.
Alaska Engineering Commission, personnel, 272; their work at Anchorage, 275.
Alaska-Gastineau mines, 78.
Aleutian Islands, development of the, 239.
All-Alaska Sweepstakes, the, 198.
Allan, Scotty, saved by his lead dog, 203.
Anchorage, a live railroad town, 273, 274.
Anderson, Peter, one of first party to climb Mt. McKinley, 285.
Andreafski, fuel oil tank at, for Yukon steamers, 181.
Annette Island, Father Duncan's work with Indians of, 13.
Annette Island Reservation of Metlakahtla Indians, 17.
Anvik, Indian settlement on Lower Yukon, 181.
Athapascans, and sub tribes, the, 44; visited on the Yukon, 117.
Ayer, Fred M., mining engineer and owner of racing dogs, 198, 199.
Baker Hot Springs, visit to the, 133.
Baldy of Nome, famous sledge dog, 203.
Baranof, Russian Governor of Alaska, 33; fur trading stations of, in California, 37; establishes first Russian colony at Kodiak, 37.
Basket work, Indian, 104.
Beach, Rex, his old home at Rampart, 151.
Bear cubs as pets, 121.
Bears, in many varieties, 267.
Belle Island Hot Springs, 133.

Beraud, G. E., noted assayer and chemist, 163.
Bering, explorations in Alaska waters, 36.
Bering Sea, size and climatic conditions, 239.
Betting on the spring ice-break, 129.
Birch, Stephen A., story of discovery of Kennecott copper mines, 290.
Boundary, U. S. Signal Corps station at, 119.
Brackett, George A., toll-road builder, 111.
British explorations along coast of Alaska, 36.
Broad Pass, a promising mining district, 278.
Brooks, De-Alfred H. estimate of gold output, 191; survey of Mt. McKinley region, 284.
Browne, Belmore, attempts to climb Mt. McKinley, 282, 286, 287.
Bryntesen, John, gold miner, 191, 192.
Burckhardt, C. A., successful garden of, 62.
Burial customs, native, 55.
Burials, in solid ice, 132.

Cadzo, Dan, and his home in the wilderness, 122.
Canadian Mounted Police, not hampered by red tape, 171.
Canneries, salmon, 21; process of dressing and canning, 26.
Cannibalism among the coast Indians, 14.
Carcross, on crest of the Divide, 113.
Caribou, abundance of, 264.
Cats, necessary in fox farming, 237.
Central heating, at Fairbanks, 145.
Charitableness in Alaska, 166, 172.
Chatanika, mining at, by steam thawing of ice layer, 159.
Childs Glacier, reached by Copper River Railway, 297.
Chilkats, advancement of the, 46.

315

INDEX

Circle City, the almost deserted village, 120.
Civilization among the Indians, efforts for, 47.
Climate, variableness of, 1, 10, 43; of Sitka, 32; Aleutian Islands, 66, 243; Juneau, 72; Skagway, 97; White Horse, Yukon Territory, 110; Tanana, 125; Fairbanks, 154; Nome, 189; Seward, 254; an Alaska woman's opinion of, 131.
Coal fields, development of the, 279.
Coast Survey, work in behalf of navigation, 7.
Cod fisheries, extent of, 30.
Cook, Captain, early explorations along Alaskan coast, 36.
Cook, Dr. Frederick, claims to have made ascent of Mt. McKinley, 285.
Copper deposits, the story of Kennecott, 289.
Copper River Railway, the country along the, 296.
Cordova on the Copper River Railway, 296.
Cremation among Indian tribes, 45, 55.
Crime, extent of, in Alaska, 172.
Cyanide process of gold extraction, 86.

Dahlia growing at Skagway, 97.
Dairy farming, possibilities in, 65.
Davis, General Jefferson C., in command of troops at transfer of Alaska to the United States, 40.
Dawson, time of opening and closing of navigation, 129; the gold rush to, 111.
Dehn, Judge, U. S. Commissioner at Tanana, on the climate, 125.
Deckey, W. A., names Mt. McKinley, 284.
Diomede Island, catch of fur sold in Alaska markets, 218.
Dog races, the Derby of Alaska, 197.
Dogs, the motive power, 197, et seq.
Douglas Island, under-sea gold mining at, 78.
Duncan, Father William, work with the Indians at Metlakahtla, 13.
Dyea, city of, now farm land, 99.

Eagle, first American town on the Yukon, 119.
Edes, W. C., on Alaska Engineering commission, 272.

Eldridge, George, explorations on Mt. McKinley, 284.
Erwin, L. T., U. S. Marshal at Fairbanks, reminiscences of, 165, 170.
Eskimos, customs and progress of the, 214; schools and self-government, 222.
Experiment station work, in finding suitable crops, 149.
Explorations by Russians, British, and Spaniards, 36.

Farming, teaching of, among natives, 49; the promising future, 60; in the Tanana valley, 148.
Fairbanks, astonishing growth of, 139; richest of gold-mining districts, 156.
Fairbanks Experiment Station, success of, 60, 149.
Fink, Albert, founder of Nome Kennel Club, 200.
Fisheries, extent of, 21.
Flowers, wild, of Southeastern Alaska, 61.
Forests, extent of, 61.
Fort Gibbon, U. S. army post, 124.
Fort Yukon, now mainly a fur-trading post, 122.
Fox farming, a growing industry, 236.
Fruits, wild, of Southeastern Alaska, 62.
Fur seal, habits and range of the, 232.
Fur seal industry of the Pribilof Islands, 230.

Game, abundance of, on Kenai Peninsula, 260, 263; hunting restrictions, 263.
Game preserve of Mt. McKinley Park, 287.
Gardening, at Nome, 187.
Georgeson, Professor, in charge of Agricultural Experiment work in Alaska, 64.
Glaciers, the world's greatest, 87.
Gold, yield from Yukon Basin, 156.
Gold mining under the sea, at Douglas Island, 78.
Goods for Alaska trade, 144.
Gray, Captain, early visit to Alaska, 37.
Griggs, Prof. Robert F., discovers "Valley of Ten Thousand Smokes," 247.
Grub staking, with good and bad results, 158.

316

INDEX

Guggenheim mines, in Iditarod district, 181.

Halibut fisheries of Southeastern Alaska, 22, 27.

Hay, high price of, in mining regions, 135.

Herring fisheries, extent of, 29.

History of Alaska and its purchase by the United States, 32 et seq.

Holy Cross Mission, on Lower Yukon, 181.

Homestead farming, possibilities of, 66; not recommended, 138.

Homesteading under the Arctic Circle, 148.

Hot springs, visits to, 133.

Hydahs, customs of the, 44; remarkable progress of, 47.

Hydraulic mining in glacial ice, 193.

Iditarod district, gold mines of the, 181.

Indian cemetery at Nulato, 179.

Indian tribes, of Alaska, the, 44.

Inside Passage, travel through the, 6.

Ivory carving of the Eskimos, 219, 220.

Jones, Dr. Lester, on troubles of the Aleuts, 243.

Juneau, impressions of, 69; as a gold-mining centre 78.

Kaltag, trading post on Lower Yukon, 180.

Kantishna, mining district of, 278.

Karstens, Harry, with Archdeacon Stuck in ascent of Mt. McKinley, 286.

Katmai, Mount, explorations of volcano on, 247.

Kenai Peninsula, horseback trip across, 256.

Kennecott copper mines, the story of, 289.

Ketchikan, the post of, 5, 8.

Kivalina, school republic at, 226.

Klukwan Indians, advancement of the, 46, 47.

Kodiak, first Russian colony established at, 37.

Kodiak Island, cattle raising on, 245; heavy fall of volcanic ash on, 246.

Latouche copper mine, discovery of, 293.

Lindbloom, Erik, gold miner, 191, 192.

Lindeberg, Jafet, gold miner, sportsman, and capitalist, 191,199, 206.

Lloyd, Thomas, one of first party to climb Mt. McKinley, 285.

Log Cabin Club, the, at Nome, 186.

Lopp, William T., pioneer in reindeer introduction, 209; Chief of Alaskan Division of Bureau of Education, 222.

Lord's Prayer, in Tsimpsean language, 20.

McGonogill, Charles, one of first party to climb Mt. McKinley, 285.

Mail service, in winter, 132.

Maksutoff, Prince, at ceremony of transfer to the United States, 41.

Malaspina Glacier, size of, 94; effect of earthquake on, 95.

Marriage customs of natives, 53,57.

Mastodon and other pre-historic animals, preserved in arctic ice, 121,219.

Matanuska Agricultural Experiment Station, 60.

Matanuska coal fields, development of, 273, 274, 279.

Mears, Col. Frederick, chairman of Alaska Engineering Commission, 272.

Meat and poultry under home "cold storage," 128

Mendenhall Glacier, reached by automobile, 91.

Metlakahtla, Indian town established by Father Duncan, 13.

Miles Glacier, reached by Copper River Railway, 297.

Mitchell, Margaret, success in gold mining, 306.

Moose, in Kenai Peninsula, 266; influence of rabbits on quantity of moose in a locality, 269.

Mosquitoes, prevalence of, 74, 180.

Mount Edgecombe, extinct volcano, 33.

Mount McKinley, highest in North America, 42, 281.

Mount St. Elias, height of, 42.

Mount Verstovia, of the Holy Cross, 33.

Mountain sheep, finest of Alaska game, 260, 266.

Mountains of Alaska, 42.

317

INDEX

Muir Glacier, movement of, 94.
Muldrow, Robert, survey of Mt. McKinley, 284.

Nenana coal fields, development of, 278, 279.
Noatak, school republic at, 227.
Nolan Mine, a cleanup at the, 160.
Nome, the City of Golden Sands, 183
Northern Commercial Company, activities of, 143.
Nulato, Indian cemetery at, 179.

Old timers, tales of the, 169.

Panhandle, the, or Southeastern Alaska, 5.
Perez, Juan, Spanish explorations of, 36.
Photography under the midnight sun, 122.
Pinnacle rocks, charting of by Coast and Geodetic Survey, 7.
Point Barrow, industrial school for Eskimos, 227.
Polygamy formerly prevalent among natives, 57.
Potatoes, good crops in the Tanana valley, 150.
Poultry keeping, difficulties and rewards, 126.
Pribilof Islands, fur seal industry of the, 230; government fox farms on, 236.
Protective coloration of Arctic game animals and birds, 269.
Pullen, Mrs. Harriet, hotel of, at Skagway, 98; makes good in Alaska, 304.
Pup-mobile, the dog car railroad, 137, 197.

Rabbits, abundance of, 269.
Railroad, government, the biggest thing in Alaska, 271.
Rainfall, excessive, at Ketchikan, 9; in Southeastern Alaska, 110; scanty at Fairbanks, 154; excessive, at Unalaska, 243.
Rampart Agricultural Experiment Station, 60, 150, 151.
Raven, legend of the, 56.
Red tape, U. S. Marshal's difficulties with, 171.
Reindeer, for native meat supply and

shipment to the States, 3, 205, *et seq.*
Resurrection Bay, early history, 255.
Reyburn, D. L., survey of Mt. McKinley region, 284.
Rhoads-Hall mine, discovery of the, 162.
Riggs, Thomas, Jr., on Alaska Engineering Commission, 272, 277.
Rousseau, General, at ceremony of transfer to the United States, 41.
Ruby, mining town on the Lower Yukon, 178.
Russian occupation of Alaska, 32 *et seq.*

Salmon, abundance of, 12; spawning habits of, 25.
Salmon fisheries of Southeastern Alaska, 21.
Schofield, G. D., owner of farm sub-irrigated by hot springs, 136.
School republics of the Eskimo, 222.
Seal, fur, habits and range of the, 232.
Seal industry of the Pribilof Islands, 230.
Seward, City of, situation and development, 250.
Seward, William H, as Secretary of State negotiates purchase of Alaska, 39.
Seward, Agricultural Experiment Station, 60.
Sheldon, Charles, explorations of Mt. McKinley region, 283, 288.
Sitka, history, climate, and location, 32.
Sitka Agricultural Experiment Station, 60, 63.
Skagway, gate to the Klondike, 96; "Flower City of Alaska," 97.
Slavery, among the natives, 57.
Smith, Jack, with Clarence Warner discovers Kennecott copper deposits, 291.
Smith, "Soapy," career at Skagway, 101.
Southeastern Alaska, the Panhandle, 5.
Spanish explorations along coast of Alaska, 36.
Steam thawing of ice, in prospecting for gold, 158.
Still, crude, used by Eskimos for making alcohol, 224.

INDEX

Stoeckl, Baron, Russian ambassador, negotiates sale of Alaska to the United States, 39.

Strawberries, success with, at Sitka, 63.

Strong, H. C., success with raspberries at Ketchikan, 9.

Stuck, Archdeacon, first climbs highest peak of Mt. McKinley, 286.

Sumner, Charles, suggests name Alaska for the new territory, 40.

Taku Glacier, movement of, 88.

Tanana, the hub of Alaska, 124.

Tanana River, heavy with silt, 137; agricultural land along the, 138, 139.

Tanana valley, farming in the, 148.

Taylor, William, one of first party to climb Mt. McKinley, 285.

Tenakee Hot Springs, 133.

Terrill, Monte, an old timer, 169.

Thlingets, and sub tribes, 44 *et seq.*; legends of the Creation and the Flood, 56.

Totem poles, and their meaning, 52.

Trade of Alaska, importance of, 147.

Treadwell mines, 78.

Tsimpsean Indians, Father Duncan's work with, 13.

Tuberculosis, extent of, among natives, 49.

Turkeys, driven in overland, 167.

Unalaska, excessive rainfall at, 243.

Unimak Island, active volcanoes on, 241; largest of the Aleutian group, 242.

"Valley of Ten Thousand Smokes," discovery of, 247.

Vegetables, production of, 3; raised by aid of hot springs, 134, 136; home gardens at Fairbanks, 142; in Tanana valley, 150; gardens along the Lower Yukon, 178.

Volcanic ash deposit on Kodiak Island, 246.

Volcanoes, of the Aleutian Islands, 241.

Wainwright, Eskimo school republic at, 225.

Walrus, more than a match for the polar bear, 268.

Warner, Clarence, with Jack Smith discovers Kennecott copper deposits, 291.

Weber, F. J., dahlia gardens of, at Skagway, 97.

Western Union Telegraph Company, early explorations, 39.

Whale meat, palatable and nutritious, 244.

Whaling industry, extent of, 244.

White, Elmer J., American consul at White Horse, 112.

White, Miss Martha, first white child born in Alaska, 303.

White, Mrs., first white woman to establish a home in Alaska, 303.

White Pass Railway, construction of the, 106.

Wickersham, James, first attempt to climb Mt. McKinley, 284.

Wild flowers of Southeastern Alaska, 61.

Willow Creek, mining town, 278.

Women, position of among the natives, 54.

Women of Alaska, the, 302.

Women's Clubs of Alaska, 308.

Wood carving, Indian, 104.

Wood pulp, timber suitable for, 61.

Yak, Tibetan, introduction of, 246.

Yukon Flats, impression of the, 115.

Yukon River, navigation on, 129, 178.

319